"While there are many accounts of enterprises successfully disrupted by their founders, what distinguishes Ron Shaich's book is his willingness to share how his relentless questioning of his companies, even on the heels of their greatest successes, took them to even greater heights. For those of us who have experienced his companies as consumers, competitors, and observers, this book finally describes how his extraordinary track record seems to repeat itself over and over again."

—BRAD BLOOM, cofounder, Berkshire Partners

"Ron Shaich is a true pioneer of conscious capitalism—a purpose-driven leader with a relentless focus on the long term and a deep love for the transformative power of business. I've long valued his wisdom in the boardroom and beyond, and I have no doubt that *Know What Matters* will be instrumental in shaping the next generation of conscious leaders."

JOHN MACKEY, cofounder, Whole Foods Market; author, *Conscious Capitalism*

"*Know What Matters* is packed with practical advice and real-world examples to help readers create businesses of value and lives with meaning."

—STEVE CASE, Chairman and CEO, Revolution; cofounder, AOL

"Ron Shaich's *Know What Matters* is a must-read for entrepreneurs, leaders, and anyone who wants to be more effective in life. Ron was obsessed with delighting his customers and coworkers at Panera long before it was fashionable to do so. Ron produced a truly amazing 70X return from his IPO in 1991 until he sold Panera in 2017. He shares how he did it and what he learned in *Know What Matters*."

—WILL DANOFF, Portfolio Manager, Fidelity Contrafund

"Ron Shaich shares his compelling journey from budding entrepreneur to seasoned CEO, navigating the professional and personal twists and turns he's experienced while seeing a compelling idea early on, building it to scale, and then persuading a lot of other people to come along for the ride. The stories in this book are chock-full of enormously valuable lessons for business builders at any stage of their careers."

—**DANNY MEYER,** author, *Setting the Table*

"When Ron said Panera Bread would move to something called 'clean ingredients' for consumers, his restaurant competitors laughed. Now, healthier ingredients at big restaurant chains are table stakes. When Ron began rolling out mobile ordering at Panera Bread, those same competitors chuckled. Now they're all making big money from selling 'clean' food via mobile ordering. In a decade of covering Ron Shaich's career at Panera Bread, I have found him to be thinking ten years in advance of everyone else and usually proven right. He has done this while staying humble, true to himself, and bringing entire teams along for the ride of a lifetime. Read this book if you want to know what true leadership is all about."

—**BRIAN SOZZI,** Executive Editor, Yahoo Finance

"*Know What Matters* is an extraordinary testament to the power of persistent transformation and innovation, even when you're at the top of your game. Ron's ability to foresee and invest in future capabilities and his willingness to take calculated risks is a blueprint for business leaders looking to keep their companies relevant and competitive. The successful transformations he has led are a powerful reminder that staying the course requires continual evolution and adaptation."

—**DYLAN BOLDEN,** Managing Director and Senior Partner,
Boston Consulting Group

"Ron Shaich is not only an amazing entrepreneur but also a planner, a deep thinker, a strategist, and a real people person. *Know What Matters* is an honest assessment of his career and the building of a great company—the ups and the downs and the challenges. And it's written in a style that is fun to read: a great book for any young entrepreneur or experienced business leader, or indeed for anyone interested in looking behind the scenes of the Panera Bread and Ron Shaich story."

—**JOSH BECKENSTEIN,** Cochairman, Bain Capital

"It's rare to find a business leader who can steer both a fast-growing startup and a large public company with equal assurance and vision. Ron Shaich has done both. *Know What Matters* is essential reading both for entrepreneurs who want to achieve scale and for large-enterprise CEOs who want to stay nimble and innovative."

—**PAUL FRIBOURG,** CEO, Continental Grain

"No doubt you've enjoyed Ron Shaich's impact on the restaurant world. Through insider anecdotes from Panera and Au Bon Pain, *Know What Matters* illustrates why Ron is the kind of visionary leader that all stakeholders want at the helm. This is a first-rate playbook on how to drive profits (as a by-product!) through process, persistence, and continuous reinvention."

—**TOM GARDNER,** Cofounder and CEO, The Motley Fool

"*Know What Matters* is a crash course in understanding the restaurant industry, with a healthy serving of powerful life lessons along the way."

—**GREG WENDT,** Partner and Portfolio Manager, American Funds

"*Know What Matters* is a primer on innovation, a playbook for execution, and a guide to real leadership, all rolled into one page-turning narrative. Ron has crafted a book not just for looking back on an incredibly successful career, but to assist—dare I say inspire—all of us in building our most meaningful future."

—**DOUG RAUCH,** former President, Trader Joe's

"There are a myriad of business books collecting dust on shelves that teach lessons about taking risk, managing and scaling an enterprise, making difficult decisions, managing personnel, and serving multiple constituencies. But none cover all of them like Ron Shaich's *Know What Matters*. Shaich takes us on his journey of meteoric growth, which led to one of the most successful restaurant companies of the last few decades, generating value for customers, employees, and shareholders. Ron Shaich walks us through the many highs and lows along the way. *Know What Matters* should be required reading for any entrepreneur or business leader thinking about expanding their enterprise."

    —FRANK ALONSO, Portfolio Manager, T. Rowe Price
    Small Cap Stock Fund

"There have been numerous books written about the history of successful companies. In *Know What Matters*, Ron Shaich not only shares the journey that led to the enormous success of Panera Bread, he also teaches us what he learned and how those learnings helped him transform the business multiple times. Also there is the human element of a CEO's journey, from the humbling lows to the exhilarating highs. Ron's greatest strength is his ability to anticipate where the world is going and execute a plan to get there. He was never afraid to make smart bets to transform the business based upon these changes and, along the way, create strong lifelong relationships with his employees, business partners, competitors, shareholders, and customers."

    —PETER SAPERSTONE, Partner, Greycroft;
    former Portfolio Manager, Fidelity Investments

"*Know What Matters* is a must-read for anyone who wants to understand how to build a successful company that can stand the test of time. Ron Shaich is a visionary who helped change the landscape of the restaurant industry, and his insightful book offers an inside look into the level of creative thinking, innovation, and adaptation that was necessary to create a business that added significant economic value for all stakeholders."

    —DAVID E. TARANTINO, CFA, Senior Research Analyst and Managing
    Director, Baird Institutional Equities & Research

"Nothing worth doing is easy, but it can be hugely gratifying and life changing. Whether you're starting your own business or leading a large one, Ron offers practical advice on how to reinvent and transform your business and yourself in the process. Figuring out what truly matters in business is also a road map for living your best life."

—**DAVE BURWICK,** President and CEO, Boston Beer Company

"Ron Shaich is the most visionary brand founder and leader I've had the pleasure to work with, and he tells the remarkable story of the creation and explosive growth of Panera Bread with compelling candor. In creating and repeatedly reinventing Panera, he describes his process of first looking into the future toward a vision of a better solution, and then working backward to identify the best path to get there. His relentless focus on identifying *what really matters* to create sustainable competitive advantage and defensible differentiation, and on embracing rather than avoiding the toughest challenges, led Panera to emerge as a category of one in a ruthlessly competitive field. The journey was not without its setbacks, however, and Ron's honest accounts of Panera's stumbles along the way, and what he learned from them, make the company's ultimate success that much more impressive. Astute readers will learn to do what this book's title promises: *Know What Matters*. And what could be more important than that?"

—**GREG FLYNN,** founder, Chairman & CEO, Flynn Restaurant Group

"Ron Shaich has written a fascinating book about his entrepreneurial journey from opening a single cookie store in downtown Boston to building, running, and eventually selling the enormously successful Panera Bread. Ron's path to the winner's circle was never a straight line, but through grit, determination, and an uncanny ability to understand customer needs and build a competitive advantage, he moved beyond entrepreneurship and became a great corporate leader. Entrepreneurs and corporate managers take note: Your return on investment from reading *Know What Matters* is exponential!"

—**JOHN HAMBURGER,** President, *Franchise Times/Restaurant Finance Monitor*

"'How do you get a group of people to share a vision of something that does not yet exist?'" Ron Shaich offers a master class for those who dare to try. He is a strategist; empath; Sherlock Holmes–like observer of the human condition; inspirational high priest; expert story-teller; loyal friend, father, and loving son. His mantra, 'Speak the truth. Know what matters. Get it done,' helps the reader appreciate that 'the essence of life and business is choice.' Time and again, Ron was able to know what mattered and what choices to make. He trans-formed restaurants as we knew them; sought 'clean food' at a time this mindset did not exist; recognized, in the early days, the value of Wi-Fi to anyone who eats out; and had the insight and courage to realize that many restaurant-goers want food that both tastes good and is good for them. 'The ability to know what matters is like a muscle that must be exercised.' Ron Shaich is a gold medalist in this rarified category, and his reflections are a shared gift to all."

—**DAVID EISENBERG, MD,** Director of Culinary Nutrition,
Harvard T.H. Chan School of Public Health

"Ron Shaich, the brilliant CEO/founder of Panera Bread, has delivered a must-read in *Know What Matters*. This content-rich book is full of lessons learned and best practices that any CEO, entrepreneur, or leader can learn from."

—**JAMES D. WHITE,** former Chair and CEO, Jamba Juice

"An industry peer whom I respect greatly, Ron Shaich has continued to ex-emplify the creativity and fearlessness required to drive transformational impact. For any entrepreneur looking not just to build within an industry but also to change that industry itself, Ron's journey and approach offer invaluable wisdom to absorb."

—**DANIEL LUBETZKY,** founder, KIND Snacks

Know
What
Matters

LESSONS FROM A LIFETIME
OF TRANSFORMATIONS

Know What Matters

RON SHAICH

FOUNDER, PANERA BREAD

HARVARD BUSINESS REVIEW PRESS

BOSTON, MASSACHUSETTS

Library of Congress Cataloging-in-Publication Data

Names: Shaich, Ron, author.
Title: Know what matters : lessons in building transformative companies and creating a life you can respect / Ron Shaich (founder, Panera Bread).
Description: Boston, Massachusetts : Harvard Business Review Press, [2023] | Includes index.
Identifiers: LCCN 2023010772 (print) | LCCN 2023010773 (ebook) | ISBN 9781647825591 (hardcover) | ISBN 9781647825607 (epub)
Subjects: LCSH: Entrepreneurship. | Success in business. | Goodwill (Commerce)
Classification: LCC HB615 .S485 2023 (print) | LCC HB615 (ebook) | DDC 658.4/21—dc23/eng/20230713
LC record available at https://lccn.loc.gov/2023010772
LC ebook record available at https://lccn.loc.gov/2023010773

ISBN: 978-1-64782-559-1
eISBN: 978-1-64782-560-7

For Michael and Emma.
Being your father has helped me learn more about what matters
than any other experience in my lifetime.

CONTENTS

Preface   *ix*

PART ONE

Living the Entrepreneurial Life

1 Future Back   3

2 Competitive Advantage Is Everything   9

3 Means, Ends, and By-products   15

4 Entrepreneurs Are Opportunists   19

5 Think Before You IPO   27

6 You Take the Money; I'll Take Control   33

7 Feeding the Growth Monster   37

8 Empathy Unlocks the Future   41

9 Discovering Today What Will Matter Tomorrow   47

10 Defining What You Stand For   55

11 Getting It Done   63

12 You Don't Own the Business; the Business Owns You   69

13 Business (and Life) Requires Hard Choices   75

PART TWO

Leading a Large Enterprise

14 Develop with Discipline   87

15 Break the Cycle of Failure   95

16 Be the Innovator in Chief   99

17 Make Smart Bets   109

18 Seek Out the Tough Stuff and Create a Barrier to Entry   119

19 Know When to Fold 'Em   125

20 If You Don't Have Control, Credibility Is Your Currency   131

21 The Doing of the Doing   137

22 Business Would Be Easier without People   151

23 Parish Priest in a Business Suit   157

24 Be Contrarian: Conserve in a Boom, Build in a Bust   163

25 Business Is Personal   171

PART THREE

Driving Large-Scale Transformation

26 Managing the Desire-Friction Ratio   179

27 Making the Transformation Operational   191

28 Finding New Runways for Growth   199

29 Coming Clean—with Yourself and Others   205

30 Keep Your Promises   211

31 Know When to Sell   223

Epilogue: Transformation Never Ends   235

Notes   239
Index   241
Acknowledgments   247
About the Author   253

PREFACE

When I retired, after building Panera Bread into a beloved national brand, one of the things I looked forward to doing was writing a book to share the lessons I'd learned along the way. I signed a contract with a New York publisher and got to work.

This is not that book.

Hopefully, it's much more than that book would have been. See, that was more than ten years ago. And my 2010 retirement was short-lived. After a brief respite, I found myself back at Panera, because I saw the need and felt the responsibility to transform the company one last time. Before I knew it, I was back working eighty-hour weeks, and my book-writing endeavors were relegated to the wee hours of the morning. Eventually, I had to admit that it was too much. I didn't have time to write a book, and it wasn't yet the right time, either. Transforming Panera yet again was taking every ounce of my time, energy, and creativity—and I didn't yet fully understand the deeper lessons that would be revealed. So, I gave the publisher back its advance and set my book aside until I really did finish my work at Panera.

Now, more than a decade later, I'm proud to be holding a finished copy of my book in my hands. My hope is that those additional years have done much more than just complete a chapter in my story—they have broadened and deepened the scope and depth of this work. They made it something more than a business book or a compendium of my reflections on entrepreneurship, leadership, and management of large enterprises. Instead, my aim is to help you frame your *own* approach to leadership and life, whether in a small startup, a large public company, a nonprofit organization, or civic society. I hope to challenge you, inspire you, and invite you to think afresh about what truly matters at work and in life—and how to get it done.

For my part, I'm still not "retired," although my time with Panera came to an end with the sale of the company in 2017—the largest deal the US restaurant industry had ever seen to that point. During its last two decades as a public company, Panera was the best-performing stock in the restaurant industry—generating annualized shareholder returns twice those of Starbucks and four times those of Chipotle; exceeding the S&P 500 forty-two-fold; and even outperforming Warren Buffett's Berkshire Hathaway.

Of course, I'm tremendously proud of those achievements. But what I'm most proud of isn't captured by those numbers. It isn't even captured by the fact that, at the height of our popularity, one out of every thirty Americans—approximately 10 million guests—visited our cafés every week. The greatest achievement that I care about was that we figured out what mattered and transformed the company, time and time again.

During my thirty-seven years at the helm, the company I led underwent four fundamental transformations, each of which revolutionized the company itself and, to one degree or another, the food service industry writ large.

First, we transformed from a nearly bankrupt French bakery to a rapidly growing chain of popular bakery cafés called Au Bon Pain. Second, we discovered a new restaurant paradigm—that would eventually become the $100 billion–plus fast-casual segment—and transformed the St. Louis Bread Company, a small chain of bakery cafés in the Midwest, into the Panera concept, which would in turn become the poster child for fast casual. Third, when that new model was still just an unfulfilled promise, we transformed the company once again by shedding our legacy Au Bon Pain divisions and betting everything on Panera's potential. Fourth and finally, when we'd reached the pinnacle of our success, we looked ahead and recognized that we were about to lose our edge—so we transformed once again, completely reinventing the company and every aspect of how we interacted with our guests.

Transformation is fiendishly difficult. Some companies never do it—especially large, established, public companies—and of those that do, many fail to do it again. But to survive and thrive in our fast-changing world, companies must keep transforming, never sitting back on what worked yesterday but always reaching for what will matter tomorrow. The fact that we successfully did this, again and again, is the crowning achievement of my life's work. The learnings that informed and were developed in that journey are what I will share with you in the pages ahead.

When people ask me the secret of my success, I often say it comes down to three things I've been able to do:

1. Tell the truth.

2. Know what matters.

3. Get the job done.

To me, those three steps are the essence of transformation. You start by being brutally honest about where you're at. Then, you dig deep to figure out a solution—to discern what matters to the people you want to impact, and how you can deliver that to them. And finally, you put it into action. That's what we did at Panera—and not just once, but multiple times during my tenure. We were active learners; we figured out how to be a better competitive alternative; and we had the discipline and commitment to see it through.

Tell the truth. Know what matters. Get the job done. That pretty much sums up how I've approached this book as well. First, I set out to tell the truth—to share my stories honestly and without glossing over the difficult and downright painful parts. Then, I attempted to distill from those stories what I learned about what matters—in business and, more importantly, in life as a whole. To *know what matters* is the hardest, and most critical, part of any endeavor, which is why I chose that as the title for the book. It's also the part that I love the most— the process of figuring it out. Last, I've dedicated significant space in these pages to describing the actual processes through which we got the job done—"the doing of the doing" as I like to call it. Unless you can execute and bring what matters to life, no amount of experience or learning will translate into real-world impact. My goal, in all of this, is to show you how to distill truly innovative learnings out of the raw material of your own experience, to figure out a better solution and then translate that into action. And then, do it all over again!

Let's be clear: I'm not here to offer you another set of platitudes about the shortest way to turn your startup into the next big thing so you can IPO and cash out. I'm here to challenge you to create a business, a life, and even a society of enduring value. Again, I hope that what you'll take from these pages will apply to much more than your business. I've always said, I go to work to learn about life. The most important lessons I've learned and continue to learn are as much about a life well lived as they are about doing business, because for me, the two are inextricable. They are also applicable to politics and civic society, and to any type of organization, large or small, that seeks to make a difference.

I won't sugarcoat the truth: building something that truly matters is hard. I can show you a smarter way to go about it, but it won't be an easier way. If you want to make an impact, you'll need to be prepared for the tough stuff. But for those of us who are called to this journey, there are few things in life that are more satisfying than figuring out a new and innovative solution and then bringing it to life. If you're crazy enough to stick with it through the inevitable ups and downs, to transform again and again in order to meet the needs of tomorrow, you'll look back and see that you lived a life you can respect. And in the end, what could matter more than that?

PART ONE

Living the Entrepreneurial Life

Future Back

I learned the most important lesson of my life as my father's life came to its end. In January 1998, several years after a lung cancer diagnosis, my dad, Joseph Shaich, moved into my apartment in Cambridge, Massachusetts. The nearby Dana-Farber Cancer Institute was the best hospital in the country, and having exhausted all other treatment options, we got him enrolled in an experimental clinical trial. This was a last-ditch attempt to extend his life, but it bought him only a brief reprieve. I was his companion through the final year of his life's journey.

I cannot tell you whether there is a judgment day "up there." But after watching my father during his last few months, I can tell you this: there is one down here, if we have time to face it. Barring sudden death or mental incapacitation, the impending final deadline forces each of us to judge the life we have lived. Regardless of whether we believe in a God, most of us, in our last months on this Earth, will give ourselves the ultimate performance review. We will ask ourselves some variation of the inevitable questions: Did I live the life I wanted to live? Did I fulfill my potential? Did I live a life I respect?

Such was the case with my father. By most measures, my dad lived a good life. A certified public accountant with his own firm and an adept poker player, he was skilled with numbers and made a good living. Even when he wasn't feeling secure himself, he provided security for his family and always made each of us feel safe. He was charismatic and he made us laugh. He taught me business and how to walk in the world. He backed me, with his smarts and advice as well as his money, when I launched my very first business.

But Dad often wasn't intentional in the way he lived. Too often, he was impulsive, making reactive decisions without thinking through the consequences and then backtracking. Indeed, he zigzagged through life, focusing on what felt right to him in the moment.

In his last year, my father had time to confront the choices he had made and not made and the opportunities he missed. By the time the end came, he had reached a difficult, but honest, conclusion—in his own words, "I screwed up. And I can't fix it now." There was nothing that I or anyone else could say to soften this truth. The father I had idolized as a kid was a broken man in those final months, and there was no putting him back together.

On the morning after he took his last breath, I sat at a coffee shop, astonished that the sun could still be rising on a day when I had lost my father. I thought about his last year, and I found myself comparing it to my mother, Pearl's, who had died six years earlier. She had less time for reflection. But it was clear to me in the last few years of her life that she was at peace with herself. Always a giver, she lived her life with a clear sense of purpose: to care for the people she loved. She knew she'd done the right thing for her. She never hesitated to make the hard choices when it came to the well-being of her family. She turned her house into a nursing home for my grandparents and dedicated herself to taking care of them.

The contrast shook me. How could I attain that sense of peace and contentment? How could I ensure I didn't end up like my father, racked with regret and remorse? Would I have the wisdom and the strength, like my mother, to live a life that I could respect?

As they departed, my parents gave me a gift, the most important lesson of my life: *Take the time now, while you still have a runway into the future, to determine whether you are living a life you will respect. Don't wait until the end.* A judgment day is coming for all of us, but it's up to us to decide when it comes, and whether it comes too late, as it did for my father.

You can't rewrite your past. But if you have the courage to challenge yourself now, you *can* write your future. Each of us can choose to use the knowledge of our mortality as a forcing mechanism to create a life we respect. This universal reality, far from being morbid or depressing, is in fact a powerful tool for accomplishing everything that we want in life and business. I learned from my parents' passing how to live *from the future, back.*

• • •

In my personal life, living from the future back involves a process I call a *pre-mortem.** It's a visualization exercise or mental simulation in which you imagine yourself in your old age, looking back at your life. I project my imagination into the future—hopefully a good long way into it. I imagine my body old and fragile, my breathing shallow, my life energy almost extinguished. I try to evoke the feelings I want to have in that moment—a sense of peace, completion, and most importantly, self-respect. Then I ask myself, What am I going to do now to ensure that when I reach that ultimate destination, I've done what I need to do?

What arises for me in these contemplations is not a list of achievements and accolades, though there are many in which I take great pride. It's certainly not my net worth, my company's stock price, or my possessions. What I will truly value can be categorized into four areas: my relationships with my family and friends; my relationship

---

*The cognitive psychologist and author Gary Klein conceived the mental simulation called the "pre-mortem." He suggests that you look into the future, think about what you want to achieve, and imagine that your efforts have failed. Because you're contemplating the reasons for why things ran off the rails *before* (rather than after) the fact, you're far more willing to confront your worst fears. The exercise pushes you to take an unflinching look at the obstacles you'll likely encounter and honestly reckon with the challenge of figuring out how best to accomplish your goals. See Gary Klein, *The Power of Intuition: How to Use Your Gut Feelings to Make Better Decisions at Work* (New York: Crown Business, 2004).

with my own body and its health and vitality; my relationship with my work and what gives it meaning; and my relationship with my God, my spirituality. Have I lived my life with a sense of integrity in each of these four areas? Have I done everything in my power to be a good father to my children, a good husband to my wife, a good steward of my businesses and assets, and a person who has left a positive impact on the world? Have I honored my body and soul?

How does one live a life that will end in self-respect? That is the essential question. I cannot wake up each morning and vow to feel that way. Nor can I manufacture it by just reacting to my desires. Self-respect isn't an end in itself; it's a by-product of realizing what matters to me and living in alignment with what I value.

Like most people, I've lived too much of my life in reaction to what happened yesterday and in anticipation of what I hope will happen today. The pre-mortem process has helped me shift the fulcrum point. I look toward tomorrow, define what I truly value, and then work backward from there to ensure that those things are happening. As a result of observing my parents as they passed, I am committed to living more consciously and intentionally during my time on Earth.

When it comes to my business endeavors, and the innovation process that drives them, I am guided by the same future-back principle, using a process similar to the pre-mortem. In business, the end point you are visualizing is not your last years but a specific goal or aspiration. You start with your desired outcome and then work backward to discern the steps that will get you there.

Take any dream or goal you have for your business—something that might be three, five, or ten years into the future. Project your imagination forward and picture the article that would be written about you or your company in the *Wall Street Journal* or in your industry's flagship publication. What would it say about what you've achieved? What would it say about how you created that success and what mattered most in creating that success? *Company X had profit growth of 50 percent over the past three years. It achieved these impressive returns by creating a product that significantly outperformed its competitors.*

When asked what contributed to this success, the company's CEO told us it came down to two decisions: investing heavily in a new design and continually upgrading product features. As you do this for your own company, you'll identify the specific objectives that will matter most to you and your customers, and the steps by which you can reach those goals.

Utilizing this future-back process again and again has forced me and my colleagues to imagine what would matter once the future unfolded in front of us. It forced us to focus on what we wanted to accomplish and how we would get there. It pushed us to recognize if we wanted to increase shareholder value, we had to build competitive advantage. To do that we had to identify opportunities and commit to initiatives that would help us exploit those opportunities. It challenged us to think year-to-year rather than quarter-to-quarter and fueled the focus we needed to stay the course. The future-back process can be boiled down to this essential directive: *Discover today what will matter tomorrow, and then bring what matters to life.*

• • •

In life and in business, intent is everything. And intent is rooted in the future. Without clear intent, we live and work by default and in reaction. Our lives are on autopilot, based on how we have done things in the past rather than how we want them to be done in the future. To create anything of value—whether it's a product, a company, a society, or a life—we must push through our default settings. And we do so by living consciously and deliberately, by making the hard choices, and by using tools like pre-mortems and future-back planning to discover what will really matter, again and again.

In my businesses, I use the future-back process for everything—for a new product or project, a company transformation, or a brand-new business investment. Personally, I take time to conduct a pre-mortem once a year. I do so methodically, starting with my ultimate goals and then working back through the initiatives that will get me there in every important area of my life—health, wealth, relationships, and spirituality. This process injects a sense of urgency into my planning, but more than that, it inspires me with the knowledge that I still have time to create the future of my dreams. How much time, I cannot know. But I do know this: if I have the courage to construct that future now, I will have a greater likelihood of having lived a successful life, which for me means a life I respect.

2

Competitive Advantage
Is Everything

"Screw them. We could run a better convenience store than these folks!"

My words carried all the conviction of an untested, twenty-one-year-old undergrad with high ideals and little respect for authority. They also carried the sting of fresh humiliation. Just moments before, my friends and I had been unceremoniously escorted out of the Store 24 convenience store directly across from the entrance to Clark University by a beefy security guard. He'd taken one look at the trio of scruffy kids lingering over the ice-cream freezer and decided we were intent on shoplifting. Deaf to our angry protestations of innocence, he marched us out into the street, where we turned to each other and vowed never to patronize that establishment again. So what if it was the only convenience store within blocks of our campus?

"Those jerks don't respect us," I declared. "Their prices are inflated, and they insult us even while they take our money. We don't need that damn store." At some point, after we'd let off steam, I had an idea. "Why don't we create our own nonprofit convenience store, right here on campus, for the students?"

It seemed like a great idea. Never mind that I didn't know the first thing about creating a business. Indeed, the last thing I wanted was to join the stodgy ranks of gray-suited corporate types. I'd been raised in a family where progressive politics was the currency of a life well lived. I can still remember accompanying my father to anti-war marches and protesting the Nixon nomination ("Tricky Dick Must Go" proclaimed our homemade sign). I'd spent a gap year after high school working as an aide to a New Jersey congressman and volunteering for state senate and even presidential campaigns. Along the way, I became the New Jersey McGovern campaign's youngest candidate for delegate to the 1972 Democratic National Convention in Miami. Politics wasn't just my ambition; it was my identity. I chose Clark for its fiercely political ethos, captured in its motto: "Challenge convention, change our world." Earnest, bearded idealist that I was, that's exactly what I intended to do.

But with a convenience store? I didn't think so, until that day on campus, when something sparked in my brain—lit by a moment of injustice, but quickly taking on a life of its own, fueled by a sense of possibility. I had stumbled on the thing that all successful entrepreneurs search for: an opportunity to create a better alternative. Or, as the late Harvard Business School professor Clay Christensen put it, to *do a better job for someone*. This is the essence of successful innovation: recognizing the "job" that a customer is trying to accomplish and helping them get it done better.[1] People aren't just buying your product or service; they're "hiring" you to solve a problem. Theodore Levitt famously put it this way: "People don't want to buy a quarter-inch drill. They want a quarter-inch hole."[2]

At that point, I hadn't yet been to business school, but I instinctively knew that I couldn't pass up this opportunity to make a difference. I could *see* a better way to help students get what they needed, at a fair price, on campus, in an environment that respected them. Plus, we could provide jobs. And yes, we could stick it to the folks at Store 24 in the process. Although I wouldn't have put it this way back then, agitated twenty-one-year-old me was envisioning a comprehensive, end-to-end solution that delivered for all stakeholders.

Over the next few days, my friends and I went through what was essentially a future-back exercise, although of course we didn't have that name for it then. We started with our vision and then worked backward through all the steps it would take to create our store. We mapped out our proposal and pitched it to the people in the administration. They were unimpressed. In their view, our chutzpah did not compensate for our lack of resources and near-zero know-how.

Once lit, however, the spark in my mind was not easily extinguished, so I persevered. As student council treasurer, I successfully campaigned to fund the store through a tax on the student body, effectively making Clark students our angel investors. The administration grudgingly gave us a space on campus, the previous home of the Faculty Wives Thrift Store. I spent the summer fitting it out.

Supplying the store was another challenge since no wholesaler was willing to do business with us. Instead, we had to wake up early Saturday and drive to a local deep-discount grocer, where we'd fill ten carts with goods to resell. I told the bemused store staff that I lived in a commune—a believable explanation, since I looked the part, with my long hair and my peace sign button. Had they known the truth, they might not have believed it anyway.

The General Store, as we named it, became my passion and my education, far more important to me than classrooms, professors, or grades. I *loved* it. Figuring out what customers wanted, changing the mix of stock, settling on the right price, hiring the proper staff. I remember hurrying out of movies on campus as soon as the credits rolled so that I could open the store for the late-night rush. We delivered brownies (no, not that kind) to dorms on our "Munchie-Mobile." To some, all of this might sound mundane, but to me it was a profoundly creative experience. For a kid from New Jersey who couldn't dance or sing, this was the closest I'd ever come to being an artist. As our customers moved through the aisles, I realized that we were orchestrating live performance art. And I was learning. Not from a textbook or a professor, but from living. From that day forward, I've always said: *I go to work to learn about life.*

My political ambitions didn't die, but they temporarily took a back seat as I immersed myself in the newfound creativity of business. In the process, I realized that business and politics were not so different.

A business enterprise is like a small society, comprising constituencies ranging from customers and staffers to vendors and funders and other stakeholders. Business challenged me with real problems that were crying out to be solved, and it offered me the chance to have a palpable impact, to make a difference in the lives of customers and team members. It could be painful, overwhelming, and exhausting, but it was also invigorating like nothing else I'd experienced.

A business is like a political primary, where voters are faced with multiple candidates, and in which you are able to win by being the singularly best choice for a slice of the total voting population. Being the best choice for a small niche is the key to success, both in business and in politics. Indeed, in a primary election, you can win with 15 percent of the vote. In the same way, a pizza joint doesn't have to be the best among local restaurants, but it does need to be the best pizza place in the neighborhood. You don't need to be everything to everyone, but you need to be number one for someone.

The General Store made a $60,000 profit in its first year. No one was more surprised than me since I hadn't set out to make money at all. I just saw a way to do a better job for the students. We were technically a nonprofit, so there was some consternation over what to do with this unexpected cash. My idea was to throw a Grateful Dead concert on the college green as a thank-you to the students. Unfortunately, the administration had other ideas, and the money ended up in the scholarship fund.

• • •

What allows a business or an enterprise to prosper? Simply put, being a better competitive alternative. Having your target customer choose to walk past your competitors to reach your establishment or product. Being a better alternative ain't complicated. It's just really hard to do. If all you do is rely on market share, on an average distribution of customers, you'll operate a low-margin, grind-it-out business. I call that "dirt farming." That's not worth spending your energy on. To grow your sales volumes and have a successful business, you need to stand out in the eyes of some group of customers—or, in the parlance of MBAs and business consultants, be differentiated.

Competitive advantage is everything. Seems obvious, but most people in corporate America ignore it every day, judging by their actions. They ignore it by focusing on cost-cutting or short-term risk avoidance, while avoiding the much greater risk that comes from losing competitive advantage. They ignore it by focusing endlessly on the results of last quarter and the next, when competitive position must be built over the long term. They ignore it by copying their competitors rather than looking ahead into the future and asking, "What will matter?" In all these ways and more, leaders destroy competitive advantage, often with disastrous consequences.

The world doesn't pay any of us to do what everyone else is doing. It pays us to figure out where the world is headed and to be there when the future arrives. Those rare businesses that can keep their focus on building what will matter—that future they envisioned in a premortem or future-back process—thrive over the long term. Whether they're Amazon or the General Store, what successful businesses have in common is that they know the jobs they're doing for their customers, and they've figured out how to do those jobs better than anyone else. They keep asking, "What matters?" and are disciplined in bringing the answers to life. And I'm not just talking about what matters today; I'm talking about what will matter tomorrow. They think future back. They're able to look down the road and see where the market is going.

The General Store went on to become a Clark institution and a model for other stores at schools across the country. Over three decades, it employed hundreds of students and served tens of thousands of customers. For me personally, the most valuable outcome of that enterprise was not the unexpected profits. It was what it revealed to me about myself. The General Store showed a kid who had a dream to change the world that he could do it, through business. It gave me the opportunity to discover firsthand that building a business is emotionally and intellectually challenging, a highly creative activity that could perhaps sustain and satisfy me for the rest of my life. And it revealed to me my own competitive advantage—my knack for seeing opportunities and figuring out how to deliver a better solution.

Means, Ends, and By-products

Standing on a busy street in downtown Boston on a scorching summer day, I held out a tray of chocolate-chip cookies to a square-jawed gentleman. "Excuse me, sir, would you like to try a cookie?" He hesitated, then accepted. "We're testing a new recipe. What do you think?"

He took a bite and brusquely rendered his opinion: "Tastes like Toll House."

That wasn't exactly the reaction I was hoping for. If my freshly baked cookies were indistinguishable from the mass-produced dough found in every American supermarket, I wasn't achieving much of a competitive advantage. But my cookie-taster was probably right. I hadn't yet hit on a better recipe—either for my cookies or for my own success and satisfaction in life.

But at least as far as the latter went, I was getting close (my baking skills needed more help). I'd bounced from Clark to Harvard Business School to a corporate job with the Original Cookie Co. (a job which I thought of as the third year of my MBA). Then, still pulled by the aspirations of my youth, I'd gone back to politics for a while. I went to Washington and helped run a political consulting firm. But while I gained a sense of purpose in working on senate campaigns, I found that I missed the creativity and dynamism I'd discovered while running the

General Store at Clark. I was torn between pursuing a life in business or a life of political action.

I knew my passion in life revolved around the process of figuring out what worked, whether opening cookie stores, creating a robust revenue stream for a progressive nonprofit, or working with those trying to take political polling to a new level. What I didn't realize then, but see clearly now, was that the question I was agonizing over—What kind of job do I want?—was the wrong one.

The right question was: What do I truly want my life to be about? I was focused on the *means*—business or politics—rather than the *end*, which was my desire to make an impact in the world. And I didn't yet understand the most important thing of all: that if I pursued that end with purpose and intention, its *by-product* would be the thing I ultimately sought—a sense of self-respect.

Means, ends, and *by-products*. A profound distinction is concealed among those prosaic terms, one that unlocks the code to designing a business and a life of enduring value, created from the future back.

I like to explain this distinction by talking about a friend of mine who suffers from type 1 diabetes. He wants to live a long and healthy life, like the rest of us, but he knows that simply focusing on that desire won't get him there. For him, longevity is not an end he can pursue directly but, rather, a by-product. The critical end he must focus on is keeping his blood glucose levels between 80 and 180. And he accomplishes that through specific means: management of insulin, sensible exercise, and eating right. The by-product of his efforts—living longer—takes care of itself.

Some things in life can be pursued directly—these are the *ends*, or goals we set for ourselves: landing a great job, getting a PhD, owning a house, running a marathon, publishing a book. We attain those ends by choosing the right *means* and following through with discipline.

Other things in life—often the most important ones—are more elusive: being in love, finding happiness and contentment, feeling a sense of integrity or self-respect. These are *by-products*. By its very nature, a by-product is a secondary result; you can't generate a by-product by focusing on it.

This is a core paradox of being human: that most of the things we deeply yearn for cannot be grasped directly. It's what the great psychiatrist and philosopher Viktor Frankl meant when he wrote that "happiness cannot be pursued; it must ensue."[1]

Frankl understood that making happiness a target only leads one to miss it. He saw happiness as an "unintended side-effect" of a life dedicated to a greater purpose. It is the same with success—in business and in life. Building a business or a life that we respect will be a by-product of the ends we focus on and the means we choose over decades.

• • •

The means, ends, and by-products framework is a powerful tool when building a business. You'll find that it helps clarify the path forward—from launching a company to innovating new products to staying relevant in a fast-changing market.

When applying this concept to business, here's the most game-changing insight I've discovered: profits are not an end; they are a by-product. If you focus on profit as the end, you fail. You can't really "make" profit. Value creation, in the form of profit or stock price appreciation, is the by-product of your efforts. And when you fully appreciate that value creation is the by-product, the end you can focus on is delivering a better and more differentiated experience than your competitors.

Sometimes people take this sentiment to mean that profits don't matter. No. They do. They are important. But they can't be created as an end in and of themselves, and if you focus your efforts on trying to make more money or raise the stock price, you will actually lose sight of the means that create the end you seek. Treating profit as an end rather than a by-product is self-sabotage.

So if profit is not the end, what is? *Competitive advantage*. I know that sounds like abstract MBA textbook jargon, but remember, it simply means that you offer something your target customer wants enough that they are willing to walk past your competitors to visit your establishment. Pursue that end with great focus; the profits will take care of themselves.

Ron's Rules for Knowing Your Means, Ends, and By-products

Too many people in business lose their edge because they don't know the difference between means, ends, and by-products. Here's how I see this critical distinction in a business context, in reverse order to reflect the fact that these are defined from a future-back perspective:

The by-product: Value creation

The end: Competitive advantage

The means: Initiatives and projects executed with discipline

This was true in the General Store, which turned a profit even though we never set out to make money. And it would turn out to be true with my next venture as well—which brings me back to that day when I stood on the street in Boston, handing out barely-better-than-average cookies.

I didn't yet understand the ideas I'm sharing with you now; I didn't know how to work from the future back and then plot my path to get there. But luckily, my business-versus-politics dilemma had been short-circuited by a commercial landlord who called and offered me the opportunity to lease a four-hundred-square-foot storefront in Boston's Downtown Crossing shopping district. I jumped at the chance to experience the freedom and artistry of running my own business again. At the age of twenty-six, I was about to launch the second entrepreneurial venture of my young life: a cookie store named the Cookie Jar. Did my cookies improve? Yes, with some help—but they were soon eclipsed by other, more innovative offerings. See, they were just a means to an end.

Entrepreneurs Are Opportunists

The Cookie Jar hadn't been open long when I realized I had a problem. A morning problem. As in, people don't eat cookies for breakfast. Every morning, I watched tens of thousands of potential customers pass me by without a glance. If I wanted some of them to come through my door, I needed to sell them what they wanted to eat in the morning. So I came up with the idea of adding French baked goods like croissants to attract the breakfast crowd. I found a small group of three French bakeries that had a great reputation for their baguettes and croissants. It was called Au Bon Pain, which means "place with the good bread." I met with the company's CEO, Louis Kane, to propose selling his French baked goods in our cafés. Louis and I quickly hit it off.

As an operator, you get to know your vendors quickly—and you know which are well-run businesses and which are not. As much as I liked Louis, Au Bon Pain was the most screwed-up business I ever dealt with. Sometimes deliveries showed up and sometimes they didn't. Sometimes I received a bill; other times I didn't. In fact, I'll bet I still owe those guys money for croissants they forgot to bill for.

Au Bon Pain was sinking under the weight of its debt. Louis and his team had opened thirteen cafés across North America and quickly shut down ten of them. Early in our relationship, I decided that despite the fact I was half his age and had limited business experience, I could fix Au Bon Pain. I would make an offer to merge our companies.

Louis was intrigued by the offer. He believed in me. His father, George Kane, thought he was nuts. So did mine. "If it's worth having, you're not going to get any of it," Dad pronounced. "And if you get any of it, it's not worth having."

I asked my father to accompany me to a meeting with Louis and his father. Dad didn't hold back. "Ron would be better off using his money to bet on craps in Vegas than doing this deal," he announced. George Kane seemed to agree with him. But in this case, the sons prevailed, and we struck a deal in which we merged my profitable cookie store with Louis's three unprofitable French bakeries under the Au Bon Pain brand. I ended up with 60 percent of the new company, and Louis and his partners ended up with 40 percent. (Amazingly, this was the same corporate entity that I transformed multiple times, renamed Panera, and would end up selling for $7.5 billion in 2017.)

I had an uncanny confidence that I could summon all that I had learned in the cookie business, apply it to the French bakery business, and take the first steps toward becoming a company builder. What was beckoning me was the chance to build the kind of food establishment that I wanted to visit as a customer and that I wanted to work in as an employee. And Louis Kane, to my eternal gratitude, gave me the space to do it—and in the process, to truly find myself.

Louis might not have been great at running operations, but he had an unmatched ability to connect with people and snap up premier locations. Suave and movie-star handsome, Louis reminded me of Blake Carrington from the soap opera *Dynasty*. He was on George Mc-Govern's power list and Richard Nixon's enemies list. One of the original alpha networkers, he was hardwired into the community. He knew everyone—from the mayor to the homeless guy protesting our café's encroachment into the park in Harvard Square. It sometimes seemed that with just three calls, he could get to anyone in the world on the phone. When we were in Paris and needed reservations at an impossible-to-get-into restaurant, Louis just called up his old friend Julia

Child, and she made it happen. He could—and would—do anything for his friends. People adored him.

In every partnership, there's an exchange of currencies. In me, Louis got a strategist and operator with the discipline and know-how to manage and grow the company. Through Louis, I got a vast network of contacts and entry into a world that had once seemed distant. In many ways, Louis and I were the best kind of partners: polar opposites who powerfully connected and who respected each other enough to let each do his thing. My weaknesses were his strengths; his weaknesses were my strengths. Louis never saw a deal he didn't like, and I never saw a deal I would do. He brought opportunities to the table, and I scrutinized them with a very skeptical eye.

I spent the first two years at Au Bon Pain digging the company out of debt, firing bad people and hiring good people, getting the money to the bank, shutting down an unprofitable wholesale business, and solving countless other problems. Within a couple of years, the company was above water again, but by no means out of danger. The food business has a brutal mortality rate. Four out of five new concepts fail, and that wasn't just a statistic to me—it was a truth I felt in the pit of my stomach every time I reviewed the P&Ls.

Au Bon Pain sold only French bread, pastries, and coffee. That was better than selling just cookies, but the sales volumes were still modest. And we were competing in a market in which customers had a plethora of choices.

To succeed, we'd have to come up with a concept that was magnetic enough to pull people in—to convince more customers to leave more money behind. The best way to do this would be to detect a pervasive customer need—something that customers themselves hadn't even articulated. That meant getting inside the heads of our customers, watching through their eyes as they went about their day, and discovering a need that was unfulfilled—a job that we could complete better than anyone else. I learned in creating the General Store and the Cookie Jar that opportunity grows out of observation. I'm a naturally curious guy, I like people, and I love figuring things out. And given the fact that I was always interacting with customers, I was in a good position to discover that innate, unspoken customer need. When it came, it took me by surprise—as true opportunities often do.

• • •

When you work in a French bakery, it's not unusual to be asked to slice a baguette. So I didn't give it a second thought when a young woman in a business suit walked into Au Bon Pain and asked me to cut the bread she was buying. But as I placed it in the slicer, she stopped me.

"No, don't cut it in slices. Cut it from top to bottom—lengthwise."

Surprised, I did as she asked, cutting the bread end-to-end, and then watched as she sat down, pulled out some items from a grocery bag, and filled her fresh, crusty baguette with Boursin cheese and roast beef from the supermarket deli counter. It looked delicious.

It was an epiphany for me. This customer didn't want a loaf of bread. She wanted lunch. I sensed, right there, that this might be important, but I couldn't quite say how. Then it happened again with another customer. And again. Soon, the message was clear. For a significant number of the people who walked through the doors of Au Bon Pain in the early eighties, the bread we sold was not the end; it was a platform for creating the sandwich they desired. It didn't take a Harvard MBA or a marketing degree to see the opportunity: sell sandwiches.

Customers were telling us that we could take on a far bigger job for them. They weren't telling us in words. No one was walking in and saying, "Damn, I wish you sold sandwiches." They were telling us with their behavior. IDEO design expert Jane Fulton Suri calls this a "thoughtless act"—one of countless ways in which human beings naturally modify and rearrange the world to make it work better for them.[1] Our customers had already found a solution to the job they needed done, and in watching them improvise that solution, I could see the opportunity for Au Bon Pain to better meet their needs.

We could sell sandwiches. And not just any sandwiches. We could differentiate ourselves from the standard American ham-and-cheese-on-white-bread model by offering a different class of sandwich. We could be the place of choice for customers who appreciated artisan, handcrafted breads and croissants and wanted to pair them with ingredients like smoked turkey, Brie or Boursin, and Dijon mustard. This was how Au Bon Pain transformed itself from a bakery into the American version of a bakery café. We would compete with fast food, but we weren't fast food. We were "good food served quickly." In fact, we became one of the country's first restaurant concepts to carve out a middle ground between fast food and fine dining. Faced with a choice between Wendy's and nothing, many would choose nothing. We offered a compelling alternative.

We targeted shoppers and white-collar office workers because we solved a problem for them: they were in a hurry, and they wanted a tastier, healthier alternative to a burger and fries. Our cafés had an upscale look and feel, with brass fixtures, black-and-white ceramic tile, white marble tabletops, classical music, and backlit, oversized photographs of our new line of sandwiches. You've seen these tropes repeated since in cafés, but at the time, I promise you Au Bon Pain looked *different* from other restaurants. All those cues aimed to deliver one subliminal message: *Au Bon Pain may be fast, but it's the antithesis of fast food*.

• • •

In the years it took to transform Au Bon Pain from a French bakery to a robust bakery café, I began to understand that an entrepreneur's most important resource is not capital. Sure, capital matters. But I don't share the mindset of the classic venture capitalist, with their focus on leveraging capital for maximum return on investment over the shortest period of time. To me, entrepreneurs are opportunists, not capitalists. In this paradigm, value is created through the ability to see opportunity—to recognize a need and a possible solution before anyone else sees it and then have the courage and creativity to perform that job for a customer. That's what it means to be an opportunist. For some, that word carries negative connotations—evoking the specter of the unscrupulous speculator taking advantage of circumstances to make a fast buck, regardless of the consequences. But I use the term in a more visionary sense.

Capital is an accessible and renewable resource. It's not that hard to obtain capital at a relatively low cost (provided you have good use for it and a distinctive enough view of the world that people are willing to invest in you). For entrepreneurs, the asset that's *non*renewable— and therefore far more valuable than capital—is our unique capacity to identify customers' unspoken needs, to see and seize white spaces in the market that others have missed. We capitalize on opportunities.

Case in point: back when I launched the Cookie Jar, I had very little capital. I'd gone to my dad and asked him for an advance on my inheritance. "It isn't going to do me any good when you're dead," I told him. "I want to start a business now." He laughed at me, but eventually agreed. I knew the total inheritance would be a quarter-million dollars, but I asked for it in three payments, because I was afraid my first idea wouldn't work. I didn't want to blow all the money on the first try; I wanted to protect my ability to find another opportunity if the first failed. So I started with $25,000 from my own savings and $75,000 from my dad.

This points to another misunderstood fact about successful entrepreneurs and creators. We're not risk-takers. In fact, we're risk-averse. The swashbuckling entrepreneur of popular imagination is just a myth and rarely succeeds. Real-life entrepreneurs develop the skill of seeing patterns to the point where they're so confident in the opportunity they see that the greatest risk would be to miss it. Venture capitalists see risks as financial. Opportunistic entrepreneurs see risk as missing out on an opportunity to meet a need.

Another pervasive myth is that the entrepreneur is some kind of novelty-producing genius. In fact, opportunistic entrepreneurs have a sensibility that leans more toward the editorial than the inventive. We don't create new things so much as we take a wide-angle view of all the ideas and possibilities that we come across; edit out 99 percent of them; focus on one bright, promising possibility; and execute against it better than anyone else.

At the outset, we may not really know what we are looking for. But we recognize it when we see it. I knew when I saw that customer making a sandwich that it was significant. Entrepreneurs are always on the lookout for moments like that. It's a never-ending search. Even as we are engaged in some other task or responsibility, we try to ensure that at least a part of our attention remains alert to the first faint signs of an emerging opportunity.

. . .

When you strike gold, you know it. The bakery-café took off like it was the best thing since, well—sliced bread! Every developer in America wanted a French bakery café in their mall. The world had changed; our once near-bankrupt, broken-down concept was hot again. I'll never forget the morning I slid open the glass doors for the first time at the new Au Bon Pain bakery café in Boston's Copley Place mall. I'd spent months desperately trying to figure out how to get people to stop walking past our door. And now, here they were on day one, waiting in line. At six in the morning. At least fifty people standing there before we opened. I couldn't believe my eyes. I could have stood in the doorway all day, drinking in this incredible sight, but the guy in front said, "Hey, man, are you going to let us in or what?" And so, I hurried back behind the counter and started selling sandwiches.

And people bought them. We'd hit a sweet spot with our "good food fast" formula. Even the stuffy folks in the Harvard Square Business Association, which had a zoning ordinance that locked out fast-food retailers, gave us a pass. Our café across from Harvard Yard, with its outdoor seating and yellow-checked umbrellas, quickly became our most successful location and was the iconic setting for movies like *Good Will Hunting*.

My dad told me I could—and should—retire to Florida on the revenue from that one café in Harvard Square. But I wasn't in it to cash out. That wasn't the by-product I had in mind. I was in it for the joy of building a business. And I was just getting started.

Think Before You IPO

It was a warm June evening in New York City, and I was in a limousine driving up Fifth Avenue when I had a sudden urge to get out. "Pull over," I instructed the driver.

In the seat next to me, Louis was confused. "Get out? What for? We're going to celebrate!" We'd just priced Au Bon Pain's long-awaited IPO. Now in his late fifties, Louis was euphoric at the prospect of a successful IPO, which would amount to a crowning achievement for his career. But I had mixed feelings about it all.

"I'm going to take a walk. I'll catch up with you later."

The limo swerved to a corner, and I hopped out onto the sidewalk. I should have been elated; it was every entrepreneur's dream to be on the brink of a much-anticipated Nasdaq debut, with demand far exceeding the supply of stock. In the past five years, Louis and I had worked so hard for this, rapidly expanding the number of our locations and our revenue. We had spent the previous few months on the road, staying in fancy hotels and meeting with bankers and fund managers throughout the country to tell the story of how we had transformed this broken little company into an industry influencer, with some of the highest unit volumes and the greatest profitability in the French bakery-café business. We placed our cafés in upscale office buildings, shopping centers, transit hubs, and airports, where we could capture businesspeople and shoppers. By the late 1980s, it seemed like every commercial landlord in every midtown from Boston to Washington, DC, wanted an Au Bon Pain on the ground floor. PepsiCo, Sara Lee, and other industry behemoths expressed interest in buying us, and when we resisted, they created or bought rival concepts to come after us. But, as I told everyone we met on that pre-IPO road trip, our genuine passion for serving our customers and our singular commitment to delivering a better experience gave us an edge over all the far-better-capitalized new entrants into the market.

I'm a natural-born salesman and performer, and there are few things I enjoy more than making a great speech and seeing people's eyes light up when they get it. I'd loved every minute of our road show, none more than the moment I looked out at an audience of two hundred prospective investors and saw my mother and father beaming with pride.

Yet when we left the bankers' offices after the pricing meeting and dusk fell over the city, my mood darkened. I couldn't quite say why, but I felt a sense of foreboding.

The car pulled away from me with Louis still in it. I loosened my tie and took off my suit jacket as I ducked into Central Park and tried to make sense of how I was feeling.

An IPO was our logical endgame. It would leave us debt free and give us access to the public capital markets to fuel expansion. It would also reward our venture capital investors, many of whom were pushing for liquidity. And it would cement our victory in the bakery-café wars, signaling to competitors and stakeholders alike that Au Bon Pain had arrived.

But intuitively, I knew this milestone wasn't the end of anything. It felt more like the beginning of something, even if I couldn't quite grasp it yet.

Sure, the IPO would make me a millionaire on paper. But what would it cost me? It would be years before I'd be able to fully calculate the price, but on the quiet paths of Central Park, contemplating, I could already feel the weight of the expectations that come with taking investors' money. I'd never had public shareholders before, but I could feel their presence bearing down on me. Tens of thousands of constituents with demands and opinions. It would no longer just be Louis, me, and our venture capital investors in control, making decisions as we saw fit. Would I be able to protect Au Bon Pain's long-term interests from the pressure to produce short-term results for the investors pouring money into our stock? Would the multitude of shareholders drive regression to the mean? And would the breadth of information we were required to provide as a public company mean that our competitive advantage would be exposed and copied by competitors?

There are downsides to going public that are rarely considered amid the hoopla that leads up to a company's debut on an exchange. An IPO is just like a wedding—everyone gets carried away in the ceremony, the promise, and the emotions of the moment. It's a culmination, long planned for and anticipated. But as anyone who has stood at the altar and exchanged vows will tell you, after every wedding comes the hard work of marriage. And being married to tens of thousands of investors is no happily-ever-after fairy tale. Inevitably, it drags you into a shorter-term focus. Your stock price, which should be a by-product of serving your customer well, most often becomes an end in itself.

But no one's thinking about that when they step up to the altar of Nasdaq or NYSE and say, "I do." I myself couldn't have fully articulated it that night when I ditched Louis to walk alone in New York City, but looking back, I now understand my feelings all too well. Cold feet.

. . .

My dark mood on the eve of that celebratory occasion was not unusual for me, but it's not because I'm pessimistic by nature. I think of myself more as a skeptical optimist. I believe in the possibility of the future, but I also know that there will be bumps on the journey.

People will often tell you that everything bad contains something good. But I believe the opposite is true as well. Buried in everything good is something bad. I can see opportunity, but I can also see the ways opportunity might get derailed. I have faith in the dream, but I also seem to be wired to worry about what could go wrong. Experience has taught me to be cautious when things seem to be going well. It's a trait that's served me throughout my life and my career in business. But sometimes, it leaves me feeling out of sync with the people around me, like I did that night in the car with Louis.

This oxymoronic state of mind is, I believe, what's behind people calling me a contrarian. I'll accept that label, but with a caveat. When people use that phrase, I suspect they think it means a person is thinking differently than others in a self-serving way—to call attention to themselves. That's not it at all. If I seem to be taking the contrarian position, it's because my locus of attention is different.

My focus is on what is going to be happening three to five years out. Louis's focus was on a successful day, and champagne corks popping. I was already anticipating the downside of what would follow the IPO. In part, I feared the loss of control and the increased accountability to short-term shareholder interests. But there was something deeper, more existential, that concerned me as well. The skeptic in me was aware that however successful we had become, we couldn't afford to think we'd arrived and take our eyes off the future.

On that day in June 1991, Au Bon Pain might have temporarily vanquished its rivals to become the toast of Wall Street, but sooner or later those rivals would catch up. We needed to be looking for our next opportunity, even as we celebrated this success. In fact, I worried we'd already lost our competitive edge, even though no one could see it yet.

As the world speeds up, companies fulfill the promise of their business models faster than ever, and so are in danger of peaking and sliding into irrelevance ever more quickly. In a world where niches are by their nature limited and competition moves quickly to copy you, the ability to transform—to develop a capacity to adapt—is the most important competitive advantage of all.

The greatest threat of all to a successful company is itself. Its systems, its functions, and its people are perfectly set up to deliver what mattered yesterday. Sure, you've discovered something special. Everyone's jealous. Competitors want to be you or buy you. Investors flock to your IPO. B-school profs write case studies about you. The folks next door act more like you every day. All of it makes you feel better and better about your company. *Aren't we great? Aren't we wonderful? Look how everyone loves us!* That's how we felt at Au Bon Pain.

But amid all this, you neglect to do what's necessary to maintain competitive advantage. That's the risk. Because what you accomplished yesterday won't help you succeed tomorrow. Yesterday is over. If you don't make the right choices today, tomorrow will find you without competitive advantage and with shrinking market share, just as my inner skeptic feared would happen to us—and sooner than anyone expected.

And yet acting today is so difficult, especially when you're on top of the world and you're winning. It's hard to relate to, but that is the moment when, in fact, you are at the greatest risk.

To avoid falling into this common trap—to escape the shackles of yesterday's success—you must continually be willing to innovate anew well before you really feel like you need to. As I always say, the time to worry about a heart attack is not when you're in the ambulance on the way to the hospital.

Eventually, that night in New York City, I rejoined Louis and put my skepticism on pause—at least temporarily. We raised a toast and celebrated how far our little bakery café had come since the day when I watched a customer turn one of our baguettes into a roast beef and Boursin sandwich. But I knew I'd need to reckon with the question: Are we able to be what the world will need and want from us, three, five, even ten years from now? And how much harder would it be to do so when we had a host of new investors demanding short-term results? There was no doubt that the marketplace would continue to evolve. But would we?

6

You Take the Money;
I'll Take Control

It was just months after Au Bon Pain's IPO that I got my first taste of what being a public company CEO really meant. I was in the middle of a company event at Jillian's, a Boston billiards parlor, when I got a call from our Morgan Stanley analyst. He sounded angry.

"Why are your numbers off?" he demanded. We were going through a bit of a rough patch and not living up to the starry-eyed forecasts of our pre-IPO road show.

That was when it fully dawned on me that I worked for this guy now—and for all the fund managers and investors in those funds who had piled their plates high with the millions of shares we'd offered in our public debut. In going public, we'd effectively taken on thousands of new partners, and together, those outside investors had more control over Au Bon Pain than I did. We worked for them, regardless of our emotional connection to an enterprise that we had nurtured for ten long years. My sense of responsibility—a responsibility that felt intensely personal to me—had expanded considerably. In that moment at that billiards parlor, I understood the heavy weight I'd felt settling on my shoulders the night before the IPO.

Our stock would rebound—and increase by 70 percent within months—but my mood would not. I couldn't seem to shake the gnawing sense of unease. As the year ended and everyone else was celebrating our success, I once again found myself out of sync with the mood of the moment. I saw our stock's performance for what it truly was: a by-product of having seen, and leveraged, a promising opportunity to operate within a (temporarily) uncontested niche in the market. That opportunity was already close to playing itself out. And because I now worked for that analyst and a bunch more investors just like him, I wasn't sure I had the support to do what would be needed to regain our competitive advantage.

Put simply, I'd given up control of my company.

"Control means that if you get in a pissing match, you stay and they go," a friend once told me. Control is the ideal for any entrepreneur. But it's hard to maintain when you're bootstrapping a business and you can see how much more would be possible . . . if only you had more capital. When you have big visions but limited funds, when Wall Street comes courting, when the buzz around your impending IPO reaches a fever pitch, it's easy to forget that for every dollar of investment capital you receive, you pay a very high price: you give up one more slice of your ability to steer and control your vision. The capacity to exert control over the company's destiny should be of utmost importance to all entrepreneurs and business builders.

With the benefit of hindsight, I have become more skeptical about raising capital—both from venture funds and from the public market. These days, if I were to be offered investment capital for any business that I believed had significant future potential, I'd be very hesitant to accept the money. My new mantra is: "You take the money; I'll take control."

But that's easy to say from where I sit. I'm not strapped for capital. I'm all too keenly aware how difficult it is for early-stage entrepreneurs to navigate that trade-off, just as it once was for me.

Control is something too many entrepreneurs take for granted, until one day they carelessly trade it away in return for a round of investment. If you're too beholden to the agendas of others, particularly investors, you won't be free to make the necessary sacrifices in the short term to protect your dream for the long term. Never forget: capital is a renewable resource. The capacity to control your future, once lost, is gone forever.

Raising capital may be necessary at certain points; I'm not denying that truth. But it should not be thought of as some annual life-cycle event for every young growth company. It's more like the choice to have a child with another person—an act that should be carefully considered with an appreciation of its tremendous, irreversible, long-term consequences.

Before taking on capital, ask yourself: What is your relationship to the business? Is your aim to sell the company and walk away with a mountain of money? Or do you see the enterprise as the fulfillment of a vision—an expression of yourself, your platform to live your dream and make your contribution to the world? If it's the latter, think hard about how to continue to hold the reins when you take on investors. You don't want to end up in a situation where you feel like "they don't get it" ("they" being the investors) and yet they're forcing your hand, maybe even forcing you out the door.

I'll never forget the tears in Steve Jobs's eyes when he was fired from his own company. For all his success, he'd lost control. If it hadn't been for the new leaders' abject failure over the next decade, he'd never have come back. Most leaders in his position never get a second chance.

There's no perfect answer to the challenge of maintaining control while also getting the capital you need to grow. Over time, perhaps we can reform capital markets so that companies are less beholden to short-term investors. In the meantime, there are at least a few things you can do to mitigate the risk of losing control.

One solution is simply to stay private and grow more slowly within your means, by reinvesting the company's profits in new products and services. Since its inception six decades ago, Chick-fil-A has followed that path. The Atlanta-based chain retains ownership over each of its nearly three thousand restaurants and is one of the most valuable and well-respected restaurant companies in America. Because the company is privately held and grew at a rate that allowed it to fund its own growth, the founding family has been able to build a business that embodies and sustains its values. This won't work in every industry, however.

Another option, if you decide to take the enterprise public and you have maintained control up to that point, is to do what Au Bon Pain did, and what other companies including the New York Times, Facebook, and Google have done: create dual classes of stock. Class A common stock, with limited voting rights, is sold in the public markets through Nasdaq or NYSE. Class B shares are offered to founders, executives, and their families. They come with proportionately more voting power and therefore the potential for more control over the company. (At Au Bon Pain, we gave our Class B shares three times more voting power than Class A—a decision I would later come to realize was not enough. I'll tell that story in chapter 20.)

Sure, you may hear from investors that they don't like dual classes of stock. And they don't. But they will accept it, I promise, if your company is strong enough and worthy of going public and you remained the controlling shareholder up until the IPO.

Whatever route you choose for your company, my message to entrepreneurs is this: believe in yourself. You know what you're doing. You wouldn't have gotten here otherwise. You created something special— that's why people want to invest in your company. Raising capital is an unavoidable reality for almost any growing business, and the options for doing so are limited. Taking on investors may be your best option. But never forget: when you take somebody's money, they become your partner.

Partners can be a good thing, especially if they bring valuable experience to the table that can help guide an entrepreneur. But partners have real rights and legitimate opinions, and they're usually not shy about exercising and expressing them. Be strategic in choosing your partners and be sure to maintain as much control as possible during the process.

In the end, there's no perfect answer to the conundrum of capital versus control. But I would urge any entrepreneur to think seriously about what they are giving up in return before going public. Don't be afraid to be a control freak—your ability to execute your vision may depend on it.

Feeding the Growth Monster

"So much for California dreaming," I thought to myself bitterly as I stared out at the blue expanse of the Pacific Ocean. On this warm summer afternoon in the early nineties, the Golden State was at its seductive best—sun-drenched, relaxed, beautiful. No wonder people and businesses had been making this westward journey for centuries, inspired by dreams of better opportunities and a better lifestyle. But for Au Bon Pain, California was where dreams went to die.

My pre-IPO fears hadn't come true right away, but eventually I was proven right. By the time of IPO, Au Bon Pain was a powerful niche business that I estimate had sustained a double-digit rate of growth for almost a decade. That's why our IPO was a success. Immediately after the IPO, we did what every public company does: we took some of our newly raised capital and invested in new store development. It wasn't long, however, before it became apparent that the very thing that made Au Bon Pain special was beginning to limit our growth.

Our ill-fated attempt to expand into California was the clearest sign of it yet. That summer, I spent a miserable month shuttering our seven cafés in the state, less than a year after they opened.

We'd become ubiquitous and popular on the East Coast, but virtually no one in California had heard of Au Bon Pain. They didn't even know how to pronounce it. The air of continental sophistication that had served the brand so well back East didn't translate in California's sprawling suburbs and malls. Au Bon Pain worked best in high-density urban locations like office buildings, transportation centers, and hospitals, where time-pressed consumers were willing to pay a little more for higher-quality food. The concept was designed to move large numbers of businesspeople and shoppers through a tight space in a brief window of time. It traded on the currencies that mattered even more to city dwellers than price alone: quality and speed.

And it depended on location above all. With Louis Kane's real-estate acumen, this had been our strength in the eighties and early nineties, but as we approached the three-hundred-café mark, we had nearly exhausted his best connections in major urban markets like Boston, New York City, Chicago, and Washington, DC. Bottom line, we were running out of locations where Au Bon Pain could thrive.

Our shareholders, however, pushed for more growth. Keep opening more cafés. Keep expanding into new markets. But growth is not just a pedal to be pushed. Growth can only build value if the underlying business model is worthy of being reproduced. Ours was a worthy business model, but only up to a point. Unfortunately, this was not what our investors wanted to hear so soon after the IPO. The growth monster, as I call it, was hungry and demanding to be fed.

• • •

To understand the voracity of the growth monster's appetite, we need to consider the question, What makes a company valuable? As a company builder, I can list many things that define a company's value. The uniqueness of its offering, its recognizable brand, its assets, its potential for impact, its market share, its intellectual property, its expertise, and its people.

But in the eyes of investors, what makes a company (or more precisely, its shares) valuable is something much more mercurial: the perception of future growth. The economic value of any enterprise is not based solely on earnings—it's based on a multiple of those earnings and the multiple is determined by the market's assessment of the company's future growth rate.

Investors pay for growth. So, God forbid you let your growth rate slow down. If you revise your expected growth rate downward, you'll see your multiple plummet and your stock price fall dramatically, even as your reported earnings remain exactly the same. Suddenly your investors are complaining, your board members are hearing about it, and analysts are demanding an explanation. It's like owning a beautiful house but suddenly discovering that your neighborhood isn't trendy anymore. It's the same house, but due to a shift in perception, its value goes down.

As a result, the drumbeat of growth is relentless for a public company. And as a leader, you must march to that drumbeat, even when it goes against your best instincts. You can't ever afford to let people think your growth is slowing. The growth monster demands to be fed, even when you're running out of sustainable ways to satisfy it. As a result, management teams often just keep blindly growing—even if the returns on those new investments are weakening—until they effectively march their companies like lemmings right off the side of the cliff.

Such is the conundrum I found myself in after Au Bon Pain went public. Luckily, if there's one thing I'm good at, it's telling myself the truth, even if my investors don't like it. I wasn't about to walk off the cliff, so I made an unpopular but necessary decision: we would protect Au Bon Pain by letting it grow only at the rate that it could sustain, and we would focus on investing in new business areas that were aligned with our core competencies.

We had, for example, expertise in manufacturing frozen dough, so we built one of the largest frozen dough manufacturing plants in the United States—in Mexico, Missouri—which allowed us to control our own supply chain and create a wholesale business supplying supermarkets and club stores. We were also experts in what I called "high-density urban feeding," but we'd run out of domestic markets with good locations, so we began looking for locations internationally, where there were plenty of cities that fit the bill.

I didn't know as we took on these ventures if either would deliver enough profitable growth to feed the growth monster and drive up the stock price. So, I continued my 24/7 effort to find an opportunity that would put us on the upside of a new growth curve. As it turned out, to borrow a line from an old song, that opportunity would meet me in St. Louis.

Empathy Unlocks
the Future

The opportunity that awaited me in St. Louis wasn't easy to find. Literally. Tucked into the corner of a suburban strip mall, with minimal signage, the small bakery café couldn't have been further from Au Bon Pain's high-visibility locations in places like Rockefeller Center and the World Trade Center.

I'd awoken before dawn to meet Mark Borland, our chief operating officer, and visit this place, and I was starting to wonder if I should have just stayed in bed. After several wrong turns, we finally arrived.

What had initially intrigued me about this little Midwestern bread company selling sandwiches, baked goods, and pastries was that it generated sales on par with the average Au Bon Pain store while paying a fraction of what Au Bon Pain paid for real estate. Seeing customers standing patiently in line as the first rays of sunlight brightened the dingy parking lot that morning told me that people were seeking the place out. Now my curiosity was piqued.

The St. Louis Bread Company had been founded in 1987 by an entrepreneur named Ken Rosenthal, who, inspired by San Francisco's North Beach café scene and artisan bread culture, vowed to bring it to his hometown. Ken and his partners had sought my advice on franchising as they tried to figure out how to expand their company, which consisted at the time of twenty locations in and around the Midwestern hub for which it was named.

My initial reaction was that he was crazy. His company lacked the infrastructure, systems, and discipline necessary to grow and manage a sprawling network of semiautonomous franchisees. At the same time, I could see why he was asking, because I couldn't ignore his sales or his prospects for growth. Which was why I showed up, bleary-eyed, at that strip mall, hoping to experience for myself whether this company might contain an opportunity.

The doors opened and I followed the crowd inside, all my senses on high alert. I inhaled the seductive, comforting aroma of fresh-baked bread. Behind the counter, the source of the aroma—a variety of warm, crusty loaves and pastries—was proudly displayed in baskets up the wall. I studied the decor—Tiffany lamps, green tile. A little dated, but homey, comfortable, and unpretentious. I listened to the tone and cadence of customers' conversations as they waited in line and sat around the café tables. It felt more like they were at a family gathering than running an errand. I noted how the manager greeted many people by their first names.

I was also struck by what I didn't hear—not a hint of grumbling or impatience, even as folks waited ten or fifteen minutes for their loaf of sourdough. If Au Bon Pain had imposed a ten-minute wait on New Yorkers, we'd have been strung up by our apron strings. Was it just Midwestern politeness? Or were the bread and pastries truly worth the wait?

When the crowd dispersed, I made my way to the counter and bought my own loaf of sourdough bread, a bear claw pastry, and an espresso drink. The sourdough was indeed exceptional: crusty, tangy, with substance and texture. The pastry was light, buttery, delicious. And the coffee was authentic cappuccino—something that was hard to come by even in New York back then. Sure enough, I spied an expensive Italian espresso machine behind the counter.

Based on what I saw, heard, smelled, and tasted that day, I sensed an opportunity. It wasn't the product of boardroom brainstorming or exhaustive market research, but rather the product of *empathy*: making the effort to feel what other people were feeling—their needs and desires, and why they were satisfied or disappointed.

Empathy is the key to innovation and the root of all learning because it's the key to human relationships. It's what allows us to connect to each other and bridge the divide between our subjective worlds. It pulls us out of our own mental models, our well-worn habits, to see the world through others' perspectives. And it's what enables us to understand the jobs we can do for our customers.

With all my senses on high alert, I was practicing empathy as I waited in line, ordered, sat down, and ate. And that practice led me to an intriguing question: Could this thriving little company be Au Bon Pain's gateway to the elusive suburban and Midwestern markets?

Rosenthal also saw an opportunity. He knew he and his partners did not have the experience to grow his business. So rather than letting his ego get in the way, he was smart enough to entertain the idea of putting his creation in the hands of an operator who knew how to nurture it, evolve it, and build the capabilities to expand it into multiple markets.

Not long after that initial visit, Au Bon Pain acquired St. Louis Bread Company for $24 million. (In my favorite twist to the story, Ken took that money and used it to become our franchisee, and ultimately grew a franchise business that was four times larger than the one he sold to us. Even better, I'm pleased to say we still love and respect each other—something you can't say about the parties in many other corporate acquisitions.)

I felt confident the magic was there in my newly acquired company. But I also knew that I didn't fully grasp it yet. Like any new business owner, I could see all kinds of things that could be improved and standardized—the St. Louis Bread Company didn't even use the same typeface for its signs or the same decor in its stores, let alone run streamlined production processes. But I wasn't ready to rush in and fix what didn't work before I understood what did work.

The truth is, I've never understood why companies acquire other companies at high prices and then immediately try to change them. I want to know what I've got before I try to make it into something else. I knew we had limited time, but we had to take *some* time to learn what magic needed to be respected and protected. So I put walls around the company and elected to study it.

My initial instinct was that St. Louis Bread Company could give us a path into the suburban market, while Au Bon Pain could go on serving the urban market. I imagined growing it to perhaps three hundred to five hundred stores across the Midwest, taking the pressure off Au Bon Pain to adapt to territory that wasn't its natural habitat.

But I wasn't yet sure, and I couldn't see much further than taking that first step. And I was okay with that—at least for a while.

• • •

If you've read this far in the book, you might think this is at odds with the approach to business I've been sharing—envision the future you want to reach and then plan backward and define the steps you will need to get there. But sometimes, in business and in life, you can't force it.

If the future you're heading toward isn't clear yet, you just need to take a step in the right direction and then pay attention to what unfolds. That doesn't mean you're drifting aimlessly—I knew my ultimate destination, my end. I knew that I was aiming to achieve competitive advantage and build a great company that provided our guests with an experience they couldn't find anywhere else. But I didn't yet know how this little Midwestern bakery would do so. So, I adopted an approach that was more like bodysurfing.

Imagine you're floating in a clear blue ocean—somewhere warm like Hawaii or Mexico. Waves are breaking and rolling toward the white, sandy beach. You know that's where you are headed, so your ultimate destination is clear. And you know that any wave will take you to shore. But not just any wave will do. You take the time you need to scout out the best wave in sight and then catch it and ride it in. And if that wave doesn't get you all the way there, you rest and wait for another opportunity to come along. St. Louis Bread Company looked like a beautiful wave, but I couldn't yet see how far it would take me. So, I let it carry me forward.

Another way I think about this approach is, *be rigid in vision but flexible in execution*. Sometimes we can't see all the steps that will get us where we want to go. But if we keep the vision clear in our minds, we can allow opportunity to unfold and adapt along the way.

It took some guts to give St. Louis Bread Company the time it needed. The pressure to find new avenues for growth was building. The monster was hungry and impatient. Just a couple of months after the acquisition, Au Bon Pain's stock reached a new high. In May 1994, *Nation's Restaurant News* awarded Louis Kane and me the coveted Golden Chain award, which recognized excellence in leadership and achievement in the food service industry. I was honored, but I knew that the work we were being recognized for was already in the rearview mirror. Ironically, even as we accepted the award, Au Bon Pain's growth rate had begun its slow but inexorable descent. A lot was riding on the St. Louis Bread Company.

something relevant beyond its home city, we needed to answer that question. If we were to innovate a new business model that would provide new opportunities, that question had to be answered—fully and deeply. That night in the bar, talking about beer bottle labels, I sensed Dwight was getting close to an answer.

"The label on that bottle is a mirror for who people perceive themselves to be," Dwight continued. "When you have people over and you want to make a good impression, you don't serve them Bud. You serve them Corona or Sam Adams." (Remember, this was 1994, and the "craft" revolution was just beginning. Today, the same point might be made with a triple-hopped IPA from the local microbrewery.) "And when you do so, you're making a statement about who you are."

I nodded, now excited by his direction. It meshed with what we'd observed over the past weeks and months. We were in search of deeper, long-term trends, not short-term fads. We were seeking the signal, not the noise. I could feel we were onto something significant.

These were not mainstream cafés we were studying. We bet that we would learn the most from those businesses that were the least like our industry's incumbents. You can't glean insight into the future from studying the status quo. You must seek out those establishments that are pushing the extremes, pleasing the most discerning customers.

The places we chose were busy, so we spent hours asking customers why they were choosing that place over others. We took note of the atmosphere, the decor, the style of the menus, how the staff worked and the way they dressed, the kinds of people who visited, the things they were talking about. We recorded details of how the artisan breads were baked as well as the ineffable feeling of heart and soul that these places exuded. We started to intuit that people frequented these artisan bakeries and cafés for more than convenience or even pleasure. Something else was at play, but we hadn't quite got it yet.

• • •

We spent countless hours debating and analyzing our on-the-ground observations. We learned by respectfully challenging each other's as-

Discovering Today What Will Matter Tomorrow

"You want to understand today's consumer? Look at the label on their beer bottle."

I was sitting on a barstool, somewhere outside of Chicago, when my friend Dwight Jewson made this pronouncement. I took a swig of my own beer and waited, curious for him to continue. Dwight was a psychologist turned researcher and strategic consultant, with a knack for decoding consumer behavior. In the mid-nineties, he'd become my most valued thinking partner in the quest to discover new opportunities for competitive advantage. Dwight and I spent untold weeks crisscrossing the country along with Scott Davis, the point man for our innovation efforts, trying to figure out what was going to matter to the consumers of tomorrow.

We understood, to paraphrase the science fiction writer William Gibson, that the future had already arrived; it just wasn't evenly distributed. Which was why we spent hundreds of hours in new-wave artisan bakeries and boutique coffeehouses on the West Coast—eating, sipping, observing, taking notes, and discussing. Our intention was to find those small pockets of tomorrow that already existed today and answer a critical question: *What will matter to more and more of middle America in the future?* If we were to give Au Bon Pain a new lease on life or turn the newly acquired St. Louis Bread Company into sumptions and wrestling with what we had seen. Through exhaustive, sometimes exhausting, but often exhilarating rounds of give-and-take, we crystallized our learnings. That night in the bar was one of many such conversations, and we were finally on the brink of a breakthrough.

The first and most obvious trend we identified was something we saw happening across all consumer categories. We recognized it as a quiet uprising: certain consumers were beginning to reject the mass-marketed products that had amassed outsized market shares. I called it "decommodification."

By the early nineties, choices in nearly every consumer category had become limited to a handful of brands. Competitive advantage was based on advertising dollars and distribution. Think Budweiser and Miller beer, Folgers and Maxwell House, or Coke and Pepsi. A growing number of customers who had grown up with these brands now felt they deserved something better. They were seeking out specialty products made the old-fashioned way.

As Dwight pointed out that night at the bar, they rejected the beer brands typically guzzled at a ballpark in favor of craft brews. They would have been offended if I'd pulled out a can of Folgers after dinner; they had begun to grind their own specialty coffee beans at home. And they didn't want Coke or Pepsi; they wanted a Snapple iced tea or an Odwalla juice or any of hundreds of other specialty drinks that were becoming available as alternatives to soda. We knew we needed to understand the deeper trend that was driving the customer behaviors we were observing.

Dwight finally nailed it that night at the bar using his deep emotional intelligence and training in psychology. He made a critical leap of empathy, looking at the beer bottle in his hand. "People don't just want a special product. They want to *feel* special in a world in which they no longer are."

We called this phenomenon "a drive for specialness." Ultimately, it became one of the most powerful trends that defined the consumer marketplace in the late nineties and into the new millennium.

As we considered how our insight impacted multiple product categories, its power and relevance seemed ever more evident. Just as the drive for specialness was happening in beer, coffee, and beverages, we realized, so it was about to happen in food.

To appreciate how profound this insight was at the time, and the process by which we came to it, I invite you to step back in time for a moment. Imagine a world in which your only reliable options for a *quick* lunch across much of the country were fast-food joints like McDonald's and Burger King. If you grew up in the sixties, seventies, or eighties, no doubt you remember it well. Back then fast food was special. (I remember attending the grand opening of a Burger King with my dad. Could you imagine that today?) Fast food offered an alternative to a lengthy dining experience. You could grab a burger and fries within minutes, for not too much money, and fill your stomach so you could get back to work.

If you grew up with a Starbucks on every block, a Whole Foods Market down the street, and Panera and Chipotle around the corner, you might find this former reality hard to believe. If you're accustomed to walking down to the local park and taking your pick among a dozen food trucks, you might have forgotten how recently those didn't exist. None of that existed in the world in which I was doing business in the early nineties. But we saw that future coming.

How would the restaurant industry evolve in reaction to these new consumer trends and how did we want to position our business so that those trends were a tailwind for us? That was the question Dwight, Scott, and I were trying to figure out.

We began our brainstorming by giving voice to what we observed. We recognized that a growing number of consumers wanted that feeling of specialness. And fast food made them feel anything but special. They didn't want to look too closely at the Formica tables, plastic seats, or paper hats on employees. They held their noses and went to fast-food restaurants even if they didn't want to because it was their only option to get food quickly—like a self-service gasoline station for the human body. These consumers felt bad about that choice, and it made them feel bad about themselves. They had a hunger that went beyond food. They wanted experiences that they respected and that respected them—indeed, elevated them and their sense of self rather than depleting their sense of self. In a society where real meaning felt hard to come by, they craved small, everyday experiences that added up to something bigger, including in the meals they ate. Their choice of food was not just a way to fill their stomachs; it was an opportunity to assert their individuality and feel good about themselves.

These were the people we found in the West Coast cafés we'd visited—places that served real food in engaging and unique environments with a side of positive energy, warmth, and humanity. We began to feel in our bones the opportunity this represented.

It was so clear to us that specialty food was a revolution reaching its time, and so far, no one had done it at scale. We were determined to be first. We felt that we had seen the future. We could imagine a food concept that elevated self-esteem but was still quick. It would be to fast food what Samuel Adams had been to Bud. And this new food concept would be built around bread—because the very same "desire for specialness" we'd been observing in most major consumer categories was happening in the bread business as well.

Bread had once been made in small bakeries by local bakers, but after World War II the bread industry was consolidated, and bread became a commodity. Brands like Wonder Bread were sold at the supermarket, three loaves for $0.99. By the nineties, part of the drive for specialness meant consumers were seeking better bread and local bakers were starting to provide it. They were producing extraordinary loaves the old-fashioned way, using traditional ingredients and methods and shunning additives, preservatives, dough enhancers, or chemicals. Artisan bread-making was a new and quiet revolution, started by pioneers like San Francisco's Grace Bakery and Vancouver's Terra Breads. Their bread put to shame the bland, factory-produced fare in supermarkets. We'd tasted the breads in those cafés we visited, and we came to believe that artisan bread could be a powerful platform that defined the authority of the specialty food establishment we imagined.

We didn't have a name for what we hoped to create, but in the years to come, as our vision began to turn into a reality and the trends we'd observed solidified, the term "fast casual" would come to define this experience. My colleagues and I, along with Howard Schultz at Starbucks and later Steve Ells at Chipotle, were among the first to see where things were going. We all connected the dots and intuited that they represented a broader trend in society and in our industry—a trend that would eventually be labeled the fast-casual sector.

For what it's worth, I don't much like the term "fast casual." I've yet to hear someone say, "Hey! Let's go to a fast-casual restaurant!" But a good innovation has a life of its own, and no matter how much the innovators may want to, they can't control the way it takes root in the culture at large.

Regardless, I am profoundly proud that I recognized what fast casual could be, and that it has ended up being a $100 billion–plus market segment and a revolution in the dining experience of hundreds of millions of people.

• • •

It's a cliché to ask, "What business are you *really* in?" but I'm amazed by how many restaurant owners and operators think they're in the food business. They're not. They're in the experience business, and food is only a part of that equation. All the time and energy spent observing and analyzing our West Coast adventures helped Dwight, Scott, and I recognize that by creating an elevated experience in our cafés, we could tap into the growing niche of people who wanted to feel better about their "quick dining" experiences. The job some customers wanted to hire us for wasn't simply to deliver a great-tasting quick breakfast or lunch for not much money. It was to serve them great food and beverages while giving them back a bit of their dignity. To make them feel special again.

Everything we discovered during this formative period resulted from answering the most important question: What matters? Unless you take the time to learn what matters, you'll miss the opportunity to discover truly significant trends, address the deepest human needs, and build something that will have real impact. Dwight's insight at the bar was the culmination of a long and focused learning journey, driven by questions such as:

> Who are our customers? How do we understand the structure and niches of the market?

> What matters to the target consumers in each niche? What do they want?

> What jobs do they need us to complete?

> And what do we have to do better than our competitors to win their loyalty?

Most leaders don't take enough time to do this learning. Learning mode is not a comfortable place to be because it means first admitting that you don't have all the answers and then gathering the patience and humility to explore many possible options. But unless you truly understand what matters to your customers, you're shooting in the dark. As your company grows, it may be tempting to shunt your market research efforts off into an R&D department or an external consulting firm. Don't. Stay directly involved. To me, getting out of the office to connect with customers is the most important thing a leader can do, which was why I made those trips with Dwight and Scott, just as I'd personally made the first visit to St. Louis Bread Company.

Most of our learning on those trips was built on developing deep empathy with customers. Empathy requires that you pull away from your own concerns and obsessions and extend yourself—emotionally and mentally—into another person's mind and experiences. This is not surface level. You need to get in customers' heads and feel the world as they feel it. It won't always make sense to you, as we tend to be stuck in our own mental models, assuming that the rest of the world thinks the same way. We are so often unwitting prisoners of our own paradigms and quick to assume we understand before we've taken the time to do so. It's little wonder so many businesspeople come up with innovations that look good on paper but fail in practice. It's because they aren't rooted in empathy.

People don't always know what they really want or need, which is why focus groups often fail to provide useful insights. A well-developed sense of empathy gets to the roots of the customer's problems. It's based on all the observation I've talked about in these past few chapters: taking note of physical details, reading body language, asking questions, listening and most importantly, watching what people do. Then, once you start to connect to something that matters, you need to be patient, step back, and look to extract the generalization—the broader patterns that might confirm the relevance of the need you've uncovered. This is the work of the innovator.

As the astute business thinker Simon Sinek has said, "People don't buy WHAT you do, they buy WHY you do it."[1] If we had stayed at the surface level and responded to product trends or made cosmetic changes to the design of our cafés, we might have hooked a few more hungry diners, but we'd never have been able to understand and then satisfy the deeper hunger that we were sensing and in the process create a whole new segment of the restaurant industry.

Even as we built on Dwight's insight on the drive for specialness, we had no idea what "fast casual" would become, but we knew we were onto something that mattered. We began to sketch out a vision of a café that would be built on relationships instead of transactions; a café that filled a bit of your soul as well as your stomach; a café that was an oasis from the rush of everyday life rather than an amplifier of it. We could imagine a "specialty food" café, built on the authority of artisan bread. We could see it, feel it, taste it. Now we just had to get the job done and bring it to life.

Defining What You Stand For

At the end of our two-year "listening tour" of the West Coast café scene, Dwight, Scott, and I could begin to conjure up a picture of what we wanted to create. It was like a collage of our favorite features—the kind of thing you might create on Pinterest today. We loved the thick-cut sandwiches from Café Intermezzo. The artisan breads from Terra. The smell of the Honeybear Cafe. We had to take what we had learned about the powerful trends that were playing out in consumer society— the pushback against commodification, the drive toward specialty and craft, and the widespread desire for community—and create from them a totally new customer experience that would land us in the path of the food industry's future.

But we worried that when the time came for others to execute on our vision, on what was so clear to us, much of it would get lost in translation. How do you capture your vision and communicate it such that thousands (and, soon enough, tens of thousands) of designers, chefs, bakers, vendors, franchisees, and frontline associates, not to mention senior management, can not only get it but make it happen just as you imagine it? In short, how do you get *alignment*?

Our first step was to create a document we called Concept Essence.

A Concept Essence isn't a business plan. It doesn't contain financial projections, market analysis, or sales strategies. All that comes later.

This document answers the essential question: *What will make us special in the eyes of our target guest?* Or, put another way, *where is our authority derived?* And it outlines how we hope our target customer will experience us. Its purpose is to break down the answers to those questions and communicate them so powerfully that anyone who picks it up and reads it will be able to execute the vision.

A Concept Essence is the emotional blueprint for how a company is going to go to market and how it intends to compete—its competitive DNA, so to speak. It illustrates an end-to-end vision of what we deliver to our guests and how. It captures the personality of the brand being envisioned. Think of it as a watercolor painting, rather than a detailed architectural plan. Because I'm not an artist, I can't paint a picture of what I'm seeing, but I can use words to sketch it in detail and thereby fuel other people's ability to envision it.

Done well, it becomes the brand's primary tool for navigating into the future—the North Star by which we plot our course and keep our course, even when waters are rough.

I did my most creative work on a document that would become the Concept Essence for Panera Bread over Labor Day weekend in 1995 at the St. Louis Bread Company café on Halstead Street in Chicago. We'd gone through months of rough drafts, but now the document needed to be taken to the next level. Over that weekend, I worked on it for sixteen hours a day, my table piled high with the notes from the observations I'd made out in the field. My aim was to crystallize the vision, using my notes as a touchpoint for how my thinking had developed. I wanted to distill the concept down to its very essence. I labored over every word. To me, they were like notes in the score of a symphony. It wasn't enough for them to be almost in harmony—every single note had to resonate, and every note had to make sense with every other note; otherwise there would be discord when a whole orchestra sat down to play them.

I'd say the words out loud, testing whether they captured what I wanted to convey. When your voice bends air and sounds become words, you hear them differently than when they're echoing inside your head. The process of speaking words aloud forces you to think about the things you're trying to communicate most deeply. When I finally started to find the right words, I could feel them resonate in my soul.

Then, I shared them with my trusted inner circle—Scott, Dwight, and our design partner Terry Heckler—and the refining began. We examined this latest draft of Concept Essence through multiple lenses and from multiple angles. Did it effectively define the concept's approach to food, design, service, and personality? How would it affect the customer? How would it affect the team members working within it? How operationally achievable was it? Most importantly, did our words capture with precision what would make us stand out in the marketplace, where our authority and credibility would be derived?

Slowly, we shared the final Concept Essence with broader and broader circles in the company, continuing to polish and perfect it. All told, we must have spent nine months working on that four-page document. And not a moment of that time was wasted.

• • •

Creating a Concept Essence serves two important purposes. First, it forces the innovator to define the future in vivid and precise terms, turning it around and looking at it from all sides. Doing this rigorously is a necessary test for the opportunity you think you're seeing. It's one thing to have a glimpse of a need in the marketplace. It's another thing to construct a persuasive intellectual and emotional vision of how to meet the needs of your target customers.

Second, a Concept Essence is a tool to sell your vision of the future to those who must execute on it. How do you get a group of people to share a vision of something that does not yet exist? How do you get them to align around it so that what they create is faithful to your original intentions? The orchestra needs a score. If the concept is muddy, sooner or later the company will lose focus. It might not happen right away, but as the effort scales, bad outcomes are inevitable.

Even as we worked on this document, a cautionary tale was playing out for us in our own company. Au Bon Pain had started out with a powerful, innovative idea, but as it scaled, it was losing the characteristics that made it stand out from fast food. If managers and associates don't have an intellectual and emotional grasp of the essence of a company's authority and differentiation, the concept will revert to the mean and lose that essence, becoming like everything else.

A good Concept Essence acts as a self-regulating device for individuals and teams throughout a company. Not only does it guide the initial creation process; it's a touchstone they can refer to again and again in decision-making as the company grows and evolves. Done well, a Concept Essence should have a long life—remaining essentially unchanged for many years, maybe decades. That's not to say a Concept Essence should never be questioned or revised—sometimes a company reaches an inflection point where such a fundamental reinvention is necessary. But it's not something to do lightly. Just as your personality may change and evolve over time, so too can a brand's, but it's a process that happens gradually over decades, not overnight on a whim.

Our country's founding fathers knew this when they wrote the Constitution—wrestling with the words and phrases that would unite a new nation. I like to imagine them working through the night—debating, testing, defending, questioning each line of a document that they intended to stand the test of time. The Constitution doesn't spell out every detail of how the nation will work; rather, it articulates the principles that underlie our laws and processes. It is not entirely inflexible, but it is clear in intent and is not easy to change. And it is aspirational—centuries after it was written we are still striving to live up to its ideals and form a "more perfect union." A good Concept Essence works the same way. A business may spend years, even decades, trying to grow into the vision that was laid out in its founding documents.

No Concept Essence document is perfect, nor is that its goal. But it should offer significant clarity on who you hope to be—with somewhere in the range of 80 to 85 percent certainty. There will always be things to tweak or adjustments to make in response to new information. But if you can get it largely right before you move into the phase of creating what you envision, you'll save yourself so much work in the long run.

Some people might balk at giving so much time and energy to words on a page. But words matter. Words precede actions. To this day, I'm certain there are folks who roll their eyes when I sit down to work on yet another version of a company's Concept Essence statement, or when I spend hours debating a particular word or phrase. But I know that getting it right is the difference between that vision coming to life as a fully differentiated concept and it becoming another copycat.

I've often been called relentless by those who've worked with me during the innovation process. And it's true—I am relentless, especially when I've locked my sights on an opportunity. I'm relentless in asking the question, What matters? And when I start to get a glimpse of an answer, I'm relentless in developing, clarifying, testing, and refining that answer until it becomes an unforgettable concept—first on paper, then in the physical world. I don't care if meetings run late into the night, if we spend an hour getting a single word or phrase just right. Good enough never is. Getting the essence right is everything.

At the height of Panera's success, we had thousands of bakery cafés. But what we really had was one bakery café, done correctly, replicated thousands of times. If we hadn't gotten that one right—in its essence— we would never have had the opportunity to build thousands.

So many times, I've seen smart, talented people jump to action without truly understanding what it is that they are trying to create. And as a result, they fail. The outcome is clichéd or irrelevant. The power behind lasting innovations comes from the willingness to continue to ask what matters—to stay with that question a little longer than it feels comfortable. If you want to create something of enduring relevance in this world—whether it be a business or even public policy—don't skip this step. Don't be afraid to subject it to the test of putting it down on paper. Take the time to truly define the solution you are imagining. Knowing what will matter tomorrow—and being able to clearly see it, feel it, state it, and communicate it to the people who you need to help

Highlights of Panera's Concept Essence

The document we created in 1996 contained our answer to the questions, "What makes us special? What makes us a better competitive alternative? From where do we derive our authority? Why do we stand out in the marketplace?" The details of what made this answer so powerful are to some extent situational, a product of the era and the market in which we were operating. In today's world, they resonate differently than they did back then. But when I read them, I can still feel the vitality that every key word held for us as we reached into the future and put our stake in the ground for a new kind of restaurant experience.

- "Bread is our passion, soul, and expertise."
- "Our food must be as good as our bread."
- "We build trust through relationships with our customers and communities. We are a club that allows our customers to feel good about themselves. We are of them. Our brand can be trusted."
- "We are an everyday oasis for our customers."

For each of these statements, we wrote paragraphs expanding on its meaning and the way in which we would bring it to life. That original document, once completed, remained our North Star for almost two decades, until the time came to rewrite it around a revised vision in 2015. This document, more than anything else, was the singular element that created $7.5 billion in value.

you bring it to life—dramatically increases the probability you will produce the outcomes you desire.

As I reread the carefully chosen words of Panera's original Concept Essence today, I find myself wondering—will readers get it? Will it just sound like another corporate mission statement posted on the wall to be ignored? Even I must make an effort to reinhabit the world in which those words and phrases have freshness, meaning, and vitality. But in a sense, that is the greatest testament to how powerful they were.

We now live in the world that was only an imprecise vision back then. Our intuition of what would matter to our future customers was right. The ripples we were sensing became a powerful tide that completely transformed our industry and the world we live in—so much so that we take it for granted, and those words feel like clichés today. And I don't think it's hubris to say that in some small way, Panera helped to create that new world—because we identified a new niche, discovered what would matter to our target customers in that niche, and were relentless in our pursuit of that future.

Getting It Done

As our Concept Essence was coming into being, Au Bon Pain continued to explore avenues for growth, though none proved sufficient to slow its decline. St. Louis Bread Company, however, was more promising. We'd begun placing some strategic bets inspired by the observations we were making in the field. We fed what we learned from those bets back into the vision we were creating.

We knew St. Louis Bread Company had the potential to fulfill the desire for specialty food, with its authority rooted in artisan breads. But how were we to create a sustainable economic model that promised a high return on investment? I knew that the only way to generate sufficient sales and a strong ROI is to turbocharge the asset—that is, to use the asset (read: the café) to meet multiple needs and ensure that customers are patronizing us at all times of the day.

St. Louis Bread Company cafés were anything but turbocharged when we bought them. They were cavernous (we used to call them "bowling alleys") and remained largely empty for much of the day, except for lunchtime, when people flocked in for sandwiches made on the exceptional bread, and the soups and salads we'd added to the menu.

One of the first bets we made was to build on our authority in sourdough bread and go beyond lunch. By adding sourdough bagels, we filled the cafés for breakfast and goosed average sales per café by approximately $5,000 a week.

Even with that positive result, the cafés were still mostly empty at other times during the day. How could we change that? One day, as I was working in one of our bakery cafés, I noticed that many customers were finishing their lunches and then . . . not leaving. I saw one woman working at a table in a corner. I walked up, introduced myself, and asked her what she was working on.

"I teach at the school around the corner," she replied. "This is a good place to do my lesson plan."

Four guys were sitting at a nearby table, their sandwiches long finished. They told me they were taking a break from their jobs at a nearby tech plant and talking sports. At another table, a man who was reading the local paper said he was catching a few minutes of alone time before heading home to his wife and kids. And at another, a group of moms were catching up over coffee before picking up their kids from football practice. A couple of them had strollers pulled up with babies strapped in—there was plenty of space around the table for all of them.

It hit me. If we could create an environment in which people wanted to sit and linger, they would naturally purchase more beverages, baked goods, and food.

To veterans of the fast-food business, where restaurants are intentionally designed to be slightly uncomfortable to encourage table turnover, inviting customers to linger was heresy. But we were looking to reinvent the status quo, not validate it. And I began to see an opportunity to build sales in the so-called shoulder hours between meals, a time when the cafés had plenty of excess capacity. Indeed, we could become more than a place for meals; we could become a venue to connect, study, conduct interviews, meet with Bible study groups, gossip with friends, write the Great American Novel, or simply catch a breath.

Once again, observing our customers' behavior with empathy allowed us to see an emerging trend. There was a need in our culture for a place that is not home and not work—a "gathering place" as we began to call it. People hungered for a place to come together.

Starbucks is often credited with mainstreaming the idea of a "third space," but its version was much more suited to single individuals, since most Starbucks cafés had just a handful of seats. Our cafés, because we had a hundred or more seats, could offer a true gathering space. We started to see that if we created the right kind of environments for people to gather—infused with positive, welcoming energy—our guests would seek us out. The price of admission would be low, a sandwich or a cup of coffee. They would come for the environment and stay for the food. We concluded that we could and should be in the community-building business. And that made real economic sense. That gathering-place business quickly added approximately $10,000 a week in sales per café.

Offering multiple customer solutions from one platform was turbocharging the asset. Taken together, these smart bets would eventually increase our average sales per café from approximately $1 million to almost $1.75 million annually and fuel a high ROI model that worked and deserved to be replicated in cafés all across America.

• • •

However, not all the bets we made paid off like this. We tried selling bread merchandise, for example, and it was a huge flop, though luckily a flop contained within a test. That luck is the result of another important principle of my approach to innovation: get it right before you replicate. It's an approach that can seem at odds with today's "fail fast," minimum-viable-everything innovation culture. Any innovator must be willing to experiment and to fail, but I'm a firm believer in taking the time to think things through, test them, and do everything possible to short-circuit problems before they arise—especially in a large, asset-heavy business like restaurants, where each new unit can cost a million dollars or more.

"Fail fast" might work when it comes to software. "Done is better than perfect" might be an appropriate mantra for Facebook. When speed-to-market is your priority, minimally viable may be sufficient. But if you're trying to build a lasting brand, to create a relationship with your customers for the long term, and you're dealing with fixed assets, you've got to put in the work to get it right up front lest you have to scrap your innovation and reengineer things later. In the real world, where tens of thousands of employees depend on you and fund managers are putting billions of dollars of people's hard-earned money behind you, crashing into rocks along the way can't be par for the course. Each false start erodes the trust of your board, your investors, and your team and hacks away at your credibility, which is a leader's most valuable currency. Credibility buys you latitude to implement your vision. Repeated missteps will eventually lead to you losing control.

• • •

By the mid-nineties, the pieces were coming together. The bets we'd made in our St. Louis Bread Company stores were paying off, and we had an economic model that was beginning to work. Key to that was the development of a physical manifestation of our Concept Essence. What should be the touch points that translated the concept into a three-dimensional space? Were there aspects of the vision that wouldn't easily coexist? What trade-offs might need to be made? Could it be built within the financial constraints of our economic model? And above all, would our customers get the message that we were trying to communicate when they walked through our doors?

We took over a café in the Stratford Square Mall in Bloomingdale, Illinois. Until this point, although we'd changed many things about the way the Bread Company cafés ran, we'd left the actual spaces largely untouched. Now, we were ready to make changes—and not just new paint colors or furniture. Our intention was to strip the place down to the studs and start over, creating a fully working archetype of Concept Essence. A bakery café that was warm, contemporary, and refined; an oasis where families and friends could gather, or office workers could take a break from the day. We didn't yet have a name for our new place, so we code-named it the Wheat Store.

The team often turned to the principles in Concept Essence for guidance. For example, we focused on graphic design rather than architectural design, allowing us to easily change and update the look and feel of the café by changing signage and decor. Scott and his team had worked closely with Terry Heckler and our in-house designer, Tony Coleman, to create a design-driven experience. At all costs, we avoided the typical trappings of fast-food chains, such as disposable plates and cheap plastic menus. Every detail—from the round tables that encouraged conversation to the comfy leather chairs by the fireplace to the colorful banners to the artfully spotlit wall of fresh bread to the warm earth tones of the decor to the real plates to the lack of uniforms—was designed to communicate integrity, warmth, and respect, to build a connection with customers and make the store feel as welcoming as home.

I met with the team monthly during the six-month build, and I reviewed pictures of the work in progress, but I chose not to visit the site in person. This in itself was a test. Had my vision translated powerfully enough through Concept Essence that they could build it without me there to translate and explain?

Staying away is not staying out of the details though. Every little thing mattered to me. In my view, the small stuff *is* the big stuff. Innovation leaders must move seamlessly from the big vision to the nitty-gritty, which brings the vision to life. Strategy without detail is impotent; detail without strategy is directionless. Sustained innovation comes from mastering the details and making incremental improvements while never losing sight of what matters and where you are going.

Even with my constant engagement and focus on details, I wasn't prepared for what happened when I first visited the completed café. I stepped into the Wheat Store and the first words out of my mouth were, "I've found God."

• • •

I don't mean to offend anyone's faith with this, but it really felt like nothing short of a religious experience. There, in suburban Illinois, was our vision—Concept Essence—brought to life in three-dimensional glory. Every detail reflected the future we'd been pursuing and debating and laboring to put on paper for more than two years. We'd worked backward from that future to create this physical space and filled it with the things we'd identified as being *what matters tomorrow*. The things our customers hungered for. The things that would allow them to feel special, connected, respected. It exceeded my every expectation.

The Wheat Store was more than a new design. It also provided a test lab in which we could bring together all our innovations and subject them to the operational realities of our business. Concept Essence was driven by intuition and empathy; refining the Wheat Store was driven by real-world experience. It was an accelerated learning process where we could see what worked and what didn't, make improvements, and confirm that they delivered the desired results. If something worked at the Wheat Store, then and only then would we be confident enough to roll out the new concept to more locations.

When we did so, it would not be to St. Louis Bread Company cafés. We elected to brand all cafés outside St. Louis as Panera Bread. Panera, as a brand name, was an empty vessel, which was perfect, as we could inject the personality we wanted into it. There is no Joey Panera. In fact, "Panera" is a made-up word—a mash-up of Latin and Spanish that we translated roughly into "time of bread." We bought into the name, intellectually and emotionally, through our logo, which personified the nourishing warmth of our brand in the form of a woman we named Mother Bread.

All of these key brand assets were born out of our original Concept Essence. And we had a three-word shorthand that summed up all of it and became a touchstone for our vision: *Share the warmth.*

Warmth. That was what I felt when I first set foot in the Wheat Store—the kind of warmth that makes you feel nurtured and special. To this day, I look back on that moment as probably the most gratifying in my business career. It far outshines the more typical highlights, such as going public or selling the company. I *loved* our new café—and so did our customers. I could hardly wait to transform the rest of the locations. And start opening more.

You Don't Own the Business; the Business Owns You

If this were a business fairy tale, we'd be close to the end now. I'd tell you the story of how we rolled out our new concept and lived happily ever after. And eventually we did—though it certainly wasn't a direct line between points.

But this isn't a fairy tale, and it wouldn't be fair for me to leave out another, darker chapter in my story. In fact, it's not even another chapter; it's the other side of the chapter I've just written—the one you just read.

All through those seemingly sunny, optimistic years in the mid-nineties when we were conceiving and creating Panera Bread, I was also confronting distrust, a flat stock price, and a fast-decelerating growth curve that I had known was coming for some time. At the very same time that I was engaged in my most creative work—studying new-wave coffeehouses, discovering fast casual, prototyping what would become Panera—I was fighting with board members who told me I was washed up, finished, and out of touch. The very same month I was writing Concept Essence, my dad told me he had cancer. The very same time that the Wheat Store was proving the success of my vision,

I was confronting the looming failure of my short-lived first marriage. And at the very same time that we were conceiving Panera, Au Bon Pain—my first child—was on life support.

In retrospect, midwifing Panera's birth looks like a happy heroic tale of breakthroughs and innovations. But those years were hard and sometimes harrowing. I was barely past forty, but some days I felt like I was twice that. Maybe I was washed up. I sure was tired. Part of me wished the board would go ahead and oust me so I could be free of this burden. It wasn't so much that I was sick of running the business. I was sick of the business running my life.

It's an uncomfortable truth about being an entrepreneur or company builder: you don't own the business; the business owns you. It's with you night and day—when you're taking a shower in the morning, when you're out on a date with someone you want to be in the moment with, or when you're taking a long-dreamed-of vacation. Most people who build businesses can neither turn off nor throttle down their commitment to their pursuit. For me, it's an addiction of sorts. I thrive on solving problems no one else can—and often those solutions begin to unfold while I'm out for a run or sitting on the beach with my business challenges right by my side.

This addiction exacts a high price. For every great quarter you get to celebrate, there are dozens of family dinners missed. For every breakthrough innovation, there's a personal tragedy that you just swallow while you keep showing up to work, every day. For every happy customer who shakes your hand and thanks you for creating something they love, there's a disappointed spouse at home who doesn't understand why you were late to dinner, yet again. For every milestone IPO or sale that proves the company made it, there's a marriage that didn't. For every day you see your vision come to life and think you've found God, there are countless nights when you wonder if there's any rhyme or reason to the universe.

The Hollywood version of the entrepreneurial story is about high-flying, confident risk-takers who beat the odds and retire young. Say the word "boss" and most people imagine a well-heeled executive, jetting between meetings, bellowing directives that faithful employees dutifully execute. Entrepreneurship and leadership in the real world are a grind—filled with disappointments, setbacks, and failure. You're constantly plagued by self-doubt. And even when your personal life is falling apart, you have to keep showing up for everyone else.

My mother's sudden death in 1992 kicked off a decade of loss and grief, during which I simultaneously felt acutely responsible for the morale and livelihoods of tens of thousands of employees and yet suffered extraordinary personal pain. I believed in Panera and the opportunity we were pursuing, but success would not be assured until the future played out. I could see the end zone, but I felt like I was trying to run down the field with eleven defensive tackles on my back. I had a failing company, a mutinous board, and a seemingly endless parade of personal trauma. I wondered if I'd ever get there, or if Panera would just get trampled into the mud somewhere midfield.

To me, these are details that need to be shared—and not just as a dramatic prelude to the eventual happy ending. The tough times are ongoing, and anyone who is serious about building a business or making any kind of meaningful, sustained impact in the world needs to be prepared to embrace that reality.

To be clear—in sharing the personal pain and heartache I went through, I'm not seeking sympathy. Believe me, I wouldn't change any of it, because it was part of an amazing learning journey that made me the person I am today. And I did some of my best work under the looming cloud of a drawn-out existential crisis. My hope is only to offer a more authentic accounting of the entrepreneurial life—both the highs and the lows—because in reality they often can't be separated.

• • •

When things are going well, everyone wants to be your friend—even the banks. During Au Bon Pain's initial growth, we'd been courted by Citizens Bank. It had virtually begged us to take a loan, and eventually we did, obtaining a $30 million line of credit to speed up our growth. The moment our same-store sales (a key metric for measuring a restaurant's vitality) went flat, however, everything changed.

We'd never missed a loan payment, but the moment our aura of growth and promise began to dim, the bank freaked out. Without warning, we were put in "workout," which is not what it sounds like. It doesn't mean the bank wants to work things out with the company. It wants to work your loan out of its portfolio. I had to endure weekly meetings with the workout group—the bank's tough guys—and hear their audacious suggestions that we use their consultants to tell us how to run our business.

The bank's sudden change in attitude seemed like a metaphor for many of my business relationships during those years. Au Bon Pain had always felt like family, with my dad on the board and my partner, Louis, like a favorite uncle. As they both battled cancer, board seats were filled by different kinds of folks. They were good businesspeople, but it was just business for them. For me, it was intensely personal.

I blamed myself—not necessarily for the limitations of the business model, but for the failure to find a new opportunity fast enough. Yes, we were "working on a dream," to quote one of my favorite Bruce Springsteen songs, but we were also working in a reality that wasn't pretty. Not only was Au Bon Pain running on fumes, St. Louis Bread Company was also bumping up against the limits of its infrastructure and operating processes as the old management team attempted to expand into new markets. I was commuting to St. Louis weekly to stop the bleeding because I felt like there was no one else I could trust with that task.

All of the harsh realities of a weakening business bore down on me, every minute of every day. I agonized over whether we'd make payroll, worried about whether I could turn the ship before we all went down. The anxiety wouldn't even leave me when I slept—it would well up in the middle of the night, jolting me awake and leaving me exhausted by the break of day.

Compounding all the apprehension and uncertainty was the utter loneliness. I had no one else to turn to. I spent solitary hours contemplating challenges and weighing options before making hard decisions no one else wanted to make. The toughest ones were left to me, and their success or failure was ultimately my responsibility. And no one could spare me the self-questioning that inevitably accompanies such decisions. Even today, after decades of success, I still grapple with this agonizing doubt.

At its best, the entrepreneurial life is filled with camaraderie and the joys of collaboration. But the hard truth is that when the winds blow against you, you often realize that you're on your own. People who cheer you on or even join you for the ride still don't carry the burden like you do.

As the board doubted me and banks worked me out, I was faced with the looming losses of the two father figures who'd had my back for so long. I watched my once vital and athletic father suffer through six surgeries and chemotherapy and then die. Louis Kane's health was failing, too, but to protect the company, the stoic ex-Marine told everyone at work that he had a gastrointestinal infection, and he could deal with it. Only I knew that in fact he was battling advanced pancreatic cancer.

All through the mid-1990s, when I took my annual break at the close of each year—usually a time of reflection and planning—I would lie in bed at night, look up at the ceiling, and ask out loud, as if someone was listening: "How can things possibly get any worse? They can't get any worse, right?" But, for so many years, I was wrong. The downward spiral continued.

This might all sound like a dramatic preamble to a lesson in work-life balance. It's not. In my view, there is no such thing as balance. There are only trade-offs. There are choices. And for me, my work has always been every bit as important as my family or personal life. But they aren't always equal. At times, one takes precedence over the other.

I don't draw a hard line between my work life and my home life. I want my kids to see the joy and pain of what I do and understand that sometimes I bring it home with me. And I want my colleagues at work to see my family popping up in the middle of my workday and being given my full attention, if only momentarily. That's why I'd often get my kids up on stage with me at the annual Panera Family Reunions. My work is an extension of my personal values, and as such, I can't relegate it to a convenient box that I can close up at 5 p.m. every day and forget. The kinds of struggles I've been describing are unavoidable for someone who is trying to authentically make a difference in the world. Of course, I wouldn't wish a decade of death, divorce, and decelerating growth on anyone. But it happens. Life happens. And through times like that, you've got to be willing to accept that you're not going to feel peace again anytime soon.

To survive the challenges of the entrepreneurial life, there's only one prescription I can offer: love the work. And I do—that's why, even in sharing these harsh realities of leadership, I'm not complaining. I love the work; I love it for its own sake. Nothing else—not the money, and certainly not the spotlight—will get you through the tough times. Those are wonderful by-products, but they can't be the end you are shooting for. Every entrepreneur who hopes to succeed must have the fortitude to endure the tough times, to remember what matters, and to make the hard choices necessary to bring what matters to life.

Business (and Life) Requires Hard Choices

There are moments in life when your whole perspective is turned on its head—when you experience what can only be described as a paradigm shift. For me, one such moment came during Christmas break in 1996. It was a couple of months after I'd walked into our completed Wheat Store and felt like I'd found God, but now I was sitting on a beach in the Caribbean—one of the most beautiful spots in the world—and feeling profoundly unsettled.

What occupied my mind that day, like most days, was my company. Specifically, the division of the company we'd now named Panera Bread. I knew instinctively that it was something truly rare in the restaurant world. Panera had a real shot at evolving into a nationally dominant brand—something only one in a thousand concepts ever achieve. It had just had a phenomenal year, posting double-digit annual same-store sales gains. The new café format was beloved by customers. But it was the second smallest division of the company, with just a modest number of cafés dotted across the Midwest. Au Bon Pain was the established, legacy brand. And Panera would require significant investment of time, energy, and human and financial capital if it were to grow into its potential. Mostly, I worried that we weren't taking proper care of this precious but still unproven gem, because it was just one division among many that needed our company resources.

Meanwhile, Au Bon Pain was flatlining and devouring capital and resources in the process. Same-store sales were negative in the third quarter. We'd poured money into a new dough manufacturing plant in Mexico, Missouri, thinking it would turn the tide, but as the company scaled back its expansion, we couldn't provide the new plant with enough volume to make it worthwhile.

The bottom line was, we couldn't access sufficient capital to revitalize Au Bon Pain *and* grow Panera, nor could our human capital successfully support both.

We also seemed to be mired in constant infighting, as team members tussled over resources. Au Bon Pain folks resented Panera people for siphoning the cash that the larger unit was generating. The Panera team griped that their speedboat of a business was tethered to a foundering old ship. The guys in manufacturing were trying to figure out why they were in the retail business. And the guys in international never wanted to call home. Although I tried not to take sides, my greatest fear was that Au Bon Pain's problems were distracting us from the once-in-a-lifetime opportunity that was Panera.

Sitting on that beach, a place where I do a lot of my best thinking, I poured out my concerns to a friend. He was quiet for a moment, then turned to me with a simple but radical question that shifted the entire paradigm of my thinking:

"What if, instead of Au Bon Pain owning Panera, Panera owned Au Bon Pain?"

The answer came out of my mouth before I could rationalize it away:

"If I had any guts, I'd sell the other divisions of Au Bon Pain, take the capital and the best people, and bet everything on ensuring Panera is able to fulfill its destiny. And I'd move down to St. Louis myself and make it happen!"

The choice was clear—if I had the courage to make it.

• • •

Leadership—and life—is all about choices. You can be a victim to circumstances and other people's agendas, or you can make a choice. The choice may not always be clear at first, and once it becomes clear, the choice may not be easy to make. But it's still yours to make. And the quality of your business and your life depends on you doing so. When you reach that deathbed moment and you're reviewing your life, you'll realize that everything comes down to the choices you made and the will and skill you brought to the path you chose.

The pertinent adage here is, you can do anything, but you can't do everything. Most people can only do a handful of things well in a lifetime. So, if you're going to do things well, you need to do less. You need to pick the things that matter and let go of the things that don't. Fewer things done well: that's the recipe for a successful business and an impactful life.

That means saying no to some things so you can focus on others. I'm often amazed by how frankly childish people can be about this need to make trade-offs. They insist they can have it all, even though ignoring the trade-offs doesn't make them go away. Trade-offs are inevitable. Choosing one thing means not choosing another. Every opportunity seized is another lost. And not choosing is still choosing—it's the worst choice of all.

If you're alive, you're in the trade-off business. And if you're in business, well, that's what being a leader or manager is. We get paid to manage the trade-offs, to make decisions, and to understand opportunity costs. Sometimes they might be small choices, like whether to hire a new team member or invest in new product development. Other times, they might be enormous choices, like the one I contemplated while sitting on that beach: selling one company so the other could have a chance to thrive.

Apple design chief Jony Ive once recalled that during the fifteen years he worked with Steve Jobs, Jobs asked him the same question nearly every day: "How many times did you say no today?"[1] Jobs's message was that if you didn't say no to something, you weren't focused on anything. That's true. But saying no in and of itself isn't a recipe for success. I believe the harder, and more important, task is figuring out what to say yes to. As leaders, it's incumbent on us to discover the one, two, or three things that will make the most difference in vaulting the company into the future and then do everything in our power to execute on those few initiatives. Do those one or two things really well and ignore everything else. Push past the distractions, pick the right stuff, and do it right. That's it. Ultimately, almost all the other stuff doesn't matter.

• • •

Sitting there on that beach, my a-ha moment made the right choice clear to me. But that clarity didn't make it feel any less gut-wrenching. In fact, it felt terrible. Au Bon Pain was still like my firstborn child, and I'd put nearly two decades of hard work into the company. I'd forged some of my most important relationships there, learned critical life lessons, and in no small sense, the company had shaped my identity. But Au Bon Pain wasn't good enough for where the world was going. And it was holding Panera back. If Panera was going to have a shot at fulfilling its potential, Au Bon Pain had to go.

I still had no idea how we'd pull it off, or if it would even work. But the only way to find out was to act. By the time I'd dusted the sand off my feet and boarded the plane home to begin the new year, my mind was made up, and I immediately felt the burden of actually *doing it*.

An entrepreneur must be a doer as well as a dreamer, and the insights you have on a beach somewhere don't mean anything until you follow through. And you might as well do it now—there's never anything to be gained from postponing making the hard choices.

Unfortunately, the choice that seemed so clear to me was not so clear to everyone else. I arrived back in the office and walked into a wall of personal and institutional resistance. Understandably so. I was pushing an upside-down logic—jettison your bigger divisions and put all your chips on your smaller division. That thinking is anathema to investors and board members responsible for quarterly results. People with whom I'd worked shoulder to shoulder to build the company were suddenly questioning my judgment and fitness to lead. And their doubts ate away at my confidence.

Still, I stood firm, and we put the company's three biggest divisions up for sale in April 1997. Analysts referred to it as "a bet-your-job decision." But it was even bigger than my job—I wanted to do right by the company and the people who worked there. And I wanted to do right by myself. It was a "bet your sense-of-self decision." I was terrified.

Au Bon Pain's stock price continued to slide, and a buyer failed to materialize. I doubted my own logic and questioned whether I really had the wherewithal to see it through. So did others. Knowing that our sale book was out in the market, the head of Au Bon Pain International had me over the proverbial barrel and pulled a palace coup. He told me he would leave if I didn't make him president of the entire company. Against my better instincts, I caved and agreed to his demand, making him president. But even that didn't satiate him. Not too long after his options vested, he walked away. Reeling from the betrayal, which came on top of the ongoing losses in my personal life and the strain of caring for my dying father, I felt beaten down and alone.

More than a year after my beach a-ha, one of our directors, Jim McManus, offered to buy my stock at $4.50 a share (split-adjusted).

Maybe it was for the best, I thought. I was exhausted and had nothing left. I agreed to his deal. But just two months after making his offer, McManus pulled out. Another blow, though I had no idea at the time what a gift it would turn out to be. I was prepared to take $4.50 a share from him. But instead I kept my stake in an enterprise that would go on, as Panera, to trade up seventy-fold to $315 a share. That would be years later. At the time, I just felt trapped, seeing the powerful opportunity in Panera but lacking the finances or human resources to fulfill that possibility while managing a company at war with itself.

More months of meetings with potential buyers all came to naught, until we reached an agreement in principle with New York–based Bruckmann, Rosser, Sherrill & Co. (BRS) to sell Au Bon Pain's businesses (except Panera and manufacturing). Even then, BRS strung us out for fourteen months and, along the way, dropped its offer price. In the meantime, I sold off our manufacturing operations to Bunge. However, it wasn't until I effectively created my own group to offer a competitive bid for Au Bon Pain that BRS stepped up and closed the deal, for $78 million.

Two long years after that night on the beach, the deal closed and Panera was the company's only division and singular focus. And yet, there was no sense of euphoria. In fact, it was one of the saddest days of my career. The right choice doesn't always feel good.

Over the course of those two years, not an hour passed when I didn't doubt my decision and question whether I had the wherewithal to make it happen. Even on the day of the closing, our general counsel, Tom Howley, had to give me a final push to sign the deal.

In letting go of Au Bon Pain, I surrendered a bit of my self. And I lost my trusted partner, Louis Kane, who had agreed to stay with Au Bon Pain as a condition of the sale—a final act of generosity that freed me to go with Panera. A year later, Louis would succumb to the cancer that he had battled so valiantly and so privately. For its part, Au Bon Pain refocused on serving hospitals, universities, and transportation centers and became a successful niche business.

In the end, selling Au Bon Pain was all about self-respect. I felt, in the very core of my being, that if I didn't give Panera my best shot, I would never be able to face a mirror and look myself in the eyes. It was, in the deepest sense, a pre-mortem decision, and it was only that thread of connection to my future self that gave me the strength to stay the course.

· · ·

Dealing with the reality of choice is powerful because it forces us to come back to that all-important question: What really matters? As you think about what to say yes to, it's helpful to prioritize against what I call the three Ts—Time, Talent, and Treasury. In other words, how are you going to spend the hours, days, weeks, months, or years of your precious time or your company's? How are you going to allocate the company's human capital—its people and their energy, creativity, emotional commitment, and intellectual engagement? And how are you going to allocate the company's financial capital? Each of these resources is limited. So make sure you're spending them on what truly matters to the long-term health of your enterprise.

Whether you're looking at an individual life or a company, how you utilize the three Ts is a real test of what you're all about. And the way you spend them will determine what your life looks like in the rearview mirror. I often think about prominent public figures or leaders—how many thousands of choices they make during their lifetimes, and yet in the end they'll only be remembered for one or two key things.

In the long run, most of the things that take up our time and intellectual bandwidth—everyday distractions like email and meetings, conferences and celebratory events, as well as short-term wins that simply pop the company's stock—quickly fade away. All that remains are the limited number of choices that really matter. And the more conscious and courageous you can be about getting the big choices right, the more chance you have of ensuring that the defining achievements of your life are the ones that leave you feeling good about yourself.

Making choices isn't easy, and a lot of the time we prefer not making choices at all. We live reactively, ignoring long-term trade-offs and opportunity costs. In the short term, we might avoid some pain and conflict this way. But in the long term, the price is profound. Through lack of use, you lose touch with your sense of what matters most deeply.

The ability to know what really matters is like a muscle that must be exercised. And the way we exercise it—the existential weightlifting of a conscious life—is by making choices and staying the course. It might be challenging, even painful at times, and you won't always be proven right. Sometimes you'll make the wrong choice. Other times you'll make the right choice, but circumstances will thwart your progress. But if you keep making choices with as much future-back vision and foresight as you can muster, you will strengthen that all-important guidance system that defines a life well lived.

• • •

Time, Talent, and Treasury. After we had sold Au Bon Pain, we ended up with about 180 Panera cafés, a debt-free balance sheet, cash in the bank, and a plan to create the future of our dreams. That was our Treasury. As for Time, I was finally free to focus solely on the one business. And being liberated from the short-term troubles of Au Bon Pain, and the competing agendas of the other businesses and their executive teams, we finally had the time to focus on the long term. When it came to Talent, I picked the best people who shared my enthusiasm for the opportunities ahead.

In my personal life, the clouds were beginning to lift as well. I had recently gotten married to Nancy, in May 1998—a bright moment in my otherwise depressing personal life in the nineties. In the summer of 1999, not long after the birth of our son Michael, we moved to St. Louis so I could begin building Panera and breathing life into the future that I imagined. It felt like a new beginning.

I was celebrating the best Thanksgiving I'd had in years in Vermont when I got a call from Bill Moreton, then Panera's CFO.

"Ron, I've got some bad news. Sorry to break this to you on the holiday, but I thought you'd want to know right away. While you were focused on the deals, our comps have gone in the wrong direction and our costs have exploded. We are out of control. We're going to miss our projections."

Ron's Rules for Adult Management

- **There is no balance, just trade-offs.** Make the trade-offs you can respect.
- **Planning successfully means making choices.**
- **Do fewer things well.** The best brands make choices. If you are everything to everybody, you are not special to anyone.
- **Accept the pain of making the tough choices.** There will be blood on the floor.
- **Push what is working, fix what is wobbling, and stop what is not working.**
- **In sum, we can do anything; we just can't do everything.**

"Really?" I was taken aback. "By how much?"

There was an ominous silence on the other end of the line.

"About fifty percent."

Just because you make the right choice doesn't mean the road ahead will be easy. We'd bet everything on a dream for the future—but it hadn't yet come into being. We'd bet everything on a company that was full of promise but lacked the infrastructure to support growth. We were going to miss our numbers by a mile. Clearly, we had some hard work to do if our crazy bet was to pay off.

But even as I stared down that challenge, I knew one thing for sure: the alternative—not making that bet on Panera—would have been a much greater risk.

PART TWO

Leading a Large Enterprise

Develop with Discipline

"Welcome to the new world, Ron," I told myself, looking out over the city lights of St. Louis, framed by the iconic Gateway Arch. "You got what you wanted—an opportunity to impact the industry with a singularly powerful new concept: Panera. Now, you'd better care for it properly and grow it right."

When I'd headed West at the turn of the millennium, having sold the Au Bon Pain divisions and manufacturing to invest everything in the fledgling, unproven, but promising concept we'd called Panera Bread, I knew it would take years to make good on the vision we'd set out to create. And when I got that call from Bill Moreton telling me we were going to miss our planned numbers by 50 percent that year, I wondered if I'd be given the freedom to see it through. We were still the same public company (Au Bon Pain Co., Inc., was renamed Panera Bread) so we were still accountable to the same investors. And investors don't have a lot of patience for poor short-term results, no matter how inspiring your long-term vision. How was I to manage Wall Street's quarter-to-quarter myopia while building for the future? It was this question that often woke me up before dawn, with a familiar sense of excitement and insecurity churning in the pit of my stomach.

I had no delusions about how difficult it is to succeed in the restaurant business. Frankly, it's almost impossible. In a couple of decades, you can go from being on every other block to being forgotten.

Bankrupt, bought, or bust. Few restaurant concepts will make it—and ones that do survive rarely thrive for more than a decade. As I like to say, the restaurant industry isn't hard; it's just hard as hell to do well. There are a hundred ways to go wrong.

I knew in my heart, though, that Panera had the potential to be one of the rare few that got it right. Since acquiring St. Louis Bread Company, we'd forged our Concept Essence; we'd added breakfast and created a gathering place and changed just about everything else. We'd become a warm and welcoming experience. In doing so, we had turbocharged our asset and increased our average unit volume from $1 million to $1.75 million. We now had a concept that *worked*. A concept that generated consistently high sales volumes and ROI across multiple geographies—from Springfield, Missouri, to Springfield, Massachusetts—and had the potential to become nationally dominant. A concept that was worthy of being reproduced, that could and should grow. The responsibility I felt was to develop it the right way.

As I shared earlier, I see growth as a *by-product* of achieving the true *end* that a business should aim for: competitive advantage. The *means* to that end is establishing your authority in your chosen niche and then leveraging that authority through smart bets that serve your target customer in ways your competitors find hard to match, thus creating barriers to entry (topics I'll unpack in detail in coming chapters). The challenge that would consume my every waking minute for the decade to come was how to lead Panera in such a way that growth would be the natural, almost inevitable outcome of our continuing triumph in the race for competitive advantage.

Growth is a by-product, not a means. I hit this point again because it is such a contrary mindset to most conventional business thinking and practice. In the common model, a high stock price is the end, and growth is a means to that end. Nail down that model as fast as possible and then reproduce it as quickly and efficiently as you can in order to raise the stock price by increasing that magical multiple that is based on your perceived growth rate. People talk about driving growth, but as I've said before, growth is not just a pedal to be pushed. Indeed, the quickest way to destroy a promising concept is to put your foot down on that accelerator and remove your hands from the steering wheel.

• • •

In those early days at Panera, we knew we were ready to grow, and we had an opportunity to grow relatively quickly. But I didn't want to rush. One guiding principle I followed was, Don't make a decision until you need to. That might sound obvious, but so many companies leap to promising dramatic growth and then trap themselves under the weight of the expectations they've created. I knew that we didn't need to decide in 2001 whether Panera would grow to be 500, 1,000, or 2,500 units; whether it would stay in the Midwest or go nationwide. We just needed to know we could keep feeding the growth monster by ensuring we had enough prospective sites to fuel us for three years ahead. Enough to keep the investors happy, while learning and then growing in a way that made sense without getting out over our skis.

To that end, we made some important strategic choices about development. One key early decision was to embrace franchising. We named the former president of St. Louis Bread Company, Rick Postle, head of development. As the former president of Wendy's and COO of KFC, Rick knew the business of franchising and brought deep connections to it. Franchising was a smart bet because it gave us fast access to local real estate and operating knowledge. It's not always a good move for a restaurant company, but when you've got your concept figured out—we had a concept we believed would work in almost every market in America—and want to scale quickly, it makes sense as part of a balanced development model. Franchising allowed us to go from opening 25 to 50 cafés a year to opening 100 to 150 a year. It was a great way to get a quick start on growth and build scale without overextending ourselves.

Franchising goes in and out of fashion in the food service industry (and others). For a long time, back in the sixties and seventies, the prevailing thinking was that company operations were the way to go. And then, perhaps driven in part by the focus on short-term return on investment and stable royalties, the trend shifted yet again, and people wanted "asset-light" models, where they owned few if any stores. Indeed, companies like Applebee's decided to franchise almost every unit and live off the royalties, while stripping the overhead down to almost nothing. These days, the pendulum has swung back, and popular concepts like Chipotle are all company owned. In my mind, it doesn't have to be one way or another; it's really a question of finding the right balance.

I think of it as being like asset allocation in investing financial resources. When the great recession hit in 2008, everyone wished they had all debt and no equity. But when the market goes on a great run, as it did over the last decade, everyone wishes they had all equity and no debt. Neither strategy alone makes a lot of sense, because your strategy needs to work long term over the entire business cycle.

The same principle applies to franchising. When a business is doing well, it's great to operate all company stores and get the leverage from same-store sales, but when sales weaken in a public company, it's great to have the stability of royalties. If you don't have both, it is harder to weather the ups and downs.

I'm opposed to an all-franchised (asset-light) model because it inhibits your ability to effectively guide the brand. You have no skin in the game, no units to experiment with, and limited resources to figure out what makes sense. If you need to make a significant business transformation, you have neither the credibility nor the capabilities to do so.

Conversely, an all-company-store model is no panacea. It requires tremendous capital in the growth phase. And franchisees, which are the longest owners of the brand, do make corporate management teams think.

So having *some* franchisees is a wise strategy. Yes, you give up some control, but you get so much back in return from franchisees. They bring local real estate knowledge, capital, and local operating skills, and they put a little tension in the system.

At Panera, we ultimately ended up with a balanced system: half franchise, half company, and it worked very well for us.

We adopted an "area franchise" model, in which each franchisee committed to opening a certain number of cafés in a market. That way, we never had more than thirty or so franchisees to deal with. Because our concept was strong, our franchisees had powerful returns on their investment and built sizable businesses in their own right, and that was a great thing for everyone.

I viewed my franchisees as my customers. And as long as their cafés were economically powerful and as long as they trusted my vision, I could count on them to do what I felt was necessary for the long-term health of the brand.

There's always some friction in these kinds of relationships, but fundamentally I think our franchisees knew we were looking out for their best interests, and we were going to deliver. In return, they were willing to follow my lead.

Another important strategic choice we made concerning our growth strategy was to develop stores in concentric circles, rather than hop-skipping across the country. Moving slowly outward into adjacent markets allowed us to leverage our supply chain and our people and, ultimately, to have a higher degree of confidence in our growth.

Growth requires discipline. Every time we opened a new café, we were investing more than a million dollars. We needed to be confident that we could deliver a 30 percent or higher return on investment on average. To do so, we built regression models that helped us determine the probability that we would deliver the necessary sales to generate that kind of return. We conducted postmortems on every opening to better understand what we were doing right and what we were doing wrong. Eventually, we instituted Real Estate Learning, a group dedicated solely to studying and understanding what would drive successful unit development and what wouldn't. Being strategic when it came to growth was all important.

These decisions allowed us to increase our unit count in a smart, disciplined way. But even as our tens of cafés became hundreds of

Ron's Rules for Growth

- Know who you are and how you're going to win before you grow. Take the time to get your concept right. You don't want to start replicating a flawed business model. Focus on your competitive advantage first. Ensure you have a plan today to be the best competitive alternative for your target customer tomorrow. Understand where your authority is derived and how that translates into a strategy for differentiating yourself in the market, what I call Concept Essence. Grow only when you have a model worth replicating.

- **Grow fast once you're confident you have it right.** When you're confident you have competitive advantage, bring in the right balance of leaders, capital, and even franchisees to grow as fast as you sustainably can. Scale matters and the winner usually takes all.

- **Grow in concentric circles.** Expanding into adjacent markets allows you to leverage your supply chain and your people and to have a higher degree of confidence in your success.

- **Utilize data and real estate learning to know what works.** Take the time to study and understand what drives successful unit development, then execute based on that knowledge.

cafés, and eventually thousands, I knew I couldn't get distracted by scale. I could never allow myself to forget that the growth we were experiencing, and all the rewards the market was bestowing upon us as a result, was neither a means nor an end. It was a by-product of the fact that we'd taken the time to create a truly distinctive concept for a particular target customer, to carve out a real competitive advantage at a particular moment in time.

And the most important thing I could do, as a leader, was to keep my eye on *that* prize—to leverage, sustain, and when necessary, evolve that competitive advantage. When it came to determining the right approach to our concept, it didn't matter how big we had gotten. Get each transaction with a guest right, and we had the permission to keep replicating. Get it wrong, and we'd suffer the fate of so many other failed restaurant concepts. Size and scale don't mean squat if you haven't discovered a better way to compete. If I didn't keep creating a better alternative that had customers walking past our competitors to get to our door, we would not succeed over the long term, no matter how many thousands of cafés we opened.

Break the Cycle of Failure

The answer was staring me in the face, in twelve-point black type. For months, I'd been asking, *Why were certain franchisees running better and more profitable cafés than we were?* At least a part of the answer was right here, in the franchise contract I was holding in my hand. I brought the issue up at the next meeting of the senior management team.

"We're hypocrites," I told the team, pointing to the clause I'd highlighted in the contract. "We require our franchisees to give the operators running their cafés 10 percent ownership in the business. Why don't we expect that of ourselves?" No one had a good answer—because there was no good answer. We knew full well that store managers do a better job when they share in the profits generated from the outcome of their work. In fact, we'd dealt with this issue back in the early years of Au Bon Pain and had pioneered a successful solution we called partner/manager. That's why we'd made it a requirement for our franchisees. But as we developed Panera and began to grow rapidly under the new brand, we'd stopped cutting in our managers for a fraction of the action in our company-owned cafés. I should not have been surprised that employee turnover was too high, the cafés were sometimes poorly run, and the result was reflected in our bottom line. It was time to make our managers partners again.

The notion of making managers partners had originally come about in response to a problem that was—and still is—endemic to service industries, where the key to success is a great store manager. But it's hard to attract good people to such roles, and if you do, it's hard to get them to stay. They're all overworked. The good ones get moved around a lot in an effort to solve the latest problem, and they burn out. That yields high turnover and low morale, which escalates the problem. And then you have to spend more money on recruitment and training, so you have even less to spend on salaries. In the eighties, I'd dubbed this situation "the cycle of failure."

Now, to operate and grow Panera successfully, it was clear that the biggest priority was attracting strong café managers who could build solid teams and run great cafés and break the cycle. How could we pay our people more and attract the kind of managers we knew could do the job? We couldn't simply write the same people bigger checks. How could we create a system that allowed good people to make more money because they moved the needle? What we came up with at Panera was known as the Joint Venture Partner program, a kind of company-owned franchise model that made store managers and assistant managers part-owners of the cafés they managed.

We charged them rent, which was simply our budgeted profit, and they shared in profits above that hurdle. We also made a commitment that they would remain with one café for five years, which gave us the stability of leadership we needed and them the stability of lifestyle that they desired. Plus, they got to benefit from their own success in improving a café through their profit distributions over multiple years.

The logic behind the Joint Venture Partner program was simple: we wanted to get our store managers' incentives aligned with ours, to increase the compensation of those who could get the job done, and ultimately maintain their engagement and commitment. The problem isn't the people—it's the system they're working within. It's management's job to create a system that encourages people to give all they are capable of giving.

It's too easy for business leaders to just assume that everyone shares their motivation to make the company successful. In my experience, most employees don't really care about the things that keep business leaders awake at night. They don't wake up and declare, "I'm so happy! We just made another penny a share for the company's shareholders!" They wake up worried about paying their own bills, taking care of their sick kid, getting through the divorce, or whatever other personal issues are weighing on their minds. So, if you want them to care about the company's financial success (which, of course, is a by-product of getting them to care about their customers and ultimately build competitive advantage), it works better if they have a stake in it. I *wanted* to pay people more, but I knew that to do so, our compensation system had to attract the people who could make a real difference in the experience of our guests and thereby unlock dollars for compensation. Our Joint Venture Partner program did just that.

For other businesses, it might look different, but the same underlying principle holds true: to get employees to engage, contribute, and exceed expectations, you need to give team members a slice of ownership. When people are incentivized as partners and treated as partners, they'll act like partners. Change the system, change the result. Break the cycle of failure and you'll create a cycle of success.

Be the Innovator in Chief

"So tell me this," the young executive looked at me earnestly across the boardroom table, "Is Panera almost as good as Donatos?"

I briefly wondered if he was joking, but it didn't take long to realize he wasn't. He genuinely didn't know the difference between Panera and Donatos, which was a pizza joint. Now, if he'd just been some guy I met on the street, fair enough. But he was a senior executive at one of the leading companies in our industry. He should have been intimately familiar with every nuance of the market. It was his job to separate the wheat from the chaff. In fact, he was in the room with me because he was considering writing a very large check to acquire the wheat.

In this story, the wheat was Panera (an appropriate metaphor), and the company looking to buy us was none other than McDonald's. This was sometime in the early 2000s, and I wasn't really interested in selling. I'd only recently shed Au Bon Pain. But I never pass up an opportunity to get a look inside the boardrooms, kitchens, and minds of my competitors. So when executives at McDonald's invited us to a meeting, I said yes right away, curious to get an inside look at America's largest food service company and find out what they might propose. I knew McDonald's was at a challenging moment in its growth. No doubt they were looking for ways to access new markets—hence their interest in Panera, which appealed to a very different customer base than the burger-and-fries crowd. What I didn't realize until that meeting was how shockingly little they seemed to understand about the business they were in.

CFO Bill Moreton and I drove deep into the heart of the company's sprawling campus in suburban Chicago to sit down with members of the senior management team and the chief strategy officer. They spoke authoritatively and expertly about franchising, about real estate, about financing, about market research, and about supply chain economics. But when it came to understanding what customers really wanted—when it came to *food and overall experience*—they had nothing to say. That's why they didn't know which business had a brighter future ahead, us or a pizza place. I remember thinking during the meeting, *These guys don't have a clue. Is it any wonder they're having all the problems they're having?* It had never been clearer to me why billion-dollar companies end up in trouble. They had lost the ability to know what matters to their customers, and to use that as a North Star for innovation. They were stuck in the past as the world moved forward. Or, to put it another way, they'd lost their connection to discovery while becoming experts in delivery.

Discovery and delivery.* Those two essential activities must be kept in balance if a company is to remain relevant as it grows. Discovery is the leap of faith that brings an innovation to life—the creative work of understanding customers' needs, seeing what matters, and seizing opportunity. Delivery is the work of running the company—making it operational, sustainable, scalable. Both activities are critical. Discovery is the lifeblood of the company; delivery is the circulation system that keeps it flowing. Discovery is what's effective; delivery is what's efficient.

The trap growing companies too often fall into is letting delivery squelch discovery. It goes like this: an entrepreneur discovers a cus-

---

*The framework of discovery and delivery comes out of agile software development. In the context of the approach known as "dual-track agile," these terms refer to two parallel tracks in a software team's ongoing development work. In their 2011 book *The Innovator's DNA*, Clayton Christensen, Hal Gregersen, and Jeff Dyer popularized the broader use of this terminology in the context of business and innovation. See also Jeffrey H. Dyer, Hal Gregersen, and Clayton M. Christensen, "The Innovator's DNA," *Harvard Business Review*, December 2009.

tomer need and creates a better solution, against all odds. Capital flows in. Immediately, there's a crying need for accounting, financial planning, purchasing. They are hired. I call them delivery people. Short- and medium-term results get better. Margins and profits go up. The business grows. You're rewarded for this, so you pour more resources into making delivery even better.

Along the way, you keep bulking up your delivery muscle while your discovery muscle atrophies. You devote resources and attention to getting work done on time and on budget. You believe you've gotten good at understanding the customer, but in fact you've sealed yourself off from new learning and, above all, new opportunities. The language of delivery dominates every conversation.

Discovery people and delivery people think differently and talk differently. The language of discovery is "Imagine if . . . " The language of delivery is "Prove it to me!" Discovery is poetry; delivery is prose. Discovery is about a dream; delivery, a spreadsheet. Ultimately, discovery people find themselves feeling uncomfortable and diminished in a company in which the focus is on delivery. Over many years, delivery effectively pushes out discovery. That's what I saw so clearly as I sat in the boardroom that day.

If you're at this point, you're already trapped—like those executives at McDonald's. Without knowing it, you have become a highly efficient deliverer of something customers wanted yesterday. You see your delivery juggernaut as a competitive advantage even as your real competitive advantage weakens. Eventually, your original vision is almost unrecognizable, a kind of hyperefficient, optimized ghost of the thing that excited people in the first place. Focus on delivery alone leads to a poorer guest experience, a lack of "specialness" that will result in disengagement from customers and transaction falloff. Ultimately, something new will come along, discovered by someone else, that will disrupt your highly efficient delivery system.

Of course, delivery matters. That's one reason why McDonald's had gotten to be the number one food service company in America. A company that busts its budgets and misses its sales targets won't endure

for long. But every successful company runs the risk of getting mus-
cle-bound by delivery. It's an easy trap to fall into. You keep optimiz-
ing and growing and getting more efficient, and before you know it,
you have a bunch of people running your company who have no real
connection to the customers, their needs, or what matters tomorrow.
Most importantly, you have no ability to discover anew, as the discovery people have fled.

Delivery feels safe. It's predictable; its processes are rational. It's
measurable. Discovery, on the other hand, feels risky. It requires leaps
of faith and is based more on instinct than research, more on patterns
than data. The tension between discovery and delivery exists in every
company and, if kept in balance, is healthy.

I took this lesson to heart as I left the McDonald's meeting and
headed back to St. Louis and our still relatively young company. It felt
like a timely reminder. We were at a stage in our growth when getting
more efficient was important. Improving our delivery capabilities was
necessary as we scaled. But as we did that, we could not afford to let
go of the spirit of discovery that had gotten us here. *Don't let it get
out of balance*, I reminded myself. *Do not take the rewards reaped from
delivery to mean you can allow discovery to atrophy. You must always
be discovering. Delivery is about your present. Discovery is your future.*

• • •

As Bill and I flew home to resume the work of building Panera, I felt
a renewed sense of purpose and clarity about my role. As our innovative company grew, it was my job to ensure we didn't fall into the
trap that had just been so clearly illustrated for me. It's up to the leader
to protect the company's discovery efforts, again and again, and resist
the corporate bureaucracy that threatens to smother and stifle those
efforts with ever more precise and efficient delivery. Indeed, I believe
that protecting discovery and fueling it should be the foremost preoc-
cupation of every company builder. I'd argue that the most impactful
role a leader plays is protecting the people who are dreaming about

where the company can be in two, three, five, or ten years, and often, fighting for discovery personally. Remember, things of value are created over time. For innovation to be truly transformative, a leap of faith must be taken, and only someone with everything on the line like the CEO can take that leap of faith and take the company with them. That's why I always say that the person holding the title of CEO must also consider themselves innovator in chief.

Top-down innovation gets a bad rap. The popular business press abounds with criticism of initiatives that come tumbling down from the peak of the org chart. And yet, take a closer look at most companies, and you'll find that organizations are still doing it that way. Why? Because it works. Or to be more precise, based on my experience, top-down works when you focus on the right stuff and bring all the convening power and focus of top management to the effort.

Don't get me wrong: I'm all for grassroots innovation and radical ideas that bubble up from below to challenge mindsets in the C-suite. I certainly don't think I'm the smartest guy in the room. I seek out ideas from every corner of the company and from customers, especially in the early stages of an innovation effort. Listening empathically is a key step in the innovation process. But in later stages, when a promising idea must be defined, tested, and iterated into a game-changing tactic, innovation works best when democracy yields to autocracy.

As a leader, I also know that there are times when I'm the only one who has the power—and the accountability to the enterprise as a whole—to overcome the internal skeptics (often a company's functional leaders) and summon the resources needed to innovate. Of course, it takes many heads, hands, and hearts to bring a new business idea to life. But when it comes to betting and executing on a game-changing, disruptive strategy, you need ownership from the top. The CEO, as innovator in chief, must take the lead in making it happen. And it's the CEO who must be held accountable for the results. Einstein once said, "If at first the idea is not absurd, then there is no hope for it."[1] Who but the CEO has the influence to convene and marshal the company's resources behind an "absurd" idea and drive it through the organization?

And what's the point of a CEO title if it's not used to ensure the company's ability to innovate?

As innovator in chief, the CEO's first responsibility is to ensure all change in the organization is linked to Concept Essence—to identify, develop, and deploy innovations that lead to competitive advantage. All the other challenges that weigh on every CEO—meeting the quarter's financial targets, dealing with investors, creating a culture where everyone gives their best—are ultimately irrelevant if you haven't figured out how you will best compete tomorrow. Of course, the CEO can't be the only one thinking about competitive advantage and innovation. The innovator in chief must create a culture where people understand that creating competitive advantage is their most important job and where they are encouraged to innovate. And that starts with the CEO modeling that attitude.

Don't delegate discovery. This message should be driven home in every leadership program and MBA class. Too many CEOs are afraid of disruptive innovation and more comfortable in the safer role of glorified administrators. The all-important work of generating new business ideas gets sidelined in a skunkworks or relegated to an R&D department. Without the sponsorship of those with organizational power, those efforts go nowhere.

The folks at IBM learned this lesson in the nineties with an initiative called Emerging Business Opportunities, where promising ideas emerged, but few ever came to fruition. Analysis of the group revealed several reasons why, but one of the most salient was senior leadership's lack of involvement. The innovative business ideas had been assigned to younger, less experienced leaders—partly out of the belief that they'd be less likely to be caught up in company convention and established ways of thinking. However, they also lacked the credibility and clout needed to give new ideas a chance at success. In response to these findings, the company changed its approach. CEO Lou Gerstner eventually appointed a vice chairman and company veteran as "czar" to shepherd the process, declaring, "It can't be just some staff guy. It has to be someone with really big shoes."[2]

An Innovation Process for Doing What Matters

Being innovator in chief doesn't mean you just sit in the corner office dreaming up visions of the future. It means being the driver of a detailed, disciplined process from vision to rollout. Innovation isn't a flash of inspiration or a momentary creative breakthrough. It's quite frankly a grind, an often-uphill struggle to bring something new into being. You have to be prepared to take on everything you need to do to solve the problem . . . but no more. When we developed the original vision for Panera, I was led primarily by instinct, but looking back I could see that in fact I'd been following a process. Ultimately, I codified the process, breaking down the steps I use to *discover what matters, bring what matters to life, and get what matters done.* It's a process I now use for any innovation, large or small, in companies I work with. Note that although the process's steps are quite distinct, they are not discrete. In practice, each step is fluid and often spills into the next step.

1. Discover what matters: Determine what job you need to complete for whom

- **Observe.** Using all your senses, tune into the everyday human behaviors that signal people's frustrations, unfulfilled needs, and desires, and thereby reveal a promising opportunity to innovate. Use focus groups and studies of competitors, as well as other industries, business models, and broader cultural trends.

- **Look for patterns and draw generalizations.** Once you've gathered this data from raw observation, you can start to look for patterns and generalize from one industry to another.

- **Brainstorm.** Explore the meaning of the patterns you're noticing. Compare notes and wrestle with what you have seen. Generate hypotheses on what will matter to people in the future.

- **Research.** Confirm your hypotheses through formal research and by looking to other industries for models. Research is the final part of the observation process, not the starting point. It serves only to confirm what you've seen directly. Research can only tell you what people did yesterday. And if you just take whatever happened yesterday, extrapolate it, and expect that world to be there tomorrow, don't be surprised when you find yourself irrelevant.

(continued)

The world doesn't pay you to read yesterday's research. It pays you to figure out what will matter tomorrow and how to be the first to get there.

2. Bring what matters to life: Capture your vision in one, two, and three dimensions

- **Identify success factors.** I think of this as a one-dimensional sketch, a single page in which you clarify and ultimately commit to the deliverables that will be required to take advantage of the opportunity you observed.

- **Rendering.** Develop a two-dimensional vision of the solution for the future you see, something equivalent to a watercolor sketch. You can see it and describe it and discuss it, but you haven't built it. You can test in your mind and discuss with others how it might serve guests, operators, investors, and so on. Continue to play with it, challenge it, and stay open. Are there secondary unforeseen consequences to certain choices? Keep discussing it until you feel confident it's at least 80 percent solid. It might take the form of a written document like our Concept Essence. It might include visuals.

- **Lab test.** Once your rendering is so vivid that you can see it, taste it, touch it, hear it, smell it, it's time to move into three dimensions and lab test the various parts or subsystems of the solution, internally, before it faces customers.

- **Prototype.** Here's where you get to truly test the full, three-dimensional, operational reality of your vision, to learn and experience how it works with guests and operators.

3. Get what matters done: roll out your innovation

- **Planning.** Determine what to roll out first, second, third, and so on (what the world can absorb when) for the minimally viable product (MVP).

- **Versioning.** Build confidence, confirm impact, and define rollout needs through larger and larger market tests.

- **Execution.** Determine who coordinates and how the full-system rollout will occur.

Discovery is the CEO's number one job and should never be delegated. Your job is not to accept what is. Your job is to change the trajectory of the business. The minute you think you truly understand the customer and can take your attention off discovering what matters, you're dead. Sooner or later, even the most brilliant and innovative concept will fall behind the times and become a competitive disadvantage.

Make Smart Bets

My dad loved poker. In fact, he loved it so much that after my mom passed away, he sold his house and moved to Las Vegas, determined to prove he could make a living playing cards. He was convinced he could beat the house. Once, after he had been playing for a while, I figured out with him how much he made in winnings over the prior year. It came to about three cents an hour.

But he beat them! He beat the "house vig" (or "vigorish," gambling lingo for the house edge). That's what mattered to him. It was the thrill of competition that attracted him to the game. He loved winning, in games and in life.

In that regard, I take after my dad. I, too, love to win (although I like my wins to net more than three cents an hour). But it's even more than that for me. I know it's imperative that as a company leader, I must win the bets I make, at least most of the time. My credibility—and by extension, my ability to keep doing the things I love—depends on it. Therefore, I don't like to gamble. I want to make smart bets. Smart bets are bets where you have an edge and the odds are on your side.

This became clear to me one time when I was visiting my dad in Vegas. I found myself wandering through a casino late at night, breathing in the smell of sweat and stale cigarette smoke, and watching people playing the slot machines. "There's no way I'd ever be doing that," I thought to myself. "The only way I'm going to be in a casino at 11 p.m. is if I own the place and have the house vig!"

To have the house vig in business, one must understand what's going to matter in the future. Leaders must have the ability to wisely stake their limited capital, resources, and reputation on those things that will give them competitive advantage. They must choose to back this project or that project. They must choose who to hire or fire. Those who win aren't just the lucky ones; they're the smart ones who make better choices. They're the ones who know that to maintain their credibility, they need to make smart bets.

How do you give yourself higher odds of succeeding when you're betting on a future that cannot yet be seen with certainty? You've seen some of the techniques in play with some of the stories I've already told. When I was observing customers and competitive concepts closely, I was building my ability to know what will matter. When we spent weeks in trendy California bakeries taking notes, we were developing the ability to make smarter bets. When we pored for months over our Concept Essence, we were envisioning a more competitive future. You have to develop skills of observation, generalization, and prediction. Interpreting, finding patterns, tracking trends, creating a rendering, testing, refining, improving—these skills allow you to see beyond the horizon. Eventually, you have the house vig and are making a smart bet.

A smart bet is not a certain one—if it were, your competitors would already be doing it. But neither is it a gamble. It's a situation where, through your own skill and commitment to observation and deduction, you have better information about what's going to matter in the future than the other players have.

Smart bets are evolutionary adaptions to your concept, rooted in the authority you've already established and its link to your understanding of the future. The best bets take advantage of existing strengths and capacities over the long term. Making the right smart bets engenders and sustains competitive advantage. Making the wrong bets or no bets at all ensures you will lose competitive advantage as the world evolves.

Successfully making smart bets requires an appreciation that things of value take time. It often takes years to appreciate the impact of a smart bet or a specific initiative. For these reasons, making smart bets isn't easy. It requires courage to invest in one, but it's not a reckless courage. If you've done the work, you've increased your odds to the point where there's a far better chance it will pay off than not, even if it's not certain and it takes time.

Smart bets drove Panera's evolution throughout the time I was leading the company. A leader must choose them wisely, knowing that there are only a handful of initiatives an organization can focus on and fully accomplish at any given time. Every failure erodes people's trust and ultimately chips away at the latitude people will give you to play out your vision.

• • •

"Free? You want to give it away for free?"

I could almost see the scenes playing out in my concerned executive's head as he considered the proposal I'd just made: giving away high-speed Wi-Fi for free. Slackers would camp out at Panera for hours, playing video games. A solo laptop user would take up a big table, while a family that couldn't find a seat would leave to get lunch somewhere else. College students would treat our cafés like a library, all for the price of a cup of coffee. Franchisees would be up in arms about costs. Lawyers would freak out about liability. Our trademark Panera warmth would fizzle in the cold glow of computer screens. All of these catastrophes were inevitable, people told me, if I pursued the ludicrous strategy I was proposing.

For those who have grown up in a world where free Wi-Fi is ubiquitous, let me take you back to 2001, only a few years after the technology had been invented. Though a few had experienced broadband at home or at the office, most people still relied on dial-up internet connections through phone lines. It seemed like a miracle to be able to get online without a telephone line and all those screechy noises. Most laptops didn't have a built-in Wi-Fi connector—you had to buy a plug-in card. People didn't even know how to pronounce it. "What do we need this wiffee thing for anyway?" was a common question from franchise owners. A few places offered it, like hotels and Starbucks, but you paid for the privilege.

Unsurprisingly, my free Wi-Fi proposal didn't seem like a smart bet at all to those around me. The doubters told me that not only was it a risk to sales and the bottom line, but it was damn near impossible to pull off. And all so we could give something away for free? But my vision for Wi-Fi wasn't about giving something away. I recognized an opportunity to enhance our core competitive advantage by anticipating what would matter in the future—the essence of a smart bet. It was a way to fulfill our Concept Essence and build energy in our cafés—and execute a jujitsu move on our competitors in the process. We'd always envisioned Panera as a gathering place—a place that was such a joy to sit in that people would come for the environment, knowing the price of admission was a cup of coffee or a sandwich. And a key element of that original vision was for Panera to be part of the revolution in how people were working. In those cafés in Portland and San Francisco, I'd seen guys in suits with big clunky laptops and pagers. I was one of them myself. I loved getting out of the office and finding new spaces to help me think afresh. Inspired by these observations, the original Concept Essence document included a section on making the cafés computer friendly. Back then, that mostly meant lots of power outlets.

When Wi-Fi arrived, I understood that the concept still applied, but it needed to mean something different. Starbucks recognized it, too. But Starbucks, like most of our competitors, didn't have our seating capacity. Its cafés had maybe fifteen or twenty seats compared to our hundred-plus. They were like a fleet of small planes that were always full; we had bigger planes with plenty of open seating. We were only full for a couple hours a day, during lunch. By offering free Wi-Fi, we could entice customers into our cafés during the quiet periods, while at the same time undercutting a competitor, Starbucks, which was making customers pay for it. That was not a bad strategy for Starbucks at the time; it served both as a profit stream and a way to discourage people from staying too long in its limited number of seats (something we didn't need to worry about).

I had a hunch Wi-Fi was the future. It was going to become a commodity. By giving it away before anyone else did, we'd establish ourselves as the go-to place for the new tribe of nomadic workers. And we'd put intense pressure on Starbucks, which, if it chose to match our free offering, would overwhelm its cafés and compress its profits, and if it failed to match us would appear greedy. In either case, it would be bad for Starbucks. That was the smart bet.

At the outset, franchisees asked me to justify this strategy that seemed so rash to them by showing them an ROI. But how do you connect giving away free Wi-Fi and embarrassing your competitor to actual sales? No spreadsheet could show that. But they wanted a number, so I literally walked around Panera cafés and observed what our laptop users were consuming besides Wi-Fi. One might just have a cup of coffee. Another had a sandwich and a soda. I figured they bought something about once an hour, and I averaged out what they were spending. I proposed that we'd make $5 of profit for every logged-on hour. It wasn't much more than a guess, but it helped to persuade at least some people.

The doubters were right about the challenge. Rolling out Wi-Fi to all our cafés was hard, and it was expensive. We had to pull T1 lines into the cafés, which added a not-insignificant monthly incremental expense to the P&L. Franchisees bristled. The IT department scrambled. We were not a company with a reputation for being high-tech, but we went ahead and built the largest industrial-strength Wi-Fi network in the country.

The doubters were wrong about the impact. Wi-Fi filled the cafés with people and energy, much as we had imagined in our Concept Essence. Now, alongside the Bible study groups and the moms having coffee together, we had students and corporate types looking for a change of scene. Pharma reps were doing interviews at Panera. Free Wi-Fi worked. I'd been right about the profound changes that were taking place, as workers were untethered from the office for the first time. They reveled in being able to set up in a comfy Panera booth with a cup of coffee and a sandwich and get their reports written or their research done. By taking on the daunting challenge of installing free Wi-Fi, we differentiated ourselves as a gathering place. In the early 2000s, any time someone said "Panera," the next words out of their mouth were "free Wi-Fi." That's differentiation. We gave people something they really wanted but didn't yet expect to get. And they loved us for it.

Of course, not all the doubters' concerns were unfounded. One guy used to literally roll a desktop computer on wheels into our café in Jacksonville, Florida, every day, using it as a rent-free office. But he was the exception. We were never overrun with freeloaders. We were just busier all day. We made adjustments along the way, such as putting a thirty-minute limit on Wi-Fi usage during peak hours, but the rest of the day, we embraced our role as the original remote office. Ultimately, my back-of-the-napkin calculation of $5 profit per logged-in hour was low. We estimated that the nonpeak business, driven by free Wi-Fi, grew to approximately 30 percent of our sales.

That one smart bet bought us years of competitive advantage. By taking on a tough challenge, we created a barrier to entry—a key principle I'll unpack further in the next chapter. The economics of Starbucks's deal with its Wi-Fi provider T-Mobile meant that it was difficult for it to evolve its pricing in response to the competitive market pressure. And even when it did switch to free Wi-Fi several years later, it still lacked seating capacity and ultimately left many customers frustrated (never good for business).

From 2000 to 2003, Panera's share price jumped some 500 percent, as we racked up nearly $1 billion in systemwide sales. Could I have predicted those numbers when I first proposed installing free Wi-Fi? Not exactly. But I knew in my gut that it was a smart bet, that it would differentiate us well into the future, and that it was directly tied to our Concept Essence, so I trusted that the by-product would be profit.

The greatest value of that investment, over time, was an unexpected by-product. I didn't see it coming; no one did. It turned out that the installation of broadband in all our cafés to enable the Wi-Fi led to faster and more enhanced credit card processing, which led to a surge in sales. Suddenly, paying with a card, which had been cumbersome and slow, became easy. And when customers pay with credit, they buy more. The average check size got bigger. Down the road, this would also become the essential foundation for a quick transition to digitally enabled ordering.

. . .

Making smart bets is a critical skill in business and in life—and one that every kid should learn. It's a skill I've worked hard to pass on to my own son, Michael, who I sometimes worry is too much of a gambler at heart. One time, during the Winter Olympics, we were watching the skiing events together. He was eager to bet his allowance on his favorite athletes, without much information to go on other than his own enthusiasm and the adrenaline rush it generated. "C'mon, Dad," he'd beg me. "Take my bet! I just know Lindsey Vonn is going to win the gold medal tonight!"

What Michael didn't realize was that the competition we were watching on prime-time American television had in fact already been decided earlier that day. I could pull up the results right there on my phone, so I had information he didn't—information that told me for sure that his favorite competitor was not going to step up to the podium at the end of the broadcast. I literally knew the future. "Okay," I told him. "I'll take your bet. I think Lindsey Vonn is going to lose tonight. In fact, I'm so confident I'll give you twenty-to-one odds." I held out my hand.

Michael's eyes lit up in disbelief. "Yeah?" I could see him mentally doing the math. He grabbed my hand and shook it quickly, as if he were afraid that I would change my mind. He ran to get his piggy bank, proudly counting out fifty dollars. He placed the bills on the table as we settled in to watch the events.

You might think this was a cruel trick to play on an unsuspecting kid. But I never intended to take his money. What I did intend to do was teach him how to think about a smart bet.

When I confessed to having known all along, he was furious.

"You cheated!"

Define Your Decision-Making Lens

Making smart bets requires that you be nimble and fast in your decision-making. Nothing weighs a company down like indecisiveness and gridlock. As an organization grows, departments expand and people work their way up the ladder, they tend to acquire tunnel vision. Their expertise within their particular function can blind them to emerging opportunities that benefit the entire company. And decision-making becomes near impossible. An organization with very strong functions is like a fiefdom: everyone can say no, but no one has the power to say yes.

To avoid a situation where one department is pitted against another, or decisions become compromises to simply minimize risk, you need a clear lens through which to make decisions together as a group, in the best interests of the whole. A good decision-making lens is focused on what matters and has several carefully prioritized filters.

To focus your lens, start with the fundamental question: What matters most to the organization and its stakeholders? In most enterprises, the answer should be some variation of *maintaining competitive advantage*. Competitive advantage is the end; everything else is the means. Good decisions are those that lead to greater competitive advantage.

To define the filters on your lens, you need to consider your key points of authority and differentiation: the ways in which you've decided to compete. For example, perhaps what differentiates you is the guest experience. Or perhaps you're competing on value. Or you might set yourself apart with a focus on quality. Your decision-making lens should reflect the concept's points of differentiation and core personality, placed in a distinct order of importance. For example, if the customer

"No, I just made a smart bet—one that was better informed than yours. I did my research, observed, and figured out something you didn't know. I discovered today what was going to matter tomorrow."

I didn't take his money, but I was glad for the opportunity to teach him an important life lesson, and I hope he took it to heart. When you make a bet, especially one that matters, with a lot at stake, you don't experience is your key point of differentiation, you should filter decisions through the question, "How will this affect our customers?" before you filter it through questions about cost. That doesn't mean you avoid the financial perspective, but that a filter is less important than the customer-experience perspective. The order of filters is driven by a clear understanding of who you are, as a brand and as a business. Here's an example of the four prioritized filters we used for decision-making at Panera:

1. How will this decision affect the experience of our guests?
2. How will this decision fit with or enhance our brand personality and authority?
3. How will this decision impact our operators?
4. How much will this decision cost?

Everyone, no matter what their functional perspective, knew this was how we made decisions. A finance person might voice concerns around cost, and this would be taken into account, but not allowed to trump lenses one, two, and three. That's the power of a decision-making lens: you avoid reverting to the lowest common denominator.

I believe every company needs its own version of this, especially as it grows and its functions become more powerful. The filters will be different, depending on the company's particular points of differentiation. Every decision must be subjected to the process, and every team member, no matter what their job title, needs to understand the whole process. Of course, this doesn't mean that decisions become easy. Every choice comes with trade-offs. The point is to make the right ones for your particular company, so that you stay aligned with what matters.

want to be flippant, and you sure don't want to be counting on luck or enthusiasm. By knowing the source of your own competitive advantage, starting from a game plan like a Concept Essence, then working hard to understand and build generalizations about what's going to happen in the future, you can in fact predict with some degree of confidence what the outcome of a particular initiative will be. Of course, when it comes to business, we can't just look up the future on our phones and know which bets will pay off. But we can learn things our opponents haven't discovered yet. Through empathy, careful observation, trend analysis, and the utilization of generalizations from one industry to another, we can improve our judgment and sharpen our powers of prediction—enough to give us a serious competitive edge. That's what powered Panera's growth in the early 2000s. Wi-Fi was just one of the smart bets we made. It was followed quickly by additional smart bets on catering, breakfast sandwiches, enhanced salads, and more—all of which fueled our same-store sales and intensified our credibility and growth.

Seek Out the Tough Stuff and Create a Barrier to Entry

I've done a lot of strange things in the service of getting my team to pay attention to what matters. One of my more unconventional management tactics involved lobbing a baguette toward one of my executives' heads. Okay, maybe "management" isn't quite the right word. It was more of a spontaneous display of frustration. And no, the baguette did not hit anyone, nor was it intended to. The point I was trying to make with my crusty missile was serious, though. Our bread wasn't good enough. And that was a big problem, because bread was never just a product to us; it was the cornerstone of our authority. Our Concept Essence declared: "Bread is our passion, soul, and expertise." "Bread" was part of our name. It had to define us. Everything we did would be measured against the quality of our bread.

To be fair, doing bread well is tough. It's devilishly difficult to make good, fresh bread under any circumstance, but to do so consistently in hundreds, eventually thousands, of cafés is damn near impossible. But that's precisely why it was a worthy challenge.

When it comes to making smart bets that create a competitive advantage, what matters is what's difficult. I *want* to do the tough stuff—I seek it out. Because if it's easy, it's not worth doing. Easy doesn't give you any sustained competitive advantage. Competitors will just copy what you've done—especially in a business like the restaurant business, where you're not protected by copyrights, where anyone can just walk in the door and see exactly what you're doing and copy it. You might as well be their R&D department. I remember a frozen yogurt company called TCBY in Little Rock, Arkansas, that was hot back in the nineties. It had a great thing going—right up to the moment McDonald's put frozen yogurt in its soft-serve machines. First to market means nothing if you only last a month. If there's no barrier to entry, there's no sustainable business model.

By having the capabilities to do the tough stuff and then successfully taking it on, you build a moat around the business—a barrier to entry that will buy you time. Barriers to entry are everything. When you make it harder for your competitors to copy what you are doing, you give yourself more space to discover the next growth opportunity. You create a mini-oligarchy, which gives you greater control over margins. By the time your competitors start bridging the moat, you will already be building a new one—working on a new and more difficult challenge. That's why Panera set out to literally bake a barrier to entry into our signature offering: our bread.

To build barriers to entry, you need to improve your capability to do difficult things, as opposed to simplifying it down to something that anybody and everybody can do. That's how you cement your authority, which is the means to gaining and sustaining competitive advantage.

A great example in the restaurant business is the Cheesecake Factory. Its complex menu offers real competitive advantage because it is hard to pull off right. Most competitors want to go in the opposite direction and simplify their menus. That's why the Cheesecake Factory has sustained its competitive advantage while so many other casual dining establishments fell by the wayside, copying each other. Mastering what's difficult—establishing your authority on that higher ground—is what sets you apart in the eyes of customers. It's what inspires them to walk past competitors and come to your door.

For us, setting ourselves apart meant the bread had to be freshly baked each day, using fresh dough. Very early in Panera's evolution, we'd decided we couldn't fall back on frozen dough—even though Au Bon Pain had invested heavily in one of the largest and most sophisticated frozen dough manufacturing facilities in the country. Utilizing that facility would have been economically and logistically much easier—but it would also have led to an inferior product and made the resulting bread easier for competitors to copy.

When we first acquired St. Louis Bread Company, it had several facilities that made the fresh dough and then shipped it out in refrigerated trucks to the stores, where it was proofed and baked. Expanding this operation for Panera was daunting—but necessary. Bread is based on yeast, a living organism. Fresh dough makes better bread, and better bread was the platform that made all our other food special. So, we recommitted to delivering fresh dough daily to *all* of our bakery cafés—no matter how many we built, no matter what the cost.

Talk about taking on the tough stuff. This meant that we weren't just in the food business; we were operating more than a million square feet of manufacturing facilities and running hundreds of trucks each day. Logistically, it was a nightmare.

St. Louis Bread Company's facilities, when they worked, produced an outstanding product. But they lacked the most basic process controls that would have made them scalable. There was little consistency in product quality or reliability in delivery. One time, a whole facility ran out of flour. Another time, they forgot to add salt, and the loaves all came out as flat, tasteless pancakes. Slowly but surely, thanks in large part to Mark Borland, John Maguire, and Mike Powell, who we brought in to oversee the facilities, we mastered the challenge of fresh dough, even as we grew.

We went on to build facilities throughout the country that would receive hundreds of thousands of pounds of raw ingredients every week, which they'd turn into dough and load onto a fleet of trucks that would travel thousands and ultimately millions of miles a year, through blizzards, hurricanes, and more, to ensure that we could bake and serve fresh bread in every café, every day.

Making fresh bread wasn't just hard; it was expensive. Building the facilities required significant capital, and it cost us many millions a year to run our fleet of trucks. We also spent dearly on our ovens. Early in the development of our concept, Scott Davis and I insisted on using artisan European deck ovens in all our cafés. They cost about $75,000 a pop. We had little hard evidence that this investment would pay off in the short term. But I never doubted the long-term competitive logic behind it. Without those ovens, we would be limited in our ability to produce an extraordinary crust and always have an inferior, easy-to-copy product.

When we declared, "Bread is our passion, soul, and expertise," we knew that if we pulled it off, we'd produce something that was difficult for rivals to match. Retail food outlets couldn't build and run manufacturing and distribution systems like ours. Smaller competitors lacked the scale and capital to mount such an effort. Industry giants would find it extremely challenging to integrate it into their complex supply chains.

But even with all of this investment, I was never fully satisfied with our bread. It did create critical barriers to entry, particularly in the early years. But it never quite lived up to the promise of our Concept Essence. In all my years at Panera, I pushed for improvements and invested in better systems and ingredients. Because it was core to our Concept Essence and our competitive advantage, I would not give up on that effort for over two decades.

What can you do that customers seek and your competitors can't deliver? In a world of abundance, what can you do that is scarce? What can you be that is special and unique? What do certain customers want that has greater authority and ultimately creates true differentiation for your enterprise? What's tough enough that it's worth doing right? That's your competitive advantage. It is a target that you must continue to clearly define and move toward with great intensity and focus if you hope to attain it.

You can never let up in this effort because competitive advantage is transient. You don't secure it once and then sit back and watch the

Ron's Rules for Gaining and Maintaining Competitive Advantage

- **Recognize that you can't please all people all the time.** Understand who your target customer is and what job they are hiring you to do. Develop a concept that's the singular best choice for some target customers on some days rather than the second-best choice for everyone, every day.

- **Define what competitive authority means** within your understanding of your concept and know how you will build it.

- **Make sure the niche you focus on is big enough to sustain you**, but not so easily duplicated that you simply become an R&D lab for larger competitors.

- **Search for the good ideas that really matter.** Otherwise, you could expend a lot of energy with a modest return.

- **Build barriers to entry.** Don't be afraid of the tough stuff. If it's worth doing, then do it and use it to build barriers to entry.

- **Get it done.** Execution is everything. If you can't actually deliver on your promises, you'll lose customers to competitors who can.

- **Accept that maintaining competitive advantage is really difficult.** One day you're the most attractive alternative on the block. The next day your target customer is walking past your door to a "new and better place" down the street.

- **Be willing to do it all over again.** Competitive advantage is fleeting. Don't wait for your competitors to pass you before seeking out a new opportunity.

profits roll in. Sooner or later, a bigger, better financed, or smarter competitor will figure out how to do what you do. The goal is not to double down forever on a successful competitive initiative; it's to postpone losing your advantage for long enough that you can innovate and evolve and continue to stay ahead of the competition. The key to thriving in a freakishly competitive world is to know what will matter tomorrow, get it done, and accomplish what others cannot—again, and again, and again.

In our era of rapid technological change, barriers to entry are collapsing faster all the time. Not only is competitive advantage transient, but as the world speeds up, the payoff from an original business model grows shorter all the time. The companies that succeed over the long term are masters at building barriers to entry.

At Panera, we knew that this was critical to our success. We'd later codify it in our cultural values as "no shortcuts." By avoiding the easy road and valuing things that were difficult, we believed we'd continue to set ourselves apart. *Get the tough stuff done with optimism and mastery*—that was our approach. The willingness to work on hard challenges for competitive advantage was embedded in our cultural DNA—and baked into our bread.

Know When to Fold 'Em

Want to know how to make a bunch of financial analysts happy? Give them free pizza. And not just any pizza—pizza they believe is going to drive growth and boost a public company's stock price.

It was early 2007, and I looked around in amazement at the almost giddy smiles on the faces of the normally dour financial professionals who had gathered to taste Panera's soon-to-be-launched new product, known as Crispani. They couldn't get enough of it! Their enthusiasm was reflected in our stock price, which rose dramatically following the new product's announcement. Market tests confirmed the positive story. Crispani was looking like a smart bet indeed. We invested in our first-ever television commercials to promote it. We couldn't wait to roll it out.

Crispani came about like many of our innovations: through observation, empathy, and generalization. In my role as innovator in chief, I never stopped paying attention to food trends. I knew that Panera had a unique capacity to take trendy niche products and mainstream them. "We observe what's happening in Brooklyn and bring it to Middle America," I always told my team. Well, one of the things that was happening in Brooklyn in those days, as well as in Portland, Seattle, and San Francisco, was artisan pizza. The cool kids weren't ordering from Pizza Hut anymore—they wanted handcrafted, authentic pies made with fresh dough and high-quality ingredients like real, fresh mozzarella and extra virgin olive oil. So Scott Davis created Crispani, a handcrafted, freshly baked, pizza product made with fresh dough and artisan toppings, baked in our stone deck ovens. It was so much better than the pizza you could find across much of America.

It seemed like a perfect play for Panera. We had established our authority in bread and could make and distribute fresh dough. Pizza was yet another way to "turbocharge the asset," I thought. We could capture a new day part—evening—the one time of day we were weakest. During its trial run, Crispani tested so well that we heralded it as the opening act in an ambitious mission to make our evening business as robust as our lunch business.

We didn't realize it at the time, but market tests can't reveal the long-term issues implicit in a national rollout. Such was the case with Crispani. All of us at Panera, and those analysts, were caught up in a classic case of "irrational exuberance." The biggest, most unanticipated challenge was how to make customers aware of Crispani's presence on the menu. People just didn't think "Panera = pizza." Or even, "Panera = dinner." Heck, even I didn't!

One evening, when Nancy asked me to pick up food for the kids on my way home, I stopped by the Cheesecake Factory. Michael and Emma were furious. Why hadn't I just brought home Crispani? I'd driven right by a Panera, and it never crossed my mind. That was the moment I realized how challenging it would be to get the possibility of pizza from Panera burned into potential customers' brains.

Though Crispani was a good idea and an even better product, we just didn't have the financial wherewithal and time to build awareness and indeed, authority, in such a crowded category without compromising the rest of our business. Soon, it became clear that's what was happening. Because we put most of our advertising spotlight on Crispani, we had fewer dollars to spend highlighting soups, salads, and sandwiches, and their sales dropped. Crispani boosted our dinner business but led to weaker sales in our lunch business. Plus, it required additional labor, which further strained our teams. Unlike all our other menu items, which could be collected at a counter, our pizza had to be delivered to the table. In retrospect, I saw that I'd focused on the wrong costs—the fixed costs, which were modest—and I hadn't been fully cognizant of the incremental labor costs inherent in rollout. As they say, it's the unknown unknowns that get you. What had the potential to be a smart bet had turned into a fool's errand.

As 2007 closed, I had to admit defeat. The numbers didn't lie. Sometimes, the smartest bet you can make is to know when to fold 'em—and do so quickly. Profit growth had flatlined and the stock price had fallen off significantly. The same analysts who'd devoured Crispani were now complaining about its unintended consequences. Shareholders were berating me.

If we'd been a private company, I'd have given Crispani more time. It truly was a great product. But in a public company, I simply couldn't justify the short-term pain.

"Let's pull it," I told my leadership team. "We've got to protect the P&L." And just like that, one of our most ambitious launches came to an embarrassing stop.

I learned a lot from the failure of Crispani. I told myself that no one wins 100 percent of the time. But it was hard to simply write it off as a learning experience and put it behind me. Crispani's demise shook the confidence of our associates and our investors. And it wasn't just their confidence in the company—it was their confidence in me. I can handle the personal humiliation of the occasional misstep, but what scared me with this was the hit to my credibility. Credibility is everything for a leader. It's the currency of the realm for leading people and bringing in investors and supporters. Failure erodes trust. And trust is what makes everything possible in business. When people trust you and believe in your credibility, and you make good on your bets, their trust increases and therefore they give you the time, the capital, and the resources to make more bets. It sets up a virtuous cycle of confidence. When you fail, the opposite occurs. And that trust takes time to rebuild. I believe I paid a price for the Crispani failure for the better part of a decade.

One of the most important lessons I learned from our ill-fated foray into pizza was about managing expectations. We got carried away with our own love for the product and talked it up every chance we got. The analysts amplified our enthusiasm. Crispani's promise took on mythical proportions. I've since learned to keep new products as quiet as I can for as long as I can. Once you drive up enthusiasm, you're boxed in by expectations. You have no room to maneuver, to learn, to course-correct. Under-promise and over-deliver.

Ron's Rules for Marketing

- **Know what marketing can and cannot do.** One of the biggest fallacies in the restaurant business is that marketing can build sustained sales growth. What actually builds sustained sales growth? In my estimation, we can correlate sales growth with:
  - The brand's authority and personality (this accounts for 60 percent).
  - The brand's credibility in the specific categories in which it competes (this accounts for 30 percent).
  - Traditional tools of marketing: price, promotion, advertising, etc. (this accounts for only 10 percent).
- **Imprint your brand in the minds of customers.** The most powerful role of marketing is to build long-term brand credibility. The focus of each marketing campaign should be to amplify the reality of the concept and the brand's long-term point of differentiation.
- **Focus your marketing on the long term.** Marketing programs that build long-term authority and credibility will have a long-term payout and a higher ROI. Marketing programs that build short-term traffic growth only (such as limited time offerings) will have a short-term payout and generate a very modest ROI.
- **Mix up the way you drive sales.** Sales can be built by driving transaction growth or increasing the average penny profit per transaction. Have a plan and the organizational capabilities to manage both.
- **Remember, marketing requires the soul of a merchant rather than simply the skills of a tactician.**

In a public company, don't talk about anything that isn't rolled out. The market lends itself to exaggeration on all fronts. You're never as good as they say you are and you're never as bad as they say you are. Learning to manage expectations is critical, and the less you can say, the better. For over a decade, I secretly dreamed about bringing back Crispani—but if I'd done it, I'd never have breathed a word of it before it was in stores.

If You Don't Have
Control, Credibility
Is Your Currency

In Irish culture, the shamrock is a symbol of luck. But when I got a call in late 2007 from Jeff Kip, my CFO, telling me that a private equity firm called Shamrock Holdings was buying up large blocks of Panera shares, I knew that Panera's luck had taken a turn for the worse. There was nothing fortunate about being targeted by Shamrock, and despite being founded by Roy Disney (Walt's brother), there was nothing funny about it either. These folks were best known for launching activist campaigns. They took down Michael Eisner at Disney. And now they were targeting us.

If you've never directly encountered activists, they might not sound like such a bad thing: motivated investors who see that a company is performing poorly and seek to influence its direction and produce better returns for investors. In reality, they're a scourge on the corporate world. They're raiding parties that show up when a company is struggling and put intense pressure on management for short-term results. They're bullies, taking advantage of weakness with no regard for anything but their own and their investors' profits. They don't care about the company, its vision, its people, or its long-term health. They don't care if they alienate your stakeholders. All they care about is driving up the stock price as quickly as possible, through whatever means they see as most effective. They wait until you're vulnerable, and then they strike.

At the end of 2007, Panera was a sitting target for activist investors. We'd been weakened by Crispani's failure, our share price had plummeted, and my personal credibility had taken a hit. I'd never encountered activists before, but I was about to discover why CEOs say that word in hushed and nervous tones. In the years ahead, I'd come to fear activists as much as any kid fears monsters under the bed. The very idea would wake me up in the middle of the night in a cold sweat.

It also made me reflect on what was probably the biggest mistake of my professional life: I gave up control of my company with the way we structured Au Bon Pain's IPO. While I'm glad we had the foresight to create a dual class of stock, we didn't go far enough. I failed to insist on far larger voting power for our Class B shares, as the founders of companies like Facebook and Google did. As a result, even though my 6 percent ownership gave me almost 20 percent voting power, I still didn't have enough leverage over the company I'd founded and nurtured to defend it against activists. Had I given Class B shares ten votes instead of three, I would have had more than 50 percent of the vote. I'd have had control.

To anyone who's still an entrepreneur, my advice to you is to think carefully about how much control you give up. If you can keep control, do it. But in the real world, most founders can't, or choose not to, because they need capital. Giving up control is still the norm.

So if you find yourself no longer in control of your company, my advice to you is to hang on to your credibility, at all costs. As I would learn during my encounter with Shamrock, if you don't have control, credibility is your most important currency.

By mid-January, Shamrock had amassed a 6.6 percent stake in Panera, which made it our fourth-largest shareholder. When I got a message that their people wanted to meet with me, I knew it was bad news. So did Panera's president, who quit that weekend. It's not unusual for senior executives to walk away on the dawn of a fight, but I hadn't expected that kind of cowardice from my team. It hurt.

I took the meeting with the Shamrock guys and heard their proposals to improve the company. They wanted to raise prices and buy back stock, paid for with debt. "Very innovative strategy," I thought to myself, sarcastically. To me, this could be risky, as raising prices typically hurts traffic growth, and debt creates long-term financial risk for the enterprise.

Next, I flew out to California and met Stanley Gold, Shamrock's CEO, for dinner at a Beverly Hills restaurant. We got along very well; we just saw the business completely differently. At one point he looked across the table at me and said, "I like you. You're not all that bad. But we know more about your business than you do." I knew he was wrong. What I didn't know was whether I'd be able to override his influence.

Sure, Panera had made some missteps with Crispani, but there was still no outsider who understood the business like I did. Gold thought otherwise. He wanted me to put Chris Kiper, a thirtysomething financial analyst from his fund, on the board. Even worse, he wanted to make him de facto vice president of strategy and innovation. Basically, Gold promised that if Chris were allowed to dictate our strategic moves, Shamrock would get off our backs.

In the ensuing weeks, Shamrock launched a bid to elect a new slate of directors and wipe out our dual-class stock, which would clear the way for it to gain far greater leverage over our board. Gold's logic was painfully clear: use corporate governance and financial engineering to push changes at Panera that would pump up the share price in the short term and thus generate a massive return for Shamrock. Such shortsightedness did not bode well for the long-term health of the business or my ability to care for our team members.

After meeting with Gold, I went into full campaign mode. My first priority was to ensure that Panera's institutional investors would back our board for another year. This was where my credibility was critical. It had taken a hit—but it wasn't a mortal blow. Thankfully, the majority of our investors continued to support me. I'll never forget when the late Jack Laporte, who headed the New Horizons Fund at T. Rowe Price, looked me in the eye and said: "You've delivered for us. We'll back you." I remember visiting the renowned Fidelity investor Will Danoff, who heads the massive Contrafund. As soon as I entered the room, he walked around the table and gave me a hug. I had been visiting Will every year for over a decade, and his support meant everything to me. The result of these relationships with my core investors was that I could be confident we had the votes and strength to take on Shamrock and reject its attempts to meddle in the company.

Having said that, I knew my leash was not all that long if I didn't deliver, as these institutional investors would be under pressure from their management to get the stock price up. So, we redoubled our effort to tighten the ship and drive up the share price in the short term in the right way.

When activists attack, you can't just go defensive. It's important to also listen to what they are asking and see what makes sense. Know what you are willing to change and what you are not. Find places to give a little and also define the line in the sand that you won't cross, even if it means you have to quit.

We focused on making smart price increases (after careful study) and put more discipline into capital allocation—which meant building fewer cafés. We'd grow slower, but better (that is, more profitably). But we wouldn't give up control of our board or layer on loads of debt.

It worked. The share price was much improved by year-end 2008, and fortunately, we had been able to bump it up without making fundamental changes to the business as a result of Shamrock's pressure. In fact, we executed some of the changes Shamrock was pushing for operationally. But we saw those things in context of our long-term plan to serve our constituents. The activists saw them as short-term means to raise the stock price.

Fighting activists isn't easy, because they have one key advantage: they don't care about the long term. It's easy to boost quarterly profits and pop the stock. All you have to do is rip costs out of the P&L by cutting back on labor and R&D and innovation. However, in the long term, those moves lead to a less competitive business that ultimately is less able to deliver for stakeholders. But the activists don't care, because by the time that happens, they'll have cashed out and moved on to their next prey, and the employees and the long-term believers like me will be left with the carcass.

Living under Shamrock's shadow was terrifying. It led me to many sleepless nights. I had poured decades of my life into my company, and I knew that there was a real chance I could lose control of its direction. It's hard to describe the pain I felt when I considered the possibility of being pushed out of the company I'd created.

By September, I experienced one of the happiest moments of my professional life. I was sitting in a franchisee meeting when my CFO passed me a note: Shamrock had just cashed out, selling its entire stake in Panera. I let out a whoop of joy. Thankfully, I'd had enough credibility to marshal a defense to the activists.

The Shamrock saga drove home a painful reality: it might have seemed like I held a lot of sway over Panera, but I lacked the power to keep the Shamrocks of the world at bay. I was reminded, once again, that I didn't have control.

It also highlighted the critical lesson that credibility is everything. If you've given up control—as most public company founder leaders have—all you have is your credibility. And credibility is very hard to build and very easy to lose. Once you take on partners in the form of investors, your creative license and ability to steer the company as you see fit depends to a large extent on your credibility. Credibility gives you air cover, so to speak, while you move forward with your medium- and long-term vision. The trick is, to maintain credibility, you have to worry about the short term, even though you know that what truly matters is the long term. This is the balancing act that the CEO of a public company performs every day: keep people happy in the short term in order to maintain the credibility to work for the long term. A public company is always vulnerable to the predations of those looking to make a quick profit, and if you neglect the short term, the activists will smell blood in the water.

Ron's Rules for Dealing with Activist Investors

- **Come from good faith.** As frustrating and even frightening as activists can be, they're part of today's corporate landscape, for better or for worse. You can't avoid dealing with them, so start out with an open mind and a willingness to listen and to talk.

- **Be a grown-up: It ain't personal.** It feels insulting to have some kid sitting in New York City try to bully you into running your business his way. It's tempting to make the activist the enemy and say things publicly that reinforce this. Don't. It won't serve you to do so, and it might just make them more determined to take you down a peg. Remember, you've got a lot more to lose than they do.

- **Know your limits.** This is a moment to ask yourself, what is your personal line in the sand? The line beyond which you will not go further. What are the things you'll never compromise, even if it means they will drive you out? Initiatives that are critical to the company's long-term health, the values that define you, the essential things that serve your core constituents: these are what you need to defend at all costs.

- **Find the win-wins.** Activists may by nature be short term in their thinking, but that doesn't mean all their ideas are bad. Listen to them; find some of their suggestions you can live with and that will maybe even benefit the company. Take action on these and celebrate the wins for everyone. Find ways to give them what they want (a boost in the stock price) without compromising what matters.

- **Count your votes.** If you don't have the backing of your board and institutional investors, you can't win against activists. Make sure you've got the votes. Visit the portfolio managers of your largest institutional investors in their offices personally, not just when the activists are attacking, but regularly. I'd suggest doing so at least once a year.

- **Leverage the crisis.** "A crisis is a terrible thing to waste," as Stanford economist Paul Romer said.[1] Use the activists as a foil to motivate and focus your team and get them in gear.

The Doing of the Doing

Why, I wondered, would Bill Allen, a friend from the restaurant industry, phone to ask me if he could fly up to Boston for some advice? He didn't need me to tell him how to run a restaurant. Bill had cofounded Fleming's Prime Steakhouse, which later became part of the Outback Steakhouse group (later renamed Bloomin' Brands). He'd overseen the process of going national with la Madeleine, a French bakery concept and one of Au Bon Pain's competitors. But when Bill came and we sat down for breakfast, he told me he was facing a new challenge. Two of Outback's founders had left the company under pressure from activists, and Bill had been tapped to take on the role of CEO of the entire company, a multibillion-dollar, multidivision public entity. *That's* what he was seeking advice on. He set down his coffee cup and said, "Ron, how the hell do you *run* a public company like this?"

Bill realized that his new role as CEO of a large company was something altogether different from running a restaurant, growing a concept, or even managing a division. And he knew that I understood that, having run a large public company for many years. During the breakfast, looking out over Boston's beautiful public gardens, I didn't pull any punches. "Leading a large public company is an exceedingly difficult task," I told him, "and everyone approaches it differently. But in the end, there's a simple test to see if you did it right, which is: *Did you get what matters done?*"

It's amazing to me how many CEOs fail that test. They talk the talk; they give speeches; they design impressive strategies; they launch initiatives. Yeah, they do a lot of stuff—they're busy, busy, busy—but somehow, they miss doing what actually matters. They get distracted chasing shiny new pennies or looking sideways at what competitors are doing. They obsess over the stock price (as if that's something they can control, rather than a by-product of getting what matters done).

I've talked a lot in these pages about how to identify what matters. But unless you can then put in place the processes and structures to ensure that what matters *gets done*—unless you can *execute*—you will ultimately fall short. Especially in a large, complex public company, where it's so easy to lose executional focus. Indeed, when people ask me the secret to Panera's success, or that of any business I'm involved in today, I'll say it's not really the innovative concept or the great products or even the fantastic people who work there. It's that we got done at least 80 percent of what we told ourselves would matter.

If you want to know the difference between a poorly run company and a great company, it comes down to that: the doing of the doing. Do they get it done? Of course, no one delivers 100 percent of what they set out to do. There are many things in life and in business that you can't control. But what you can control is what your organization focuses on and how it uses the three Ts: Time, Talent, and Treasury. Each is limited, so you want to make sure you're spending it on what truly matters. If you do this well, you *can* consistently deliver what you've set out to do. That's the hallmark of a great company in my book.

I often say, management is about ensuring the company delivers the plan; leadership is about ensuring the plan is right. Both are essential to success, and both are part of the CEO's job. When it comes to management, the CEO must design processes to ensure that you spend your Time, Talent, and Treasury on what your team agrees is most important for attaining and sustaining long-term competitive advantage. In running a big organization, it's too easy to fall into reaction mode— you just get up in the morning and do whatever is on your plate that day. You lose sight of the bigger picture—of where you're trying to go, and why it matters. A good, focused executional system gives you traction. Vision is great, but without execution, vision won't amount to much. Vision plus execution generates transformation.

The topic of execution is so important it deserves a book of its own (and indeed, a great one has been written, *Execution* by Larry Bossidy and Ram Charan, which has been a powerful influence in my own development as a manager and which I recommend). But if I were to boil execution (or "the doing of the doing") down to the essentials, I'd describe it the same way I described it to Bill Allen that day over breakfast: it's about getting the right people in the room at the right time, focusing on the right stuff, and then measuring your progress on the journey. The system is set up to ensure you have a closed-loop process with clear ownership and clear deliverables. The assumption that underlies it all is that structure is a CEO's best friend. Let's break that down.

· · ·

Focusing on the right things means knowing what matters—something we've talked about a lot in these pages. It means determining what initiatives the enterprise must get done in a given time frame to build toward a Concept Essence and attain competitive advantage. Once you've gone through your future-back process and identified those critical initiatives on which you must deliver, those should drive everything. In my companies, we call them Key Initiatives (KIs) (see the sidebar "Ron's Rules for Identifying Key Initiatives"). They're not just things you happen to be doing; they're the central focus around which you organize the activities of your whole company for the next year. They're your work plan.

KIs should be seen as those few things that matter most to accomplish an organization's medium-term objectives. They can be multiyear in nature but represent what must be accomplished next year to move the company forward.

We began the KI process by soliciting input from the organization, and then I personally wrote the first draft, and often the second and third as well. I allowed my senior leadership team to review the KIs, edit them, and then prioritize them. It was often noted how many versions of our KIs were created, and the fact that we sometimes created thirty or more versions speaks to how important it was to get the KIs right. Every word mattered when we drafted them.

Each KI was color-coded. Gold KIs were the limited number of initiatives (two or three) that we had decided the company (and its CEO) *must* ensure got accomplished in the next year. I often thought of our gold KIs as initiatives that, if we failed to accomplish them, I should fire myself. They were that important. Red KIs (three or four) were ones that we really *should* make progress on in the year and we should not feel good if we didn't. And black KIs were those initiatives that mattered but were not as important.

For each KI, we delineated the specific projects that served as the work plan that would allow us to deliver on the initiative. As we drafted our KIs, we tried hard to be clear about which project came first, which came second, and which came third if we hoped to accomplish the initiative.

Once you have your KIs, the next question is, Who's going to get these things done? An initiative or project without accountability won't get completed. In my companies, each initiative has both an executive sponsor who is generally accountable and an initiative leader who is personally responsible to organize, direct, and coordinate the cross-functional team working on the initiative. Each project that supports a KI also has an individual assigned as responsible for the project. Once the team knows who the decision-maker is on any given initiative or project, then everyone on the team can offer an opinion safely.

I think long and hard about who I will hold accountable for what initiatives. In fact, my criteria (and the criteria I suggest for every CEO) when assigning key accountabilities are that the CEO must have a confidence level of 80 percent or greater that the individual assigned to lead the work has the capability, wherewithal, and time to get it done. If you don't have that kind of confidence in your leaders (and in my experience, CEOs often don't), you need new team members.

Ron's Rules for Identifying Key Initiatives

To get clarity on your Key Initiatives, work from the future back. In so doing, you can distinguish between means, ends, and by-products.

- **Describe the by-product.** This is where you want the organization to be in two to five years, your long-term vision for the impact you want to have. This is an outcome you can envision, but you can't create directly. It's a *by-product*, so the next question is, Of what?

- **Describe the ends.** Work backward: What would the company have needed to do to achieve the impact you just described? What initiatives did it pursue and complete? What smart bets did it make? These should point you toward the specific *ends* that you can pursue, and they will become your KIs over the next one to three years.

- **Identify the means.** Once you've made the hard choices about what KIs you're going to focus on, you can break down each one in order to clarify the *means* that will get you there. This includes delineating projects that underpin successfully completing each KI; assigning each KI an executive sponsor and KI leader; creating a cross functional team; setting a cadence of meetings to ensure that the team has the time to do the work and there are appropriate reviews; and identifying metrics by which you'll judge whether you're on track (see the sidebar "Ron's Rules for Meaningful Metrics"). In this way, you assign Time, Talent, and Treasury to each KI in order to ensure you succeed.

In sum: It's hard to execute effectively if you're not clear about means, ends, and by-products. When you work backward in this way from your desired outcomes, the building blocks of your operational plan become clear. Your KIs are the essential *ends* that you're working toward in order to attain and sustain competitive advantage. Their *by-product* will be the company's long-term success. Everything else you do (besides the simple maintenance tasks that you do to just keep the lights on, which I call accountabilities) is the *means* you've identified to deliver on your KIs. If you can be clear about these distinctions and build your strategy and executional capabilities around them, you will get what matters done, at least 80 percent of the time. Which is more than most companies ever do.

At Panera, to reinforce the message of accountability, I'd sometimes walk round the table and stand behind the executive in question. Placing my elbows on their shoulders, I'd lean forward, letting them feel my weight. "You're going to get this done, right?" I'd ask, all the while pressing down on their shoulders. "Do you feel the weight of that responsibility?" That's the way I want my teams to feel when they lead an initiative or take on a project.

• • •

Once you've identified your KIs and assigned them to team members, the next question is, How do you organize time to ensure the work gets done? You've got to get the right people in the room at the right time. And I mean that literally—if it's important, it needs to be scheduled in the calendar, because what gets scheduled gets done. I'm not ashamed to say that I'm a slave to my calendar. How you spend your time, and how your people spend their time, is one of the most impactful decisions a leader can make, and a good leader should never be vague or undisciplined about that valuable resource.

A Master Calendar is foundational to any good execution system. It allows you to allocate time against what matters. A Master Calendar structure is built by looking at the next year and allocating time appropriate to your KIs. It lays out a regular cadence of meetings over the course of each week, month, and year. Included on the Master Calendar are KI working meetings, KI review meetings, strategic reviews, performance/P&L reviews, large team meetings to review where the team is on the journey, and one-on-ones between the CEO and his or her direct reports. Once the Master Calendar is constructed, it's applied month-to-month as the year unfolds. The objective is to stick to the Master Calendar structure and not let events control how management spends its time. I know meetings get a bad name in organizational life, but that's because people don't know how to have effective meetings. Done well, however, meetings accelerate our progress. The key is to be highly intentional about who is meeting, how often, and

why. The Master Calendar might seem excessive at first glance. But once people get used to it, they love it. It creates structure for their shared work life, and it ensures that everyone stays aligned and focused on what matters. (See the sidebar "Ron's Rules for Creating a Master Calendar.")

. . .

Of course, once you've identified, assigned, and scheduled your KIs, then you have to get down to the doing of the doing. And how will you know you've done it? You do that by establishing the right metrics to ensure that you did what matters and by continuing to appropriately adjust your course.

Metrics could be numbers but aren't always. Your metrics need to represent, in a concrete sense, what success looks and feels like. A metric is a mechanism to know whether you got done what you set out to do. Too often, metrics aren't connected to the *ends* people are working toward. Tracking the wrong metrics can make everyone feel like they're doing their job when they're not. If your goal is to have a good vacation in Florida, your metric needs to reflect whether you had a good time. Tracking how many miles you traveled doesn't tell you if you hit your objective. Time spent in Florida doesn't tell you. In the same way, many companies assign undue significance to numeric metrics. Unless you have a comprehensive set of metrics that directly relate to what you're trying to achieve, you could be deceiving yourself.

Remember, people respect what you inspect. If you don't measure something, it's hard to convince people that it matters. You can get up on a stage and make a speech declaring, "We're about 100 percent customer satisfaction," or "We're about serving high-quality food." But if you don't measure it, and people know that their supervisor or boss will be judging their performance based on how much they're able to cut food or labor costs, then your declarations are baloney.

In sum, we must measure the things that matter. And we must do so consistently, throughout the organization. For every Key Initiative,

Ron's Rules for Creating a Master Calendar

The Master Calendar is one of the pillars of my operational system, and it includes different types of meetings that need to be scheduled with regularity:

- **KI working meetings/KI reviews.** These are team meetings built around each KI. They might be held weekly or bimonthly. These meetings are focused on getting KIs done, making decisions on a KI's projects, checking progress against the metrics you've identified, and so forth.

- **Strategic reviews.** These are infrequent, perhaps once a year, but they offer a chance to check that you're still heading in the right direction. Are you working on the right KIs? Are you making progress? Are you getting done what matters most? Do new projects need to be identified, or new leaders assigned?

- **Performance reviews.** These are meetings (often monthly) to review the organization's results against desired outcomes.

- **Alignment gatherings.** These are larger meetings, perhaps with the entire executive leadership team, or the top two tiers of managers, or even the entire company. They might be held monthly, every few months, annually, or even every two years, depending on the size of the gathering. The purpose of these meetings is to unite people in the organization's larger story (see chapter 23 for more on this).

- **One-on-one meetings.** These are an opportunity for aligning with direct reports, making sure everyone is connected and sharing the same perspective on what matters and how to get it done. These might happen once a month or more frequently if the relationship requires it.

Functional meetings, such as marketing department meetings, are not on this list, because I don't believe they're central to an organization's work. The meetings that matter are focused on specific projects or initiatives and are, by nature, cross-functional.

Ron's Rules for Meaningful Metrics

How do you know you're achieving what matters? How do you define "done"? By creating metrics that represent, in a concrete sense, what success looks and feels like. These don't necessarily have to be numbers. To create a meaningful metric, ask yourself:

- **How will we judge ourselves?** What can we point to as direct evidence that we are making progress on what matters?

- **Who will judge us?** Often, this is the more important question. How would our key stakeholders consider our progress?

This might lead you to create a metric that is not a number, but a question, with a rating scale attached. "In the eyes of _____, to what degree have we achieved _____?"

it's critical to identify metrics that will give you meaningful guidance as to whether you're making progress and achieving your aims. Then, you'll have not just vision but visibility.

To succeed in any long-term initiative requires that everyone has a sense of the bigger picture—not just the immediate ends you're working toward, but the longer-term objectives and by-products you seek. To ensure that understanding, it's wise to measure your progress as the journey unfolds and indeed to know where you are in that journey at any point in time.

In the case of a business enterprise, I utilize Concept Essence and a high-level, five-year financial plan to understand our trajectory. At Panera, we had a five-year financial plan that we reviewed every quarter. This long-term financial model existed so that our most important leaders (both the board and senior management) could have a shared expectation of our multiyear journey and a line in the sand to judge where we stood in the journey at any given time. We also used it as a forcing mechanism to help people appreciate the financial implications of various initiatives and to better distinguish what initiatives mattered most to creating the future we desired. I like to think of such a five-year plan not as a commitment to be delivered but rather as a gauge to know where we are on the journey.

Like many organizations, we utilized one-year financial plans as well to properly budget costs consistent with future expectations for sales and profit, create incentive plans, and most crucially to manage our commitment to each other and our board and Wall Street. It was another tool to understand where we stood in the journey, albeit in a shorter time frame.

The key to proper short-term (one-year) financial planning is to define in advance the degree of difficulty inherent in the plan. To do that, we created three different versions of the financial plan. We started with the management plan, in which we held ourselves to a degree of difficulty of seven on a ten-point scale (this meant it was tough, and we'd likely hit it only one out of every three years). This represented our challenge to ourselves. We then buffered the management plan down by X dollars per quarter to create what we called the board plan. The buffer allowed us some room for the unknown unknowns. It represented our commitment to the board and was used for our short-term incentive plans. Its degree of difficulty was five on a ten-point scale, with the understanding we would hit or exceed it on average every other year. Last, we developed our street (as in Wall Street) plan. For that, we'd buffer the board plan down further by X dollars per quarter. Its degree of difficulty would be three on the ten-point scale, with the objective being that we hit the street plan three out of every four quarters. (It was our desire to hit the street numbers almost every quarter and only occasionally miss them, so we kept investors and analysts guessing.)

Another valuable tool we used when developing one-year financial plans was to plan out full-year sales but hold back final approval of general and administrative overhead expense increases for the last two quarters of the year. We did that because we knew that once we approved the cost increases, we would never be able to get them out of the budget and we would have far better knowledge midway through the year as to whether we had the sales and profit required to support the increased level of overhead.

I firmly believe that the annual financial planning process should start with a top-down, externally sensitive target. In the case of organizations I ran, we started with a one-year financial target defined by top management (CEO and CFO) based on a limited number of key inputs (in our case, it would be store count and same-store sales) and with a fulsome appreciation of what was necessary to maintain our credibility with the street and our long-term five-year financial plan. It would be presented to the senior team in an annual planning meeting, during which we would explain it, allow our team to push on it, and ultimately seek their support for it. Our intention in that meeting was that everybody in the senior leadership team was operating from

Ron's Rules for Smart Cost Management

Cost control is fundamental to a successful business, and it was central to the discipline we utilized at Panera. These rules kept our costs in check:

- **Remember: One dollar of additional cost necessitates three dollars of additional sales to pay for it.** Put another way, saving 100 basis points of cost is the equivalent of reducing required sales growth by a whopping 300 basis points.

- **Challenge any cost that grows year-over-year faster than revenue.** Cost discipline today protects the organization from getting ahead of itself and being required to reduce head count or reactively reduce operating expenses tomorrow.

- **Reducing variance from standard reduces waste.** Reducing waste is smart cost management.

- **Keep cost savings in context.** Cost saving isn't an end in itself. It pays for what really matters. Cost savings pay for innovation and allow for investment in quality and service that are central to the customer experience.

the office of the CEO—as if we were all sitting in a helicopter flying at about ten thousand feet.

Once the senior leadership team signed off collectively on the target, we did a bottom-up, department-by-department budget. This went deep and was highly disciplined, with multiple inputs. The focus was on understanding the components of our plan and determining what changes in overhead expenditures would make sense and why. Then we would compare that bottom-up budget with the target (without exception, they were off by tens of millions of dollars).

The CFO, planning team, and I would then conduct meetings with each departmental leader and compare their bottom-up plan to target. Our intention was to ask each leader to explain to us where the cuts should be made in their department or elsewhere to reach the target we had all signed up for. This process of comparing bottom-up departmental budgeting to a previously agreed-on target certainly brought focus to what mattered as we contemplated next year's expenditures.

In some cases, there was an inability to reach agreement, and as CEO I made the final decision. I found people understood that in total the plan needed to work, and they appreciated clear direction. In the end, they knew my objective was to form a workable plan for the entire company and to ensure that we never got out over our skis and allowed our overhead to exceed conservatively budgeted sales and profit.

• • •

Execution is "the missing link between aspirations and results," Larry Bossidy and Ram Charan write in their classic *Execution*. "As such, it is a major—indeed, the major—job of a business leader."[1] Bill Allen knew this, which is why he asked me to breakfast to seek my advice. Good execution starts at the top.

A leader may be the innovator in chief, but that doesn't mean they can neglect execution. Execution is so fundamental that it must be part of the leader's explicit responsibilities to ensure that it's done well. And to do that, you need to design a detailed executional system that fits your organization, driven from the future back.

When you're trying to manage from the future back—to engineer a specific by-product, by focusing on an end through a series of means— you need to keep checking that it all adds up. And that means having the right focus and getting the right people in the room at the right time, with the right metrics and a clear understanding of where they are in the journey.

It's not enough to just have leadership thinking this way. *Everyone* in an organization needs to be connected to the big picture—to be willing and able to step out of the limited perspective of their role and hop into the metaphorical helicopter and consider the company and its progress as the CEO might.

As I told Bill Allen, there's no one "right" way to execute—just as there's no one right way to run a marathon or climb a mountain. The systems I've used, and continue to use today, are those that have proven effective in my companies for achieving what we set out to achieve. In the end, what's right is what gets you where you want to go. What's right is what gets what matters done.

Business Would Be Easier without People

There are some lessons, in business and in life, that we learn once and never forget. And then there are others that we seem to need to learn the hard way, time and time again, before they stick. For me, one of the toughest lessons to learn took the better part of three decades. It dogged me throughout my years at Panera. Perhaps I'm still learning it. To explain, let me take you back to the first time I learned the lesson.

It was 3 a.m., and I was in the Au Bon Pain kitchen trying to convince a drunk baker that he needed to follow a schedule. This was back in the early eighties, when I was a brand-new entrepreneur, not long out of business school. I was working ninety-hour weeks, figuring out how to run three bakery cafés. And a big part of that was figuring out how to deal with the folks who worked at those cafés—some of whom, like that baker, relied on various substances, both legal and illegal, to get through the long hours of the midnight-to-8 a.m. shift. I'd inherited these people when we merged Au Bon Pain and the Cookie Jar, along with a bakery full of broken-down equipment. I brought in my auto mechanic to fix the machines as best he could (one such fix involved a coat hanger that almost electrocuted one of the bakers). But at twenty-seven, I was at a loss as to how to deal with human dysfunction. As I patiently tried to show the drunk baker how to use the schedule, a thought occurred to me that would come back again and again in the years that followed: *business would be a hell of a lot easier without people!*

I know, you think I'm joking. And I am—but only partly. Business really would be easier without people. The business side of business—the strategy, the processes, the execution—is easy, relatively speaking. Yes, it takes smarts, persistence, vision, and careful calculation. But it's rational and for the most part predictable. When it comes to making a business work, however, you need help. Which means *people*. Dozens, hundreds, thousands, even tens of thousands of people. At its high point, Panera had more than a hundred thousand team members. And what makes it so difficult—but also so much more interesting—is that each person has their own psychology, humanity, priorities, motivations, and needs. And then, as if that wasn't complicated enough, they all have to relate to each other and find ways to work productively together.

The lesson I struggled to learn, back then, was this: people are who they are, and you're not going to get very far by trying to make them who you want them to be. Fundamentally, people don't change that much. Sure, you can offer opportunities to learn and grow, and some people will decide to take them. But a leader's responsibility is not to make a person succeed. A leader's responsibility is to create a direction for the organization and provide the space within which individuals can step up and perform, should they choose to do so. Some will. But some won't—like that baker, who was never going to get his act together and give a damn about much more than getting through his shift and going home to sleep it off. No amount of coaching from me was going to change him. In his case, meeting him where he was meant accepting this fact and firing him. In other cases, such extreme measures might not be required. But the lesson still applies: people are who they are, so your best bet as a leader is to meet them where they are, figure out what makes them tick, and create systems that let people see that it is in their interest to help fulfill the organization's goals.

In the years after I fired the drunk baker, I learned a lot about how to manage a business and create systems that incentivize people. But

I still too often found myself trying to get people to be who I wanted them to be rather than accepting the truth of who they were. This was particularly true when the people in question were people I'd worked with for years and built relationships with.

Such was the case with one executive who'd been with me since before the birth of Panera. I loved him as one can only love a fellow traveler with whom one has shared the highs and lows of a long and arduous journey. And yet, after more than a decade, I struggled to confront the uncomfortable truth that he just wasn't getting his job done anymore. He seemed to have checked out, overwhelmed by the responsibilities of a role that had outgrown him. I kept thinking I could get him to change. I pushed him, waited for him to step up, and felt frustrated by the situation, perhaps even a little let down. I found ways to cover for him, doing parts of his jobs myself. The last thing I wanted was to fire an old colleague. So, I avoided it for much longer than I should have. Eventually, we mutually agreed he should leave the company. But I let it fester too long, and I regret that decision. In fact, one of my greatest regrets or failings as a leader is that I should have fired more people faster.

As I matured as a leader, I got better at having those honest conversations in a more timely manner. Sometimes it's uncomfortable. But sometimes it's a relief for all involved. Oddly, I've received many thank-you letters from people I've fired over the years. Former employees I asked to leave have later told me that they learned more about themselves and how to run a business while working for me than at any other time in their career. You can fire someone and still respect each other.

A leader must be as honest as possible—but you can do this in a kind and caring way. When you tell someone that they're not doing the job, you're transferring the responsibility onto their shoulders, rather than shouldering it yourself. Maybe they improve. Maybe they leave. Whatever the outcome, they own it. And you own the greater responsibility for serving the interests of the organization and its stakeholders, not just making the individuals who work there feel better. And as our late

COO Mark Borland used to say, "The good of the many is more important than the interests of one person."

Of course, not all honest conversations result in someone being fired. Sometimes, speaking the truth can improve relationships. Getting difficult dynamics out in the open can break the pattern. Acknowledging uncomfortable realities can clear the air and allow people to find creative solutions. And because human psychology is complex and sometimes hard to predict, I'm a great believer in getting professional help with such matters. I always say that therapists belong in the C-suite. Over the years, I've sought the help of organizational psychologists to assist with all kinds of delicate human conundrums, including some that were personal to me. I also turn to therapy outside of the office to help me understand myself better—to shine light on my own blind spots and defenses and the ways in which they may be getting in the way of creating the life I want, both in and out of the workplace.

One of the things I've learned about myself is why it took me so long to learn how to fire people faster. I was too wrapped up in being a caring leader. I used to think that "servant leadership" meant treating my team as a family. I cared enormously about their well-being, sometimes at my own expense or the expense of the organization's interests. Why was I so reluctant to let these people go? Experience comes from banging your head against a wall, I guess. It was only later in my leadership journey that my understanding of servant leadership deepened. Servant leadership isn't about being nice at all costs. It's about being *helpful* at all costs. And radical honesty is a much greater service to people than simply being kind.

In the end, the deeper lesson I've learned from my decades of working with hundreds of thousands of people is this: business *wouldn't* really be easier without people—it would be impossible. I could not have fulfilled my dreams for the company without the energy, creativity, commitment, and hard work of others. And yet, people are complicated, messy, quirky, and unpredictable. And that includes you. So, *deal with it*. Be lovingly, brutally honest, first and foremost with yourself, and then with those you work with. If there's anything that will make an organization work better, it's that.

Ron's Rules for People Management

- **Don't disagree on what matters.** It's okay for team members to disagree on the solution to a problem. It's not okay for team members to disagree on vision, mission, or values.

- **It is not a leader's responsibility to ensure that a person succeeds.** A leader's responsibility is to set the expectations and provide the opportunity for individuals to step up and perform, should they choose to do so.

- **The good of the many is more important than the good of the individual.** If it comes down to a choice, put the interests of the organization and its stakeholders before individual interests.

- **Play favorites.** Take care of the people who help you get done what matters.

- **Know who can do what.** The people who know what is wrong often can't fix a problem. The people who can fix the problem often don't know what's wrong. Smart management is about listening to the people who know what's wrong and empowering those who can fix it.

- **Ensure your people stay in their lanes and get their jobs done.** A culture of blaming other individuals or functions accomplishes nothing.

- **Ask yourself: If people are the key to your success, are you willing to pay them right?** A good leader doesn't just give lip service to the importance of people; they put their money where their mouth is.

- **Be honest, even if it leads to a team member's departure.** They may even thank you later.

- **Beware of bureaucracy.** Run a large company that operates like a small company not a small company with the bureaucracy of a large company.

Parish Priest in a Business Suit

The hotel ballroom was darkened, but I was sure that if I could have seen the faces of my executives, I'd have caught a few eye rolls. "Here he goes again," they were no doubt thinking, as I clicked "play" and the giant video screen lit up. By this point, they were accustomed to my habit of opening meetings with inspirational videos that had no immediate or obvious relationship to the business of running bakery cafés or selling sandwiches. On the screen, a lean, middle-aged man in khakis and a black polo shirt got down on the floor in front of his audience and banged out an impressive set of push-ups to illustrate his claim that he felt in good health despite a terminal cancer diagnosis. The video is known as *The Last Lecture*, by Randy Pausch, a professor of computer science at Carnegie Mellon University. In this powerfully uplifting speech, given just a month after his diagnosis and less than a year before he passed away, Randy talks about how we cannot change the cards we are dealt, only the way we play them. And the way he chose to play them was to live a positive, fun-filled life, rather than losing himself in complaints and victimhood. It's a message that we've all heard, but there's something about hearing it from a man who literally has months to live that drives its meaning home with great power.

When the speech ended and the lights went on, not a single eye was rolling. A few people may have been surreptitiously wiping away tears.

I was deeply moved myself, and I'd heard the speech a half-dozen times. As I stepped up to the stage, I could feel that the mood in the room had changed dramatically. It was serious, introspective, and the weight of big questions hung in the air. It felt more like a church or a temple than a quarterly leadership meeting. And that's exactly how I wanted it.

I've always considered my role as leader to be more like a parish priest or a rabbi. Every time I stepped up to address the company—whether it was a crowd of thousands at one of our Family Reunions, a group of several hundred leaders at one of our quarterly Circle of Warmth meetings, or my top team of twenty or so executives—the Leavening Committee, as I called them—I felt like I was giving a sermon. Of course, I wasn't trying to push religion on anyone, but I always considered meaning-making to be an essential part of my job.

People are looking for a sense of meaning, in their life and their work. Meaning is what motivates us—the sense that we're part of a bigger story, part of something that matters. Meaning occurs when we understand where we came from, where we are, where we want to go, and the "why" of the journey. And the leader's job is to share that story, again and again, like a priest who shows up every Sunday to offer perspective and context. I want every team member, no matter where they sit in the company hierarchy, to know that they will participate in a regular series of meetings designed to connect them to the broader journey of the company, help them learn the game of business, and help them deal with whatever pain and uncertainty they may be experiencing along the way.

It's easy to get lost on the journey. We know that some things are more important than others but we lose sight of them all too easily. Our day-to-day tasks, myriad distractions, short-term anxieties—all of these can easily overwhelm us and obscure the path we're on. We lose our way when we're in crisis; we lose our way when we feel good. And much like a minister or rabbi helps people avoid succumbing to momentary desires and fears to focus on living a good and meaningful life, business leaders must be ready to help people avoid overreacting to short-term pressures or successes and to focus on the organiza-

tion's long-term health and impact. Often, this means bringing your team up when they're feeling down and defeated, and encouraging humility and healthy skepticism when things are going particularly well. This role gets more difficult to play for a leader as head count grows. When people's roles become more specialized and there are layers and layers of management between leaders and team members, you can't take for granted that everyone is feeling connected to the meaning in what they're doing. Indeed, with size, it becomes even more important for the CEO to recognize that one of their most important jobs is to create meaning and provide context and perspective for the organization.

Besides these meetings, I also delivered my "sermons" in writing, in the form of companywide memos on holidays like Thanksgiving and at times of national significance. I'd use those opportunities to create a sense of pride in who we were and what we did and to foster unity in the face of competition. I always tried to remind people of the goals and values we shared. I also used my letters to highlight team members who could serve as examples to all of us.

My sermonizing wasn't limited to our team members. I took the same approach in our quarterly earnings calls, and I kept up a regular cadence of meetings with our most important investors, analysts, vendors, and other external stakeholders. All of these stakeholders were connected into the same narrative of meaning and purpose that Panera represented. All of them looked to me for that long-term perspective of where the company was coming from, where it was today, and where it was going in the future, and I considered it critical to keep their eyes on that horizon. It was a strategy that served me well during times of uncertainty, like the Shamrock activist attack in 2007–2008 when our investors chose to maintain their faith in me and in Panera.

While every speech I gave was different, the underlying storyline was always the same: "Here's where we've come from," I'd remind people. "Here's where we are today. And here's where we could be tomorrow—*if* we get a few important things right." There was always an "if"—a moment to let my audience feel the consequentiality of their own actions, the weight of their choices. "We have this possibility in

A Schedule of Meaning-Making Meetings

It's essential to create a regularly scheduled series of meetings dedicated to providing a holistic perspective, a long-term vision, and a sense of meaning. At Panera, which was a large public company with over a hundred thousand employees, I relied on a schedule of gatherings of different sizes to accomplish this. I use similar formats with many companies today, although the names are different, and the size of gatherings varies depending on the size and stage of the company.

- **Family Reunion** (every two years). This was a companywide gathering (which often felt like a revival meeting) for everyone from store management upward.

- **Franchisee Meeting** (three times a year). This was an opportunity for our franchisees to gain perspective on where the company was going and provide their input.

- **Circle of Warmth** (quarterly). This group of 150 to 200 people represented those who worked on customer-facing innovation initiatives. They had to present their work in front of their peers and, more importantly, sell their ideas to the operators.

- **Leadership** (quarterly). These were the three hundred or so most senior people in the organization, generally with P&L responsibility. It was an opportunity for them to get in the helicopter, so to speak, with me and senior management, and see the company and its journey holistically and longitudinally.

- **Leavening Committee** (monthly). This was the top twenty to thirty people in the company, the ones who made the company work. In many companies this is called the executive leadership team. We would use this meeting to review major strategic and operating decisions, and the team would have the opportunity to challenge them.

our hands" was the message—"and it's up to each of us to bring it into being." In a sense, the essence of pretty much any great sermon ever delivered is this: consider what matters and then reflect on your choices.

No matter what the faith tradition, a good sermon essentially aims to connect the dots between past, present, and possible futures (in this

world or beyond). A good leader, like a priest or rabbi, must be able to make people feel the relationship between yesterday's decisions, today's challenges and opportunities, and tomorrow's promised outcomes. Sometimes it's an inspirational tale, one that can pull people toward a bright possibility. Other times, it might strike a note of caution, even fear—warning people of the consequences if they fail to step up and deliver. Whatever the plotline, the leader must be an expert storyteller, skilled at the art of uniting and inspiring people through the power of narrative.

Humans are storytelling creatures. We learn through metaphors and allegories. As cognitive scientist Mark Turner writes, "Narrative imagining—story—is the fundamental instrument of thought. Rational capacities depend on it. It is our chief means of looking into the future, of predicting, of planning, and of explaining. . . . Most of our experience, our knowledge, and our thinking [are] organized as stories."[1]

Narrative is woven through the fabric of every culture, and corporate culture is no exception. The stories we tell about the work we're doing, why we're doing it, and who we're doing it for are what elevate our everyday tasks and inspire us to give more. When people understand where the company is coming from, where it is today, and what the future could look like under different scenarios, they feel more motivated to step up and do their part in creating the best possible future. That longitudinal perspective connects everyone to the key drivers of the business and links them together in a shared mission, no matter how small or specific their part.

My intention, every time I stepped up to a microphone or sat down at a boardroom table or wrote anything, was to instill a culture of responsibility throughout the company. Culture isn't some piece of paper stuck on the wall in the HQ. Culture is the animating story of a company. It's "the way we do things here." I wanted people to feel obligated—not to me but to each other, to our shared mission and vision. I'm often reminded of the saying: people don't die for a country; they die for the guys in the foxhole next to them. That's how I wanted our people to feel. In my parish priest role, I was building a culture of connection, accountability, humility, humanity, and appropriate foresight. Not just among the executives but among folks throughout the company—the people who made things run day to day.

Most leaders accept too little from their people. Just check out the perennially miserable metrics on "employee engagement." If team members are giving only a fraction of their energy and commitment at work, that's on the leader. If morale is low and people are just showing up for a paycheck, that's on the leader.

Give people a bigger context. Tell a better story. Make their work mean more than the bottom line. The leader's job is to give people a reason to do more than is expected of them, not less.

That doesn't mean simply being a cheerleader. Sometimes it means being transparent about hard truths, naming the eight-hundred-pound gorilla that no one wants to acknowledge. But a good priest or rabbi can deliver such messages in a way that relieves everyone of the burden of denial and makes them feel more empowered and accountable for solving the problems they face. When you can contextualize a challenge or a moment of crisis—connect it to choices made in the past and to possible transformations in the future—you give people a sense of ownership, agency, and purpose. And if people are engaged in this way, if they experience a sense of meaning in the job they're doing, it will be felt throughout the organization.

No matter how busy I was with my own projects and initiatives, no matter how much pressure I felt from external stakeholders, I never neglected this parish priest function. Indeed, drafting speeches, preparing for meetings, and writing memos took up a significant amount of my time—some people, no doubt, thought it was too much of my time. I wrote—and rewrote and rewrote—my own stuff. But I know without a doubt that providing context, thought-provoking perspective, and meaning is one of the highest-leverage activities a leader can undertake.

Be Contrarian: Conserve in a Boom, Build in a Bust

How many CEOs began their 2008 annual shareholder letter with the declaration that it had been a great year, one of the strongest in the company's history? Not many. For most businesses, that year was an *annus horribilis*, one they would happily consign to the garbage can of history. The economy collapsed, the stock market fell more than 30 percent, and those companies that survived the carnage did so by gutting their workforces and cutting back on all fronts, leaving them weakened and hurting.

Yet when I sat down in the spring of 2009 and typed the words "Dear Stockholder," my heart was full of gratitude and pride for what Panera had accomplished in the difficult year behind us. After the Crispani challenges and the Shamrock activist attack, we'd only gotten stronger. We had met or exceeded our earnings targets in each quarter of 2008. Our stock was up 50 percent, which made us the best-performing restaurant stock of the year. Indeed, by that point, we'd been the best-performing stock in the restaurant industry when measured over the prior decade. Panera not only had stayed the course, but had come out ahead. Why? Because we did the opposite of what most people in our industry were doing.

One thing that will be no surprise to readers by now is that I am a contrarian. If everyone is in favor of something, I'm probably headed in the opposite direction. When others are celebrating, I'm worrying, and when others are worrying, I'm looking for the silver lining. It's not because I'm trying to do the opposite of everyone else for its own sake. It's because I'm trying to live into the future when everyone else is fixated on the present moment. I'm not focused on what is happening today; I'm trying to discover what will matter tomorrow. I'm thinking future back. A company will always perform better or worse than its expectations. I know what's happening behind the scenes, so I know, at least to some extent, what the future will look like. And that knowledge gives me the confidence to make decisions against the grain.

This future-back perspective, as I've already shared, is fundamental to my approach to both life and business. But its importance is heightened during more extreme circumstances, positive or negative. From a future-back perspective, it's wise to be cautious when everyone else is investing like crazy, and to make smart investments when everyone else is pulling cash out of the market. This is an underlying principle of value investing, espoused by leaders like Warren Buffett and Charlie Munger. But it's wisdom that rarely seems to make it into business operations. I believe it works there as well. *Conserve in a boom; build in a bust.* And nowhere was that advice more dramatically relevant than in the boom years of the early 2000s and the bust of the Great Recession.

During the boom years of the aughts, Panera grew with caution. We tried to be realists, knowing that this era of irrational exuberance couldn't last forever. To paraphrase Rudyard Kipling, we kept our heads when everyone around us was losing theirs. We applied discipline and safeguarded our resources. We protected and harbored our debt capacity. Real estate was sky high, along with construction costs, so we curbed our growth, not wanting to get locked into lengthy leases at inflated prices.

Others overleveraged. I watched while my competitors built as if there was no tomorrow. It seemed like people would pay anything to get that perfect location. By the time the recession hit in 2008, they had limited financial capabilities. All they could do was react to the recession and cut costs. And when you try to maintain the P&L by rip-ping out labor hours and cutting food cost, the customer suffers. In fact, I view such cuts as a tax on the customer. Longer waits, dirty tables, slower service, and more frazzled team members all add up to a negative customer experience that will undoubtedly undermine al-ready falling sales and intensify a cycle of decline.

We, on the other hand, went into the recession with a powerful con-cept, competitive advantage, and a strong balance sheet. This allowed us to sidestep the pressure everyone else was under and to avoid falling into reaction mode. Our concept was still worthy of growth, and we knew it. I looked around at the closing stores and the reaction of our competitors, and what did I see? Opportunity.

That may sound mercenary, but it makes good business sense. I wasn't lacking compassion for the economic pain or trying to capi-talize on others' demise. I was seeing an opportunity to create value where others were temporarily unable to do so—value for the company and its shareholders, yes, but also value for the customer and the strug-gling economy.

We did this in two ways. First, we invested labor into the guest expe-rience when everybody else was cutting labor, thereby driving further competitive advantage and pushing our same-store sales up strongly. Second, we doubled our growth rate. As our competitors hunkered down and simply tried to survive, Panera bulked up by building more bakery cafés. Real estate and construction are priced on a spot market basis, but leases and investments are often locked in for fifteen or more years. So, we leveraged the recession to lease more desirable properties and build them out at lower cost. The result was that some of the high-est ROI cafés of Panera's last two decades under my leadership were built during the recession.

In my view, the worst time to grow is in a boom. The best time to grow is when everybody is retreating and costs are down.

We also used the recession to recruit A-level talent. While many companies were issuing pink slips, we were hiring. Truly exceptional people, many of whom worked for competitors, were ground down by the uncertainty that comes with store closures and staff cutbacks. As a result, many flocked to Panera.

These and other strategies had one aim: build that moat. Shore up competitive advantage and create bigger barriers to entry. The recession gave us the opportunity to leapfrog competitors. When it eased, we felt confident that they would find it far harder to catch up. And it worked.

Fast forward more than a decade, and I pursued a similar strategy in 2020 during the Covid-19 pandemic. Today, I'm an investor in several powerful restaurant companies. What did we do when the lockdowns began, when restaurants were forced to close their dining rooms and fight for survival? We expanded. We leased real estate, hired more people, and invested in cafés when everyone in the industry was acting like no customer would ever want to eat in a restaurant again.

Contrarian thinking is not for the faint of heart. Going against the herd is also often going against one's own impulses. In fact, there's one strategy I wish we'd employed back in 2008, but unfortunately Panera's board at the time didn't have the strength to pull the trigger. At the low point of the recession—the weekend after Lehman Brothers collapsed—I called a board meeting. In just a few weeks, the stock had gone from almost $60 a share to $36. But Panera was still strong, and we had suitable cash and debt capacity. To me, this was an opportunity to apply our written stock buyback plan, which stipulated that if the stock fell to a certain level, we would buy up large swaths of the company.

The way I saw it, if the market was going to completely collapse and the economy entered freefall, we'd all be cavemen and it wouldn't matter anyway. But if the market was going to eventually recover, our potential upside would be huge. To me, the buyback was the very definition of a smart bet—a bet on the future of a company we knew better than anybody else.

Unfortunately, my board didn't back me. The board members were reacting to their personal fears and stock losses, and thus were too focused on the immediate environment. They weren't able to focus on understanding where the company would be in the future and inform their decisions with that understanding. Ultimately, they passed up an opportunity to buy shares for $36 that would end up selling for almost ten times that amount less than a decade later. It was a significant price to pay for putting short-term fears over long-term perspective.

Except for that missed opportunity to buy back stock, Panera's contrarian strategies before and during the Great Recession were a great success. Such thinking is by no means unique to me or the companies I've led. But it's rare. The most successful companies in our industry and beyond have all utilized contrarian thinking, applied consistently over the long term, to build competitive advantage. They know that following the herd is, at best, just running in place and, at worst, going backward. They think for themselves. Each of these companies is obsessively focused on being the best competitive alternative in their target niches and steadfast in their commitment to determining today what will matter tomorrow. And that's why they'll still be winning when tomorrow arrives.

In retrospect, the wisdom of this contrarian approach seems obvious. But in the moment, it is neither obvious nor easy. In the midst of a bust, it's hard not to retreat into a risk-averse mindset. And it's even harder, in the midst of a boom, not to get caught up in the party. When lenders are throwing interest-free money at anyone who asks, it's tough to stay disciplined. One of the keys to successfully keeping your head is to focus forward, on the future that is yours to seize, and resist the temptation to look sideways at your competitors and mimic their tactical decisions. "Thou shalt not covet thy neighbor's concept" is a good rule of thumb for the restaurateur, or any business owner for that matter. We lose competitive advantage not just because we're reacting to the economic climate, but because we're simply mimicking other companies.

Jealousy and envy are deeply embedded in human nature, and it's understandable that we tend to look across the street at our competitors and wish we had whatever they're selling that has customers lining up down the block. When we see something succeeding, of course we're tempted to copy it. In this way, concepts begin to look more and more alike, and companies move further away from focusing on being the best competitive alternative for a particular group of customers. Before you know it, yesterday's favorite is suddenly an industry has-been.

Copying success doesn't work. The problems of Subway illustrate this point. One year it focused on great bread. The next year it focused on being the place for low-carb items. The third year it focused on being the freshest alternative. Ultimately, the recession hit, and Subway cut prices in a last-ditch attempt to differentiate. By trying to be everything to everyone, a concept ultimately ends up standing for nothing. By focusing on the short term and responding to the fad of the year, Subway destroyed any authority—and as a result, any real competitive advantage—it had.

To avoid this fate, you have to mean something to your target customer. The best brands make choices and are not all things to all people. If a brand is everything to everybody, then it's nothing special to anyone. You can't be changing every day because you see that the guy next door is finding success with a particular offering. In a way, resisting the urge to chase others' success is contrarian, too. You're saying, "That works over there, but we're not going to do that." Remember: the success you can see today is really the product of yesterday's strategy. It doesn't point you toward tomorrow's competitive advantage. I used to love it when people copied me, because they were making all the mistakes that we made last year while we were focused on how we would be even better next year. It was a sure sign they weren't going to be ahead of us to the next big thing.

Looking sideways will distract you from the hard but essential work of looking forward—striving to discern what will matter tomorrow. Avoid the industry chatter and the industry meetings where everyone pats each other on the back. Have the discipline to resist short-term zigging and zagging. Even when you're under intense pressure—from turnover in leadership to overleveraged balance sheets to the ever-narrowing short-term focus of investors—you still must face the reality that you will accomplish little if you don't maintain your focus on the future, your authority, and your long-term competitive advantage.

It will take courage. However, you will ultimately fail if you don't discover and execute today what will matter tomorrow.

. . .

As I sat down in early 2009 to write that 2008 shareholder letter, I reflected on all these things. I felt proud of our fortitude as I typed the opening words: "2008 was a great year—one of the strongest in our history." However, the tone of the letter quickly shifted to a tone of caution. Ever the contrarian, I was already looking ahead to the next challenges on the horizon. We'd sustained our competitive advantage through the rough waters of the recession, and we'd grown significantly. "In my view, this size and scale represents as much risk as opportunity for a company like Panera," I told our shareholders. "Why? Panera grew and prospered because it represented a better alternative to its guests. It was 'special' enough that consumers went out of their way to visit Panera. Typically, size is the enemy of special. In fact, too often, in many companies, size is the forerunner to mediocrity."

As I looked ahead to 2009 and beyond, this was what kept me up at night. In the decade since I had sold Au Bon Pain to bet everything on Panera, we'd gone from being a small Midwestern company with a few dozen cafés to a national brand with more than 1,300 company-owned and franchise-operated bakery cafés, and one of the largest food service companies in the United States. We were no longer the scrappy upstart; we were the incumbent. As our cafés proliferated, how were we to keep Panera special? What would matter next?

Even before the proverbial ink had dried on that shareholder letter, my mind was many years in the future. I knew that the world I was writing about was already shifting—we just couldn't see yet exactly how it would play out. I didn't yet know what our KIs should be. But there was one thing I knew for sure: doing what we'd been doing yesterday, however successful that strategy had been, would not secure our success in the world of tomorrow.

Business Is Personal

There were many things that made me proud of Panera in the fall of 2009. The way the company had come through the great recession. The culture we'd created. The food we served. The value we'd produced for shareholders. The awards we'd received. And the fact that fast casual, for which we were the poster child, was now the fastest-growing segment of the industry. But if I had to boil it down to one single thing, it would be this: I founded a company that my then-ten-year-old son desperately wanted to be a part of. So much so that he had spent his summer washing dishes and making coffee at our local Panera rather than playing Little League.

Michael's love for Panera also symbolized something essential: that no matter how big the company grew, it was still personal to me. It was part of my fiber—fused with my sense of self. Which was why, when I stepped onto the iconic stage at Nashville's Grand Ole Opry theater, the venue for the company's 2009 Family Reunion, I began my speech by showing a video of how Michael spent his summer vacation—helping out at his local Panera. See, I wanted to talk about pride in our company and how we maintained that well into the future.

As the video ended, I had tears in my eyes. No doubt the four thousand team members who packed the auditorium just thought I was being sentimental. But there was a deeper reason for my tears. The truth is, that reunion was a bittersweet moment for me. What I knew, but those in the audience did not, was that I intended this to be my last Family Reunion as CEO. I'd recently made the decision to retire—but had not yet announced it. So, the speech was something of an unspoken farewell. Soon, I would hand over the CEO role to my trusted colleague Bill Moreton. But until then, I still had the chance to shape Panera's story, to remind people where we had come from, where we were, and where we could go in the future. I couldn't tell them yet that I wouldn't be there with them when that future arrived. But I could still play a part in defining it.

I worked on that 2009 speech for literally hundreds of hours. That's how much it meant to me. I wanted to infuse every word with my love and affection for the people of Panera and the company itself. I wanted those listening to feel as proud as I was of what we'd accomplished—and to feel intensely responsible for where we needed to go.

I also spoke of the pain and difficulty inherent in every creative process and every personal journey. I reminded everyone that the odds had always been against us. I challenged them: Is our success by chance? Absolutely not. I wanted every person in that room to feel personally responsible for the journey we'd taken—and accountable to the one we would continue to take. Indeed, I wanted them to feel the burden of everything that was at stake if the company were to stumble now—the livelihoods, the investor capital, the franchise owners, the guests. I raised the specter of failure—of losing our shared dream—and the potential for success.

"Creating value tomorrow is completely dependent on the choices—on the bets—we make now," I said, looking around at the animated crowd, feeling their energy and commitment rising toward me like a great tide. Evoking the metaphor of our company as a ship on the stormy sea, I called on them to "sail on" and reminded them that our future was in their hands. "It's yours."

WE...ARE...PANERA! The chanting crowd of thousands of people echoed my words back to me, every person on their feet. Stamping and clapping, many of them had tears in their eyes, and the warm surge of love that radiated up toward the stage far eclipsed the heat of the lights overhead. The words on the teleprompter were a blur through my own tears, but I knew them by heart. I had honed every phrase until it rang true in my soul. The rhythm of the words, the resonance of their meaning, beat inside me like a drum, building to a climax. As the applause echoed through the cavernous auditorium, I felt more like a preacher leading a revival meeting than a CEO addressing a company gathering.

I know that, on paper, our company jamboree probably comes off as hokey. But when the crowd's triumphal chant echoed back, I can assure you it was a near-religious moment for me. By the time my family and Panera's leadership team joined me onstage, tears were streaming, unchecked, down my face. Bill Moreton leaned over and whispered in my ear, "Ron, are you sure you want to leave?"

It wasn't too late to change my mind. I hadn't announced it yet. For a moment, enveloped in the emotion of the moment, I wavered—but not for long.

"Yes," I told him, with more conviction than I felt. "We're going through with it." As I stepped off that stage, I knew I'd done everything I could, in that moment, to set the course for a positive next chapter in Panera's story. But what would be the next chapter in mine?

For me, as you can tell by now, there's never been a hard line between my work life and my personal life. Different leaders may take different approaches to the equation we call "work-life balance," but I think it's fair to say that for most company builders—whether they're entrepreneurs nurturing their own idea or business builders turning a good company into a great one—work is intensely personal. It's a source of meaning, satisfaction, and fulfillment.

I believe that a high degree of personal investment and an intense feeling of responsibility are essential elements if you want your leadership to be truly impactful. That doesn't mean every leader should work eighty-hour weeks and skip family dinners. But it does mean that the growth and vitality of the company should be central to your own vision for your life.

For me, it had always been that way—until 2009, when I started to wonder whether my life path and Panera's might lead in different directions. To be clear—it wasn't that I cared less about the company. Quite the opposite. It had never felt dearer to me. But other passions were stirring in me as well, and perhaps it was time to see where they might take me.

Every year, over the holiday season, I take the time to reflect on the narrative of my life: where I've come from, where I am, and where I want to be in the future—relative to relationships and family; health and body; work and finances; and spirituality. Then I practice my future-back method, just as I do for the business, to map out the Key Initiatives that will take me to the future I want. I walk myself through the choices and the trade-offs and reaffirm my commitment to getting done the things I believe will most matter to creating the tomorrow I desire.

For many years, however, there had been one goal I wrote down that I'd never made good on: the desire to have another experience beyond running the company. I yearned to take everything I'd learned at Panera and apply it on a larger scale. I'd already made some steps in that direction that year—like developing a nonprofit venture known as Panera Cares. The first of these "pay what you can" cafés was set to open, and I longed to devote more time to the project. And beyond Panera—beyond the restaurant industry—I was pulled to explore whether the lessons I'd learned about leadership and running large enterprises might translate into civic society. I watched Barack Obama speak at Grant Park, and I felt uplifted and inspired to take everything I'd learned and contribute it to the rising wave of hope and change in America.

As long as I was CEO of Panera, I knew it was crazy to even contemplate such a thing. Being CEO was all-consuming, and I needed to give myself the space to find new ways to make an impact. After all, I'd never set out to build a business for its own sake; I had set out to live a life I could respect. To seize opportunities and develop solutions that meet the needs of real people. To bring value into the world. And to spend my time on things that really matter—to me, to people I care about, and to the larger society.

These were the reasons behind my 2009 decision to retire. Ironically, on the very day I made that "Sail On" speech, while sitting in the green room getting ready to go onstage at the Grand Ole Opry, I'd received a call from the Obama White House about a job in the administration. This was it. This was the opportunity I'd been waiting for. What better moment to throw myself into a new passion, to offer my learnings and my skills to our new president? And I knew that this was *the* moment: If I didn't do it now, I'd never do it.

Despite these powerful incentives, saying goodbye to Panera was one of the hardest things I'd ever done. These people were my family, and I'd grown up with the company. As big as it had gotten by 2009, it still felt like one of my children. Yet it seemed like the right time. The financial crisis was in the rearview mirror and the company was well positioned to continue to thrive.

How would it feel to live without that responsibility for Panera? Until I took the leap off that high-dive board, I couldn't know. But there was one thing I did know for sure: I wouldn't fully respect myself if I didn't give my undivided attention to my own unfinished story.

PART THREE

Driving Large-Scale Transformation

26

Managing the
Desire-Friction Ratio

"Ron's a great CEO, but you know what he's really terrible at?" The comedian paused for effect, looking around at the crowd.

"Retiring!"

Everyone laughed, including me. I didn't mind being the butt of a few jokes at the Panera Family Reunion. After all, it was true. My retirement had been so short-lived that it came to be known as "Ron's Summer Vacation."

Initially, I'd followed through on my decision, leaving the company leadership in the capable hands of Bill Moreton in May 2010. But putting down my intense sense of personal responsibility for the company had proven harder than handing over the keys and the title. I might have thought I was ready to let go of Panera, but Panera still had a grip on my heart.

The truth is, I never left entirely—I stayed on as executive chairman, working on customer-facing projects and acquisitions. The day after I stopped being CEO, I'd opened the first Panera Cares café, so my workload, if anything, had increased. I was passionate about the pay-what-you-can model and testing its potential to help alleviate food insecurity, and I saw it as a chance to marry good business practices with a not-for-profit cause. I quickly found myself in St. Louis working a hundred hours a week on the project, as well as responding to a flood of media interest (the launch got over a billion media impressions). Ultimately, we added Panera Cares cafés in Detroit, Chicago, Boston, and Portland, Oregon.

I was also pursuing my political interests. The White House job hadn't panned out—they needed to press forward before I was free—but I was finding new ways to make a difference in Washington. I helped create the political activist organization No Labels, which focuses on reducing hyper-partisanship in Congress, and gave a lot of speeches about the negative impact of short-term thinking in our capital markets and civic society. For the first time in decades, my mind was free from the tyranny of quarterly earnings, budgets, shareholder pressure, staffing, same-store sales, wait times, and all the rest. I was liberated from the constant concern about whether we might be losing our competitive edge. Or, I would have been—if I hadn't kept showing up at Panera to get my lunch.

At the time, about one in thirty Americans ate in our Panera cafés every week. Now I was one of them as I traveled the country. I got to see, as a customer, all that made our bakery cafés distinctive—the lust-worthy food, the warm atmosphere, the soul-affirming energy. But from this fresh perspective, I also saw the chinks in our armor that came, in part, from our incredible growth. And I couldn't ignore what I saw.

Case in point: my go-to sandwich was the Bacon Turkey Bravo. But I knew I'd have to suffer a little to get it. Back then, in 2010, there was only one way to order. I'd have to find a space in the crowded parking lot and then stand in a line with a dozen or so other hungry folks. When I eventually reached the front of the line, I'd tell a cashier what I wanted. The cashier would enter it (correctly, I hoped) into a terminal. Then I'd head over to what I not-so-affectionately liked to call the "mosh pit." Here, a crowd of guests milled around waiting for their buzzers to go off and figuring out where to find the various elements of their orders. Food in one place. Condiments and utensils in another. Sodas over here. Coffee over there. Confusion everywhere.

"I order the same thing five days a week. Surely it shouldn't be this hard to get a simple sandwich," I thought. But what was I to do? Complain to management? I couldn't really blame this mess on anyone else, since I'd been in charge of its creation.

Clearly, it was just too hard for our customers to enjoy the things they loved about us. I'd seen too many just give up and walk out. Even I found myself avoiding our stores as often as I went in. A strange mix of embarrassment and frustration came over me as I hesitated outside the door, my son, Michael, by my side. Michael loved Panera almost as much as I did. But he'd also be the first to tell me everything Panera was doing wrong as we waited for our lunch. I took his criticism personally, even though it wasn't my job anymore. The company was like my third child, and I felt its successes and failures acutely, even after retiring.

Every day I kept encountering ways in which that ordering system didn't work for my personal needs—and undoubtedly the needs of millions of other customers. If I was asking myself, "Is this sandwich worth the pain of getting it?" I could be sure other customers were, too.

For example, I can remember the challenges of getting food to go for my kids on their way to school. To earn myself double brownie points with my wife, I'd offer to get the kids breakfast and lunch at Panera. Because I was always running late, I'd call up the café from the car, ask for the manager (because I knew I could trust him to get my order right), and tell him exactly what I wanted. A toasted everything bagel for Michael's breakfast, and Asian Sesame Chicken Salad with extra wontons for his lunch. A Cinnamon Crunch Bagel for Emma's breakfast and plain turkey sandwich for lunch. For me, a Power Breakfast Sandwich, a Thai Chicken Salad for lunch, and a "Shaich Special" (which everyone knew was a caramel latte with two pumps of caramel, not three, and extra foamy skim milk). I'd ask the manager to read the order back to me—I didn't want anybody embarrassed when the kids and I opened our bags.

When we arrived, I'd double-park out front, give Michael my credit card, and he'd run in, grab the food, swipe the card, and run back out with the bags. It took all of thirty seconds. The first time we executed this, I thought, *this is fantastic!* And then I thought, *it's fantastic for me.* But what about the millions of other people who wanted to take out food at Panera each week, but who didn't found the company and have the manager of their local café on speed dial? If Panera could find a way to take their order and simultaneously prepare their food as they were traveling to the store and have it ready when they arrived, wouldn't that save everybody a lot of time and pain? And wouldn't it reduce the number of people in line at our cafés and waiting at the mosh pit?

There were many other occasions when I found myself frustrated. One day, I was right on time for a meeting with the president of Clark University. He was already seated. My schedule only allowed thirty minutes for a brief meeting (in which he undoubtedly was going to ask me for yet another donation). So, I couldn't afford to spend ten min-utes waiting in line and then picking up my usual, four-day-a-week breakfast—a blueberry muffin and cappuccino—as that would take up one-third of my meeting time. *If only I could just hit a button some-how and have my regular order simply delivered to the table as I began the meeting*, I thought. Unfortunately, that system didn't yet exist at Panera, and all too often, I chose to go without breakfast.

On other occasions, I was stuck at home and wanted Panera. I'd be engrossed in something I was writing, and before I knew it, it was lunchtime. Getting Panera would mean getting in the car, driving to the store, parking, waiting in line, playing the "find your food" game in the mosh pit, and then driving home again. *If only Panera could deliver lunch to my door*, I'd think, as I sighed and instead reheated last night's Indian takeout.

I knew for sure I wasn't the only one with this frustration. One day in a senior staff meeting at Panera's offices, I looked out the window and saw a delivery guy from Jimmy John's sandwich shop coming into the office. Intrigued to see who had ordered the sandwich and why, I left the meeting, to the bemusement of the entire team, and followed the delivery person upstairs until we arrived on the third floor, where a guy in the IT department claimed the order. "Can I speak with you for a moment?" I asked after the driver left. He looked scared, like he thought he was about to get fired. "It's okay," I told him. "I'm just curious—how come you ordered a sandwich from Jimmy John's when there's a Panera on the other side of the parking lot and we give you a 50 percent employee discount?"

"I'm on help desk," he replied. "Don't you get it? I can't leave."

As I thanked him and left him to enjoy his lunch, I thought, "Why can't Panera do this job for our IT help-desk technician—and millions of others who can't or don't want to leave their desks or homes?"

Frankly, I felt embarrassed by our limitations and inflexible systems. But that personal discomfort was compounded by a recognition of the larger implications of what I was feeling. These weren't just small inconveniences for me, my kids, or the IT guy, when we wanted lunch. They were potentially fatal flaws of the company I loved. They were weaknesses that had emerged as we grew and as the world evolved that a savvier competitor could exploit to gain competitive advantage.

• • •

The question "Is this sandwich worth the pain of getting it?" captures a powerful calculus at work in every customer's heart and mind. I've come to call it the "desire-friction ratio"—how much a customer wants something relative to how hard it is to obtain that thing.

Desire is simple to understand—it means the customer wants what you're offering, they're drawn to it, they lust after it, they can't stop thinking about it. Friction is more complex, because it takes many forms, but essentially, it's anything that makes it more difficult for your customers to fulfill their desire. It might be too expensive for their budget. It might be the negative energy they get from employees who don't care. It might just be too far to drive, or maybe when they get there, it's impossible to find a parking spot. It might be the complexity of an ordering system. All of these factors drain time, energy, or money from the customer. That's the definition of friction.

To improve competitive advantage, you need to increase desire while reducing friction. It's critical to work both sides of the desire-friction ratio. It's not enough to have a product people crave; you also have to make it accessible to them. The most successful businesses get the ratio right: higher desire and lower friction than their competitors. If the desire-friction ratio is out of balance, you might not notice right away, because your most committed customers will put up with the increased friction for a while. But sooner or later, it will start to out-weigh their desire, and they'll go across the street, especially if savvy competitors find ways to reduce friction.

An example of a company that has triumphed in managing the desire-friction ratio is Amazon. Its innovations—such as one-click or-dering, free Prime delivery, and no-cost, no-hassle returns—took al-most all the friction out of the online shopping process. Meanwhile, with its individually tailored recommendations and breadth of prod-ucts, it worked the desire side of the equation very effectively as well.

• • •

The frustrations I felt in 2010 were indicative of the fact that Panera was facing a looming existential crisis—but the company didn't know it yet. More and more people desired our food, but it was simply too hard to get it. The long lines and the mosh pit created a level of fric-tion that was competitively unsustainable. As Panera's sales grew, its desire-friction ratio was tipping in the wrong direction. As a company, we had not come to terms with this reality. In my final year as CEO, I too had failed to see the signs. When I retired, I thought everything was going great.

Perhaps this was because on paper, it was. We'd fought off the ac-tivists, weathered the financial crisis, our same-store sales and prof-its were growing, and our stock was up more than 50 percent. But as I contemplated the problems I saw from my new vantage point as a customer, I realized we'd fallen victim to our own success. We were now generating sales volumes we could barely keep up with and under-delivering on speed, accuracy, and service. A business can ride the momentum of past success for a while until the cracks start to show. But eventually a desire-friction ratio that gets out of whack will trip you up. What made us successful yesterday wasn't going to sustain us tomorrow. If Panera was to remain competitive, the company needed to fundamentally rethink how it interacted with its customers—how they ordered the food they craved, and how that food was delivered to them.

As I wrestled with these issues, I was reminded again of the hard truth that the entrepreneurial life owns you, you don't own it. Your company's challenges and opportunities are with you always, regardless of whether you're sleeping, showering, or playing with the kids. Regardless of whether you say you've retired. As that fall turned into winter, I began to contemplate the challenges and opportunities for Panera, and a vision began to take shape. The vision emerged because in the various experiences I've just described, I didn't just bump up against what was wrong with the company—I could also *feel* what was needed. And despite the fact I knew getting there would be daunting, it energized me like a shot of caffeine on a sluggish morning.

It reminded me of how I felt back when Scott, Dwight, and I were touring coffeehouses on the West Coast and dreaming up a new kind of food service that came to be called fast casual. Once again, I was observing intently with all my senses. My own experiences were data points added to those of fellow customers in each store I visited. As I pieced together my collage of observations, I felt like I could taste where the world was going. I started to glimpse a transformed Panera. A place where customers could seamlessly order what they wanted, when they wanted it, in the way that was most convenient to them. Rapid pickup. Delivery to the table. Home delivery. Office delivery. A place where the latest technology was harnessed to optimize the entire Panera experience for the particular needs of each guest, removing much of the friction.

It came together most clearly for me on a trip to San Francisco that winter, when I visited a company using technology to enable a better guest experience in a way I'd never seen before, and I could imagine the same for Panera. The vision that was taking shape in my mind was summed up in two words: *speed* and *joy*.

The night I flew home from that trip, I was so wired I couldn't go to bed. I opened my computer and typed the question that would define the next decade of my life:

How would I compete with Panera if I wasn't Panera?

My fingers flew over the keyboard with all the glee of someone about to create a master plan to vanquish a competitor. As I imagined my fictional alter ego taking advantage of Panera's weaknesses, I recognized a whole host of opportunities to transform those weaknesses into strengths, build competitive advantage, and further differentiate our brand. It was, in a sense, a pre-mortem for the company I'd created—a future-back vision of what it could become next. Three days and almost ten pages later, I had a plan to make that vision a reality.

But it scared me to think about how the company might pull off yet another massive transformation. The transformation I was envisioning was nothing short of existential. It was a new Panera. Panera had always proudly embraced the "late adopter" label when it came to technology. As I'd been fond of reminding my team, we were in the food business, not the tech business. Now, I'd written a vision for Panera that would put technology at the very heart of our efforts to compete—positioning Panera as "the Amazon of the food industry." Previously, I'd seen technology as a cost to be reduced, an enabler of operations at best; now I was seeing its potential to transform the guest experience. I'm not afraid to change my mind, and I believe it's okay to learn and evolve. However, I was aware of the dissonance many would hear between this vision and my former stance, so I opened the memo with these words: "Don't use my words to argue with me. As a learning person, I am fully capable of disagreeing with earlier statements I have made."

Technology could remove time and inaccuracy, two of the biggest causes of friction, from the system. Customers didn't want another app; they wanted things that made their lives easier. I invited readers of my memo to imagine a future in which our guests had several painless options for getting their food. They could order online and have their food ready when they arrived in the café, skipping the line altogether. They could order on a mobile device or an in-store kiosk and have their food delivered to the table or they could get the food delivered to their front door or catered to their office. No long lines. No inaccuracies. No mosh pit.

But to do this, we were going to have to rethink everything and invest massively in new technology. Of course, technology alone wouldn't create this future. For too many companies, technology becomes a rat hole. They invest huge amounts of money in systems that fail to impact the customer experience. If we were to succeed, we would need to go all-in on ensuring that we delivered a fully integrated and seamless user experience. It wouldn't be done in a few months—this was a multi-year commitment that would cost hundreds of millions of dollars.

I was excited by the vision but under no illusion that it would be simple. Panera wasn't a nimble startup anymore. With thousands of locations and over a hundred thousand team members, transformation at this scale is a daunting prospect, too much for many leaders. Those who still feel the creative urge are more likely to start fresh than attempt to change an industry incumbent. It's tempting to just go back to the garage, ally with a handful of rule-breaking innovators, and conceive the next, big, crave-worthy, restaurant concept. Although that has its own challenges, it's perhaps easier than helping a big public company pivot to grab tomorrow's opportunities. If we failed, the fallout was unthinkable. We'd lose billions of dollars of investor capital and the confidence of our franchisees. We'd fail hundreds of vendors, tens of thousands of workers, and millions of customers every week who relied on us.

I didn't know if it could be done, but I wanted Panera to try. And I began to wonder if I should offer to help Bill with this effort. I was an entrepreneur at heart, no matter how big the company grew. And for an entrepreneur, there's no better feeling than figuring out where the world is going and how you can get there ahead of everyone else. If you can discover today what will matter tomorrow, and then come up with a plan to ensure that your company is already there when the rest of the world arrives, you've found the magic that animates the most creative minds of our time. As I typed that ten-page transformation memo, I felt more alive than I had in months, maybe years.

I had to wonder if Bill would take offense at my memo. Sure, I was still Panera's largest individual shareholder, and it still felt like "my" place. But Bill was the CEO, and I respected that reality. He and I were close, but the past six months had been an awkward and painful exile for me. It was strange to not be invited to important meetings, or to watch Bill heading out to dinner with the executive team while I sat alone at the bar. I cared about Bill tremendously and wanted to honor the agreement we'd made, but I just wasn't very good at being retired.

The first step, I decided, was to share the transformation memo with him. Bill, in his infinite wisdom and generosity, asked me to come back and work on it.

That spurred new worries. Was I ready to jump back into the fray? And in what capacity? Would Panera's stakeholders trust Bill and me enough to allow us to play out this vision over the next several years, or would they demand short-term returns that might compromise our ability to bring that vision to life? Was I ready to put my other dreams on hold—perhaps for good this time? Was I prepared, once again, to bet my credibility and my legacy on a future I could only see in my mind's eye? In the end, I knew I couldn't risk not trying.

At first, my return was confusing. I was still officially executive chairman, but what executive chairman works eighty-hour weeks? Ultimately, we reshuffled to more accurately reflect reality, and Bill and I became co-CEOs. I once again had the power and authority to drive a major transformation.

In sharing the leadership role with Bill, I gave up some degree of status and individual authority, but I also freed myself from the daily burden of tasks other than innovation—in my view, a CEO's most important role. In a way, I had the same job I'd always had but with half the responsibilities. I didn't have to be the one showing up at the Franchise Roundtable, giving yet another speech, leading earnings calls, or talking to analysts—all necessary activities but ones that got in the way of doing what I truly loved and believed created value. Now, I had one project: reimagining the future of the Panera guest experience and reinventing our cafés to deliver that better experience seamlessly. It was an enormous and daunting project, to be sure, but it was also an exciting one. I now had the time to indulge my love of creating and my talent for figuring out solutions to customers' problems.

I felt some regret about the roads not taken, the unfulfilled political ambitions, the set-aside "retirement" projects. But the choice wasn't that hard, and the reason can be summed up in one word: impact.

In Panera, I had a platform for immediate impact. In Panera, I could see a way to directly change the lives of millions of people—perhaps in a small way, but nevertheless in a powerful way. And that's what I cared about: changing lives. I never set out to build a business; I set out to seize opportunities and develop solutions that meet the needs of real people. To bring value into the world. And to spend my time on things that really matter—to me, to people I care about, and to the larger society. To leave the world a better place than I found it. In short, I set out to live a life I can respect.

Politics was tempting, but I knew I had neither the credibility nor the influence to truly make a difference there anytime soon. At Panera, I did—and I could see exactly what that difference would look like. I couldn't walk away from that calling.

Making the
Transformation
Operational

Almost two years to the day after I'd "retired" from Panera, I was back
where it all began: serving sandwiches. Only these weren't sandwiches
that a customer walked up to the counter and asked me to make; they'd
been ordered through our new digital kiosk. I could hardly believe that
I was working inside the world my memo had described—at least in
prototype form. We'd put together the first "Panera 2.0" café at a location in Braintree, Massachusetts, and in the summer of 2012, I was
basically living in it. Together with our COO, Chuck Chapman; our
technology consultant, Blaine Hurst; and a couple of other key team
members, I was running the store and, in the process, testing and refining our new digital ordering systems and the production systems
that supported them.

We'd invested heavily in getting to this moment—more than a year
of design, testing, redesign, and retesting. We'd chosen a store at the
Landmark Center, right next to Fenway Park, to build a laboratory to
test rapid pickup and delivery. I delivered Panera's first-ever delivery
order myself, to my own home, two blocks from the laboratory. (I was
only a little disturbed that Nancy and our kids chose not to tip me.)

Only once we were satisfied the systems worked in the lab did we integrate them into the store in Braintree with real customers. Given the investment to get to that point, I calculated that every order we took at that Braintree café cost us over a hundred thousand dollars. But we were determined to get it right there before we scaled. So we worked the store ourselves, testing the systems, tracking the results, working to resolve issues. There are some problems you won't understand unless you are physically impacted by them. You can go to a dozen meetings about a particular feature and still have no sense of what it feels like to be the operator using it, or the customer receiving it. It's essential to experience the innovation yourself, to iterate, and then iterate again. And to do it daily so you move through the iteration phases quickly. We rebuilt that entire store several times to get the systems and flow right. It was an exhaustive, and exhausting, process.

And yet the transformation kept getting bigger. When I wrote the original transformation memo, my vision had centered around access: creating multiple new ways for customers to order and receive their food, enabled by technology. But getting the ordering systems right turned out to be just the beginning. Early in the transformation, it became increasingly obvious to me that we were going to have to transform everything else about how we produced and delivered that food as well. While making my annual father-son trip to watch the NCAA Final Four Basketball tournament with Michael, in Houston in 2011, I visited a local la Madeleine French Bakery & Café. It had recently launched mobile ordering, and I was eager to test it out. I placed the order from my phone, drove to the store, and looked around for the rapid pickup location. But all the customers seemed to be waiting in one place. Irritated, I got in line, and when I got to the counter, the guy took my name and told me they'd get started on my order right away. "Wait a minute," I said. "What was the point of ordering on the app?"

Too many companies will make changes to one aspect of the business without ensuring that every other aspect of the business is integrated. They'll add an app or upgrade their website but leave everything else just as it was. And then they won't be ready when the new app brings an increase in business. Such was the case with la Madeleine. This problem also played out at larger companies like Starbucks. As we were designing our integrated digital ordering system, Starbucks was rapidly rolling out mobile pay, but it left its production systems untouched—a decision that, not too many years later, came back to haunt it, just as I'd predicted, when it couldn't keep up with the volume of its digitally enabled sales. At Panera, we recognized that if digital ordering worked, we'd have to fix production systems, which were wholly unprepared to cope with a significant increase in demand.

It's not something I'm proud to admit, but our café managers had always brought the sales volumes down to what that they could handle by limiting the number of cash registers open. Running only a couple of registers meant the lines got longer but the volume was manageable. This strategy is a dirty little secret for so many restaurants. Some customers would get frustrated and vote with their feet by going elsewhere, but the kitchen would be able to keep up. However, with digital ordering, lunch would spur a flood of rapid pickup orders all at once, and the order board would light up like a Christmas tree on Christmas morning. Unfettered demand would hit the store and we'd have no way to throttle it. There was no point building digital ordering systems that hoped to create speed and joy if the orders they generated fed into a production system that couldn't keep up. It became clear that the transformation we were undertaking needed to reach deep into the back end of the business if it were to succeed.

When people draw a hard line between strategy and operations or between technology and operations, they create a false dichotomy. These things work in tandem. You can't be truly strategic if you're not deeply immersed in the operational realities of your vision. Just as an architect needs to also understand the physical demands of construction, a visionary innovator must also understand the realities of execution. If the architect doesn't know how certain materials will affect the job, and what might be the unforeseen consequences of putting this room next to that, or situating the home in a particular spot, it doesn't matter how elegant and original the plans are—the house won't work. If the innovator doesn't understand what is going to be required of the company to deliver the vision, it doesn't matter how elegant and original the strategy is—it won't work. In our case, my fear was that our transformation to digitally enabled ordering would lead to both uncontrollable volumes and inaccurate execution on orders. This last point was another reason why Panera needed a production system overhaul.

· · ·

Don't you hate it when a restaurant gets your order wrong? I do. *I'm sure I said hold the cream. And that dressing was supposed to be on the side. Do I just eat it, or do I wait another ten minutes for a replacement?* Moments like that are frustrating for the customer and embarrassing for the server. So, you can imagine how I felt when I learned that over a million Panera guests got the wrong order, every single week. That's one in seven customers. Worse still, the people in charge of accuracy didn't think it was all that bad. They proudly informed me that they had a plan in place to raise the accuracy half a percentage point in the next five years: from 88 percent to 88.5 percent.

To me, this wasn't just a matter of metrics. It was a matter of integrity. It was excruciatingly painful to me to think that we were failing our guests so often. How would you feel if your pilot told you he was going to crash on one out of every seven of his landings? Of course, an incorrect sandwich is not a catastrophic loss of life, but it is a systemic failure, nonetheless. When companies talk about integrity, they often mean things like how well they're living up to their values, how transparent they are about their financial dealings, or whether the CEO is keeping his nose clean. Worthy concerns, all, but why aren't operations mentioned in that mix? To me, operational integrity is every bit as important. If a company can't deliver what the customer orders and pays for, consistently and predictably, then it fundamentally lacks integrity. Bottom line, a system that is out of integrity is simply not working. And sooner or later, a company that lacks integrity will lose customers' trust and, with it, competitive advantage.

Operational integrity means, put most simply, that the company *works*. It works for its customers. They can count on it to deliver. They can feel confident that what they order, how they order it, and how many they order is going to be what they get, and they'll get it in the time committed to. Quality operators protect the customer from the company's foibles, rather than protecting the company from the customer's demands.

Sounds simple, but it's not. To create operational integrity, companies must create end-to-end processes that help them to deliver what guests ask for—100 percent of the time. Not 88 percent, or 88.5 percent. It's the businesses that can be counted on to execute exactly as ordered that win the war for competitive advantage. Operational integrity is about whole and complete systems that enable us to keep our promises. No excuses.

If the best thing I could say about Panera's execution was "we don't suck," that wasn't good enough. I quickly came to realize that our production systems would need a complete overhaul if the transformation we were undertaking was to succeed. In theory, digital ordering might help accuracy by removing a human element, but it would also encourage customization, which made the orders more complicated for the kitchen. Our production systems had to be able to handle that—which meant building new capabilities into the business for the future we were anticipating.

Capabilities matter because they limit how much you can transform. Much of what happens in a particular store on a given day is decided by the systems and the processes and the people built into it. You can change the access and double your number of orders, but that won't change sales if you don't have the capabilities to handle the additional volume. You can't truly deliver for the guest unless you have an integrated solution.

Transformation isn't just about rolling out new products or services; it's about putting in place the capabilities for an integrated solution for the guest long before they are needed. That means thinking ahead about the people, technology, and systems that are needed for the future you're envisioning—and putting your money behind them. There is pain before gain. As I always say, you must make a deposit before you can make a withdrawal. That's the way it works at the ATM, and that's the way it works in business.

In 2011 and 2012, that meant designing new production systems and hiring and training extra production labor to handle the increased orders we were expecting before those higher volumes arrived. And Bill and I were already concerned that our cafés, in an effort to boost profitability, were understaffed. So our COO Chuck Chapman and I made plans to put seventy hours a week of additional labor into the stores. That cost money and would have raised objections, so we solved the problem by using labor hours we expected to save from the use of the new digital ordering systems.

• • •

If you desire to achieve excellence in any field, it helps to know what excellence looks like. I've never hesitated to seek out the gold standards of what I'm trying to achieve and benchmark myself against them. For operational integrity, this is exactly what I did. In business, the highest honor that a company can receive for its quality management is the US Commerce Department's Malcolm Baldrige National Quality Award. In 2010, K&N, a small nine-unit barbeque chain out of Austin, Texas, received the Baldrige Award in the small business category, so I looked it up. The first thing that caught my attention? Its accuracy scores. In 2011 it delivered 99.8 percent accuracy. And sales were twice the level of its franchisor. I was impressed. I wanted to see firsthand what allowed it to achieve this level of operational integrity, so I headed to Austin and sat in its Rudy's Barbeque restaurant and observed. I returned several weeks later to meet with their leadership. After that, I brought the team working on Panera 2.0 to Austin. Then I brought down my senior team. I even sent some of my team to work in K&N restaurants (and convinced it to send some folks to work in our cafés). After all these visits, I knew exactly how K&N had achieved its success.

I learned from K&N how to use total quality management (TQM) to upgrade our operational systems to achieve higher levels of accuracy. TQM shined a light on our problems and gave us a path to solving them. Briefly, for those unfamiliar, the process begins with identifying failure points in a system, followed by a review and revision to remove the points of failure. Metrics are applied when and where the process fails rather than just being used to review outcomes. You adhere to best-in-class systems and processes and encourage continuous improvement.

For us this meant we created integrated kitchen display systems to allow team members to see orders as they were coming in. We redesigned the layout of our kitchens and the processes they utilized multiple times. Ultimately, we received a patent to use video to review the accuracy of execution, sandwich by sandwich. At one point, I used to joke that Panera's production lines were among the most-watched TV, midnight to 8 a.m., in India. In so many ways, everything about food production at Panera needed to change if our digital transformation was to be a success.

• • •

When I rolled this production overhaul into the Panera 2.0 vision, I made one thing abundantly clear: we had to stop making excuses for accuracy scores like 88 percent. I wanted to stop apologizing to our own team members. I didn't blame them for our poor performance. I blamed me. We provided them with inadequate systems and still expected them to get the job done. We expected them to be heroes. But a good company should create systems and processes that make the average guy a hero as opposed to relying on heroes to run our business.

From this perspective, it was amazing that they got the order *right* six out of seven times. Our lack of operational integrity as a company was our failure to build systems that were not just workable for the customer, but as good as our people. I intended to change all that. And so we went to work reenvisioning our entire production system. By the time I was serving sandwiches in the Braintree store in the summer of 2012, those sandwiches were being made in an entirely new production system that was up and running in the back rooms of the café.

The enormous overhaul of our back-end systems, the focus on operational integrity, and the additional hiring we had to do to meet our anticipated demand—none of this had been part of my initial ten-page transformation memo. The journey had begun with observing our customers—including myself—and envisioning a revolution in digital access. But that led me back into the heart of production, to envisioning a revolution in execution. It was a much bigger transformation than I'd initially imagined. And it was about to get even bigger.

Finding New Runways
for Growth

Steve Jobs is reported to have said, "If you define the problem correctly, you almost have the solution." I might take issue with the "almost" part; in my experience, defining the problem accurately helps you to *see* the solution more clearly, but delivering on it is another matter. It's also been my experience that the definition of a problem evolves with more knowledge. Sometimes, it is only in attempting to design a solution that you discover new dimensions of the problem. And too often, defining one problem leads you to see other distinct but related problems.

That's what happened with our Panera 2.0 transformation. By 2013, we were making progress on solving the first set of problems I'd identified (our flawed ordering and pickup system) and the next set of problems that had revealed themselves in that process (our inadequate production systems and limited capabilities to ensure accuracy). Solutions were in test.

Once we'd tested and refined our solutions to these problems at our first prototype café in Braintree, we pushed out the Panera 2.0 concept to two more Boston-area stores. We also started to plan for a test in an entire market: Charlotte, North Carolina. I watched each of those first few stores like a hawk, waking up at 6 a.m. every day to check prior-day sales. Early results were promising, but we had a long way to go. Converting a few cafés was a significant task. But converting more than two thousand Panera cafés, at a cost of at least $75,000 per café (and closing each café to execute the transformation), was an unimaginably daunting, not to mention risky, task. So . . . we had to be sure we got it right before we began rollout.

Further, my satisfaction with our progress was tempered by an additional problem for the company that was now coming into focus. When I thought about the long term (and I'm always thinking about the long term!), I didn't see enough runways for growth over the coming five to ten years to fuel the $10 billion company Panera would need to be to sustain its stock price. We could roll out our Panera 2.0 initiative and continue our existing rate of café unit growth, but that wouldn't be enough. The growth monster was rearing its ugly head once again.

I firmly believe that there is a way to solve every problem. The question is whether you are smart enough and diligent enough to find that solution. In 2013, I challenged my team with the following questions: What are the ways we can extract more sales out of the zip codes we are already in? Where are we leaving money on the table? We had credibility in soups, salads, and sandwiches, and we'd built and tested digitally enabled ordering. Were we missing opportunities to expand our growth into adjacent businesses by leveraging our competitive authority to meet new needs? Or, as Bill Moreton used to put it in those days, how could we "hoover" up more revenue in each zip code we served?

With Panera 2.0 so early in its rollout, the last thing we needed was more new initiatives. But I knew if we didn't create new runways for growth now, it wouldn't matter how well we rolled out digitally enabled cafés. Without growth, the stock would flatline.

So even as the 2.0 transformation lifted off, we set out to identify new runways for growth via several billion-dollar-plus business opportunities. Top of the list was large-order delivery, which we called Catering; small-order delivery, which we simply called Delivery; and Panera at Home (consumer packaged goods), which was selling Panera-branded products like soup, macaroni and cheese, or salad dressings, through other retailers.

Catering was a good example of sales ready to be hoovered up. Panera had what we believed to be the largest catering sales in the industry at the time, but that was a fraction of the total market. I figured that catering represented an extraordinary opportunity to leverage our competitive advantage with soups, salads, and sandwiches and to build a dominant market share in a highly fragmented market.

The problem, however, was that our catering business was being run out of the back of our already busy cafés. And service in those cafés would suffer when associates had to leave the front counter to help catering customers. Our stores were rejecting half of the catering orders being called in because they just couldn't fulfill the demand. We couldn't grow the catering business from the back of a retail café. We'd leveraged the back room as far as we could.

I began searching for models of other businesses that had solved a similar problem. This process of looking for generalizations from one industry that can be applied to another is at the heart of discovering today what will matter tomorrow. In this case, I found a model in an unlikely sector: office supplies.

Staples had once been predominantly a retail business but transformed itself to essentially become a centralized B2B business, which is where most of its value was now derived. Could Panera do the same thing? I hired several Staples executives, led by Dan Wegiel, a former top executive at the company, to lead a similar transformation at Panera. We launched an initiative to build "catering hubs," which could fuel the growth of catering while relieving the pressure on the cafés. One hub could serve the catering needs of multiple cafés, which would also reduce sales volatility in each individual café that was making catering a difficult business to execute well. We could train specialized salespeople and create strategic partnerships with B2B sellers and credit card companies. In effect, Panera created a B2B model for catering.

Delivery was another potential $1 billion–plus runway for growth. We estimated food service delivery was a $44 billion industry, and I wanted a piece of it. It had frustrated me that delivery had been sidelined from the initial 2.0 prototype in an effort to speed its roll-out. I still wanted to be able to order my favorite sandwich at home (not that I had many days at home anymore; I was virtually living at the office). Jimmy John's had launched "Freaky Fast Delivery," which led to billions of dollars in systemwide sales in 2013. Panera should be able to compete for that business. We knew we could do it because we already had the digital ordering systems in place. But we wanted to do it *well*. Simply put, we wanted our delivery drivers to give people the same self-esteem boost and fast-casual experience that our cafés gave them. Our drivers needed to represent our brand, connect to the customer, and care about their experience.

To understand how we could do delivery better, we studied successful models, including Domino's and Papa John's. I flew out to Grand Rapids, Michigan, where one of our franchisees also owned a group of Pizza Huts. I convinced her to let me tag along with one of her delivery drivers for a few days. I watched how the poor guy struggled to find the locations of his customers. As a result of that on-the-ground observation, Panera was one of the first companies that brought in GPS technology to assist delivery.

We also created prototypes for what I called "Delcos" (Delivery Company) which were basically Panera locations without the seating and gathering place. These units offered to-go, delivery, and catering, but no dine-in. The idea was to fill in between retail cafés and capture more dollars from that zip code without the investment of opening a full store.

We also began developing a vision for entering new trade areas that had historically not been Panera's sweet spot, like universities, hospitals, and transportation centers.

Another important runway for growth was the consumer products business, which we called Panera at Home. We had already had surprising success selling Panera-branded products at other retailers like Target, Sam's Club, and Costco. But if we were to grow this business to $1 billion, I knew we needed to commit to it more deeply. That meant bringing in new leadership that had consumer product skills.

All these initiatives got underway in 2013, putting even greater pressure on a company already burdened by the first phases of its enormous Panera 2.0 transformation. Yet we couldn't stop there. We also needed to keep investing in the human capabilities that would support all of it, and more, into the future. If we didn't put in place the human capabilities to get the job done, none of it would mean anything. In part, that meant continuing to invest significantly in our technology team, as we needed it to become a competitive advantage.

As this was going on, it became clear to me that it was past time to rebuild Panera's senior management team. Too many of our leaders just weren't up to the task that was now theirs. They cared about the company but hadn't truly grown with it. I had to admit once again that I'd been avoiding the issue and had left it for Bill to deal with when I "retired" in 2010. It was time to take care of that unfinished business—and I couldn't afford to wait until we'd finished all the other aspects of the transformation to make those changes.

In the middle of all this, Bill Moreton shared with me that a personal matter was curtailing his ability to travel. We agreed that it made sense to change roles again, with me taking on the role of sole CEO and Bill remaining my partner as our executive vice chairman. My short-lived retirement already seemed lifetimes ago, although in truth it had been only three years since I'd stepped down and then drafted my transformation memo. Back then, I'd thought that I was describing a large and daunting digital transformation—one that I wasn't sure Panera could pull off. Now, I saw that memo as the opening salvo in a long and drawn-out battle to reinvent the company to compete in the world of tomorrow. Digital access and operational integrity were the first stage. Creating new runways for growth was the second. Strengthening our management capabilities was the third.

Now I wondered what new problems—and opportunities—would reveal themselves. I didn't have to wait long to find out.

29

Coming Clean—with Yourself and Others

"Ron, you're full of shit."

These words came from my worst critic—me—as I rode down an escalator in the Philadelphia 30th Street Station, in the fall of 2013. I'd spent the past hour eloquently arguing to an important investor that Panera was doing just fine.

Jason Schrotberger of Turner Investments had challenged me on our same-store sales, which were still positive but not nearly as strong as they used to be compared to the rest of the industry.

"It's not that bad," I assured him. "We're still doing better than most of the industry. And we're investing in the future. Give me time. Let me do my job. Large-scale transformation doesn't happen overnight. Once we get Panera 2.0 rolled out in enough cafés, you're going to see the impact."

I'd made this speech countless times over the past year (both to myself and to others), as same-store sales languished and Wall Street gleefully predicted Panera's demise once again. I'd held firm. I'd been convinced that if we could hold off the doubters long enough, roll out Panera 2.0, put in place new runways for growth, and strengthen the organization's human capabilities to get the job done, the fruits of our work would start to show. But that day in Philly, as I loosened my tie and stepped onto the escalator, I was forced to admit that I was kidding myself, and I wasn't being honest with our investors. It was time to come clean with myself and fix another root problem. Once again, the transformation was about to get bigger.

The truth was that our lackluster same-store sales growth—a key measure of our competitive advantage—wasn't just a temporary lag. The problem in 2013 was more existential. We were becoming less differentiated. *We were losing competitive advantage—like a tire leaking air.* And competitive advantage was the end—the holy grail we were always working for.

Much of my effort in the early stages of the Panera 2.0 transformation had been focused on removing friction. How could I make it easier for customers to get the food they craved? This had begun with digital access and expanded into the production system overhaul. Now, I realized that I needed to look at the other side of the desire-friction ratio as well. Did customers want our food as much as they used to? Were we still offering something that was relevant? Greater capacity wouldn't help us if we didn't have demand. I had to figure out how to reignite our brand differentiation—how to make people crave the Panera experience enough to walk past our competitors and come through our door.

Admitting this truth hurt. It felt like the company had gone through major surgery, recovered, done months of physical therapy, learned to walk again, started to get in shape—and then discovered it needed a heart transplant. I was confronting the need to rethink our Concept Essence—the one thing that never changed at Panera. For twenty years, we'd held true to that document as our identity, our North Star, and the standard we strive to live up to. It was an article of faith. It was our vision for how we attain and sustain competitive advantage, and it had proven again and again to be powerful and relevant. I once spent eight hours at a Panera Family Reunion taking three thousand people through a Talmudic-style study of our Concept Essence! We'd stuck with that vision and never mimicked what our competitors were doing or tried to be the "flavor of the month."

But after two decades, it was becoming clear that we needed to be willing to reinvent how the company competed at the most essential level.

The pressure for this reinvention came from both sides. We were being "middled," as they say in the restaurant business. On one side, we had fast food, which was out to eat our lunch—literally. Businesses like Wendy's and Applebee's had watched our success and were determined to copy what we were doing—at a lower price point. On the other side, more specialized fast-casual concepts like Sweetgreen were pushing a new "craft" ethos—using our playbook and attempting to "niche" us just as we once niched fast food by specializing in elements of what we did, such as soups, salads, or sandwiches.

It reminded me of what happened to Sears. It started out as "America's retailer," selling everything from electronics to sports equipment to suburbanites. But when specialty big-box stores followed in those subcategories, suddenly Sears didn't have authority in any category.

Even without these market pressures, the fact was our Concept Essence had become dated. In the mid-nineties, it was a radical idea to create a dining experience that helped people feel good about themselves, to highlight artisan bread and to serve up lunch with a side of self-respect. To offer food that excited customers, in environments that engaged them, served by people who cared. Those ideas still mattered—but by 2013, people expected those things and even took them for granted. And as society had grown more educated and informed about nutrition and health, the bar had been raised (in part by us) for what it took to make customers feel the way we wanted them to feel. We still wanted to elevate self-esteem and support an aspirational lifestyle, but the definitions of those terms had changed. It was time for us to revisit the most fundamental questions that shaped our identity: *Where is our authority derived? What are we the best at? What will matter to our guests tomorrow? What ultimately matters to ensure we maintain competitive advantage?*

Yes, we were still in the midst of rolling out digital ordering, creating operational integrity, finding new runways for growth, fixing management, and more. But we needed to add *yet another* new initiative to our already overflowing plates of transformation. It was likely the most important one of all. In January 2014, I gathered the best minds I knew to embark on a yearlong Concept Essence reinvention. Strategic consultant Dwight Jewson and I had a sense of where it would take us, but intellectual integrity required that we do the hard research. It began where every innovation begins: observing customers, practicing empathy, and looking for patterns and generalizations we could extract.

The process yielded a fascinating insight: our guests were in conflict about their diets. They wanted to eat well, but they also wanted to enjoy their food. They wanted food that was good—and good *for* them. Our research indicated that this customer represented about 20 percent of the market—a huge slice of the population. Anyone who could own that niche was going to win. And I knew these people well because I was one of them.

Having recently turned sixty, I'd come to the realization that I needed to eat more consciously and thoughtfully if I were to continue to live the long, vital, and healthy life I hoped to. I learned that I was close to being prediabetic, a discovery that prompted a radical reevaluation of my own diet. In the process, Panera's medical adviser, Dr. David Eisenberg, put me on a continuous glucose monitor and told me to eat at Panera every day for a week. He wanted me to understand how Panera food drove up my blood sugar. I was shocked at what I found. I wanted Panera to be somewhere I felt good about eating. But if so, it was going to need to evolve.

A greater focus on health was not a radical departure for Panera. From the company's conception, we had set a course to offer the antithesis of heavily processed, commercial food. For decades, we'd worked hard to provide our customers with food they could trust and transparency that instills confidence in their choices. In 2006, for example, along with Chipotle, we made a bet that people would pay more for antibiotic-free chicken. We believed it tasted better and was better for our customers, so we took the bold step of making it standard in all our restaurants. The chicken initially cost us significantly more per pound, but it was worth it. Not only did it produce a better product; over time it helped change the marketplace. No major chain had committed to antibiotic-free chicken before, and today, everyone including Chick-fil-A and McDonald's, uses antibiotic-free chicken. Simply put, our actions changed the economics and upped the ante for the entire industry.

We were also one of the first national restaurant companies to begin removing artificial trans fats and the first to voluntarily post calorie counts on all our menu boards. Most of the restaurant industry resisted this idea. As I said at the time, "If you're embarrassed about what's on your menu, maybe you should change your menu, not hide it." We were convinced this was a better way to compete—and the right thing to do. It wasn't just about improving our competitive position. We wanted to be part of fixing the enormous problems in our nation's food system and our industry.

I believe that those of us in the restaurant industry have a moral duty to address the problem of food insecurity (which we attempted to tackle with our Panera Cares cafés) and the health problems created by our broken food system that contribute to our health-care crisis. In Panera's case, we were serving over 10 million people each week and we had over a hundred thousand associates who counted on us. We had an obligation to lean into the problems as we saw them and to use our scale and power to take on the toughest challenges. It was the right thing to do for our self-respect. And it was the right thing to do for our business.

In 2014, as we reworked our Concept Essence, two words came to the forefront: *craveable wellness*. The intersection of desire with health. I wanted our cafés to feel like they were brimming with an abundance of beautiful food that was also good for you. If we could pull that off, we'd deliver on the promise of our original vision—to elevate our guests' self-esteem. As we worked to bring our new Concept Essence into focus, I couldn't yet see what it would take to pull it off. But once I understood our vision for transformation, I knew we had no choice but to get it done.

Keep Your Promises

I pulled my car into the garage of my Brookline, Massachusetts, home and stepped into the darkened house. Silence greeted me. It was August 2014. Nancy, Michael, and Emma were vacationing in Manchester, Massachusetts. More than three years in, I was still mired in the complexity of Panera's transformation and was unable to get away from work to join them. Panera 2.0 was now being tested in several markets. We were working on our various new runways for growth. And we were deep in the process of rewriting our Concept Essence.

But profits were weighed down by the cost of the transformation, and same-store sales growth was still modest. Across the company, tempers were fraying, and I was struggling to hold it together at the end of one of the toughest days of that period of my life. Alone in an empty house, exhausted and emotionally drained, I put down my briefcase, but I could not so easily put down the weight of the day's events.

That afternoon, our new chief financial officer had abruptly resigned, giving us two weeks' notice, after only about a year on the job. He'd begged for the job for years, but here he was jumping ship because he couldn't be certain the future was going to be as good as the past. A typical short-term investment banker, I thought bitterly. No senior executive in such a critical role had ever before given me two weeks' notice. But that's what happens when you're in the thick of transformation and you don't know if it will work. You find out who's loyal and who's not.

Our CFO's defection was another body blow to me, and to a company that was already staggering. In the second quarter of 2014, Panera's same-store sales drifted upward at an anemic 0.1 percent rate. We were aiming for 5 percent. At our big summer meeting, I personally apologized to the top three hundred people in the company for our results. I had assured them that our same-store sales would improve, but I was wrong. Over the summer, we had to cut estimates for our same-store sales and reduce our earnings-per-share projections even further. Ultimately we downgraded our guidance for the full year. Predictably, headlines like "Why Panera Bread Is No Chipotle Mexican Grill" and "Is Panera Bread a House of Cards?" followed. We'd invested so much in our transformation efforts, yet we still had little to show for it.

The problem was that the scope of the transformation just kept getting bigger and the timeline for rollout was getting longer. To convey the scale of the undertaking, I used to tell people that if we converted one store a day, it would take seven years, working seven days a week, to convert the entire chain. I knew we wouldn't see results right away, but I also knew shareholders wouldn't wait forever. My commitment never wavered, even as the task ballooned. I often thought about one of my favorite quotes, from the legendary football coach Vince Lombardi: "We didn't lose, we just ran out of time."

I told shareholders to prepare for slower growth, significant investment, and weaker earnings. I told team members they'd need to bear with us as bonuses, which were based on earnings and getting hit by the cost of the transformation, got smaller. And I told myself I could fight my way through this. But time is a nonrenewable resource. And one glance at the day's business news was all it took to remind me that Panera's investors could get impatient, and more members of the senior team could buckle under the pressure. Would they continue to trust me for long enough to let me finish the job? Or was I running out of time?

Sitting in the empty kitchen the night my CFO quit, I wondered if it was all worth it. Should I have just stayed retired and let Panera continue doing things the way it always had? What had possessed me to take on this burden again—to go back to working eighty-hour weeks trying to transform the whole company? And could I make good on my vision and the promises I'd made to our customers, our people, and our shareholders?

My phone rang, startling me out of my morose reverie. The screen told me it was my daughter, Emma, then ten. Turned out she too had had a tough day and wanted me to come out to Manchester and put her to sleep.

"Daddy, would you come up here and say goodnight?" she asked.

It was an hour-plus drive, and I was shattered and emotionally drained. I hadn't slept more than four hours a night in months.

"I'm sorry, honey," I told her. "I can't. It's too far and Daddy's had a really long day." But even as I said the words, I realized I couldn't refuse her request. So I got back in my car and made the drive. As I was tucking her in, she told me about her worries and her disappointments that day.

"Tough days do happen," I told her, "but they don't continue forever." I promised her that when she woke in the morning, the sun would be out and life would feel brighter. As she fell asleep, I realized that the pep talk was as much for me as for her.

It takes courage and vision for a leader to embark on a major transformation in a large, established public company. But that courage and vision truly gets tested when the transformation doesn't unfold quite as you'd expected. It's almost inevitable that it will take more time, more resources, and more fortitude than you could have imagined to complete a major transformation. There are always too many factors beyond your control. As a leader, if you're personally invested in your company and its future, be ready to endure some dark nights of the soul. That night when I drove out to see Emma was one of many that I recall from summer 2014. Countless times, I'd wake before dawn, check the sales numbers, and then lie awake trying to figure out how I could take the pressure off the team and the company. I was keenly aware that this was the most comprehensive transformation any large company in our industry had ever undertaken. I was sure I was about to lose the company, destroy my credibility, let everyone down. On a few such mornings, I'd get in my car and drive down Boston's Route 9 on my way to work, half-thinking to myself that a heart attack would be a welcome respite from the burden. I truly felt, at least in those brief moments, that I'd rather die than break the promise I'd made—the promise that was Panera.

Every company, at its core, makes a promise—a covenant with each of its stakeholders. When we make promises, we're pledging our intent to act. To our customers, we had promised that we would successfully execute our initiatives to deliver the food they were paying for and the quality experience they'd come to expect. To our associates, we promised a great place to work, a way to make a good living, and opportunities to advance. To our suppliers, we promised a fair deal. To our franchisees, we promised a strong and dynamic brand with long-term relevance. To our communities, we promised to be a positive force for change and a contributing member of society. To our shareholders, we promised financial performance worthy of their billions of dollars of investment. All these people were betting on me. The promises I'd made to them weighed heavily on my shoulders.

The morning after I gave Emma (and myself) that pep talk, the sun did indeed come up, but by the time it did, I was already on the road, headed back to the office for more of the hard work of transformation. I knew that what I'd told Emma was true, but it was going to take more than a good night's sleep before my new day would dawn, and I—and the rest of the world—would finally see the results we were working for. Would I ever be able to draw a line under this transformation and say, "We're done"?

I felt a little less bleak than I had the night before in my empty kitchen. I knew that my old and dearest friend, Bill Moreton, was ready to fill in as our interim CFO until we hired a new one. That's loyalty, that's friendship, and that's what generates the love I feel for Bill. If it weren't for people like him, I'd never have been able to stay the course myself.

Our CFO wasn't the last to leave. Several more of our top executives left before the end of the year, long-serving leaders who had done much to fuel Panera's success. Each had their own reasons for leaving. Even so, they were jumping ship right in the middle of the transformation. I couldn't help but wonder if they saw something I didn't. Was I unwittingly steering a sinking ship? And how would we fill their roles and get the work done? In town hall meetings and management off-sites, I shared my own worries and vulnerabilities and encouraged people to talk about theirs. I told them they could count on me to take the punches and keep coming back, to use every ounce of strength I had to see the transformation through. I knew that we were in danger of losing the positive story that united us, as people became increasingly worried about the short term. I still had faith in the potential we were pursuing, but it wasn't entirely in my hands. I didn't own enough of the company to control its destiny. And I should have known that in this moment of intense vulnerability, all that blood in the water would once again catch the attention of the sharks.

• • •

In March 2015, I took a rare break from work to honor my annual tradition of attending the Final Four college basketball tournament with Michael, in Indianapolis. We were out riding bikes together on a cold, windy Friday afternoon when a message arrived: some investment fund we'd never heard of, named Luxor, had nominated two directors to our board within one hour of the deadline to nominate new directors. I felt like I'd been dropped down an elevator shaft. I knew this feeling all too well—the clench in the pit of my stomach, the bitter cocktail of rage, fear, and indignation rising in the back of my throat. Activists.

"Here we go again," I thought grimly. The text effectively ended the father-son vacation. My body stayed in Indy, but my heart and mind had left. I sat through the games frozen in thought and then flew home after the weekend to deal with the crisis. The activists brought the

usual long list of demands. Predictably, one of the guys they'd nominated to the board was in his thirties—a bright but cocky young man
named Noah Elbogen.

"I'll be damned if I'll let this kid tell me how to run my company,"
I vowed. I wrote a strongly worded letter that essentially said, *If you
push me, I'm resigning.* But I never sent it. Instead, outwardly, I tried
to be courteous and open-minded. I knew I'd have to work with these
guys, and there was nothing to be gained from throwing a tantrum—
at least, not in public. I'd learned a lot in my last tussle with activists
in 2008. This time I was better prepared. I think they were surprised
at my willingness to meet and talk. Activists expect to be made the
enemy. But I've learned that being respectful but firm and taking them
seriously is a better approach.

Privately, I was fuming. I hadn't spent the past few years working eighty-hour weeks only to have these punks come in and derail
our transformation for a quick buck. I knew what was important for
Panera, and I got clear with myself that I would not budge on aspects of
the business and our strategy that truly mattered. I'd rather be forced
out. These would be my lines in the sand. In any case, I knew from my
annual visits to our investors that I had their support, so I was ready to
stand up to the threats.

To appease the activists, I gave them some wins on issues that
were less important to me. Some of their demands were actually good
ideas—even things I wanted to accomplish—so I used the activists as
leverage to convince the board to accept them. These initiatives included increasing our debt load to one times EBITDA, and an agreement to buy back our stock. These weren't things that compromised
our core transformation initiatives or changed our relationship with
our customers. So I embraced them. I also agreed to put out a press
release saying that Luxor had been influential in helping us make that
decision. It didn't cost me anything to let it have that victory. But I held
firm on the things that mattered to the integrity of the company and
its long-term transformation, and I was not going to put the activists
in our boardroom.

Behind closed doors, I used the activists as a foil to rally our team members. As Stanford economist Paul Romer put it, "a crisis is a terrible thing to waste."[1] I had no intention of wasting this opportunity to unify my team by giving them a common enemy. And make no mistake—Luxor was the enemy. That summer, our family went on safari in Africa. It was hard not to draw a dark parallel between the lions and leopards stalking and hunting unsuspecting impalas, antelope, and water buffalo, and the activists who ruthlessly ambush vulnerable prey.

Upon returning from my trip, I invited Noah to address our top three hundred leaders. He delivered a dry, prepared speech telling them why they needed to drive up ROI. At the end of it, I handed him a Panera apron, saying, "I know you really want to be running the company, but you'll have to start by running a store." He took it as a joke, but when he'd left the room, I ran him up the flagpole, describing my safari observations and decrying predatory investors. I got the crowd so riled up with the fear of working for Noah that by the end they were chanting in unison, "F___ you, Noah. F___ you, Noah." It was a cathartic moment that we all needed at that difficult point in our long transformation.

I should mention that over the nearly two years that Luxor would remain investors, I actually came to like and respect Noah (though I couldn't tell anyone). He was bright and he cared about Panera and was enthusiastic about being a part of it. His suggestion to use reverse auctions was a good move that would save us tens of millions of dollars. I was a little sorry to say goodbye to Noah when Luxor cashed out, though I couldn't admit it at the time. (Fast forward a few years, and I asked Noah to become a partner in my new venture, Act III. You never know what will come of befriending your activists!)

Our transformation continued, unabated. In May 2015, shortly after Luxor attacked, we took a major step in delivering on our reenvisioned Concept Essence. We publicly announced a commitment to "clean food"—which meant food that was free of artificial colors, flavors, preservatives, and sweeteners. To throw down the gauntlet and focus our team, I made a public announcement of Panera's intention to remove all artificial additives from the standard bakery-café food menu by the end of 2016. We published what we called the "no-no list"—more than ninety-six ingredients that we planned to remove from existing menu items and/or never use in the future. That got the team's attention, and the media's. Now all we had to do was deliver.

Keeping this promise was a challenge. We had to break down each ingredient, which in many cases meant going back to the supplier, or the supplier's supplier, sometimes all the way back to the farm, to figure out what was in the food. We had a team of ten working on this, over several years. And many of the new ingredients we used to replace the artificial ones had a shorter shelf life, which meant we had to ramp up food safety practices. As an example, our popular Broccoli-Cheddar Soup went through dozens of revisions to remove all the artificial ingredients without sacrificing the taste and texture that customers loved.

In the end, not a single menu item remained unchanged. Out of 450 ingredients, 122—27 percent—had to be reformulated. Plus, we had to retrain all our staff. They couldn't pour the salad dressing out of a bottle anymore; they had to make it.

With our new Concept Essence in place, we intensified innovation in operations, food and bakery, marketing, and store design. We also launched a national advertising campaign built around the slogan "Food as it should be." The only good thing, I sometimes thought to myself, was that all of this kept me so busy that I just didn't have time to worry about the damn activists. I was simply too absorbed in the challenge of following through.

I stayed focused because the alternative to successfully transforming Panera was so much worse. We'd end up needing a *turnaround*, which is an ugly thing. You might read about dramatic turnarounds by heroic CEOs like Steve Jobs's improbable resurrection of Apple or Lee Iacocca's stirring rescue of Chrysler. But successful turnarounds are rare. More often, as consultant Gary Hamel puts it, a turnaround "is transformation tragically delayed."[2] Tragic indeed—because had the company had the courage to engage in innovation before it hit a crisis point, it might have never needed the rescue. And as former Nasdaq CEO Robert Greifeld comments, massive reorganizations are "more often than not the result of a miscarriage of leadership . . . an admission that management hasn't been doing the hard work of continually improving the business."[3]

I was reminded of this in the midst of Panera's transformation when I read the news that JCPenney's CEO Ron Johnson had been fired. Just a couple of years earlier, he'd arrived at the flailing retailer wearing the glow of his former employer, Apple, and full of big ideas and lofty promises to shake up the company's moribund culture and put it back on the right side of the growth curve. But the hoped-for transformation failed to happen quickly enough, and Johnson was unceremoniously booted. I couldn't help but feel that the drubbing he received in the business press was missing the larger lesson: turnarounds are long shots. The real culprits were those who had managed the company over the past decade and allowed its competitive position to erode so badly.

Johnson's ouster reminded me once again that transformation might be a long, hard, and painful process, but it's neither as hard nor as painful as an emergency turnaround. Don't avoid the inevitable. Be a realist and innovate and indeed transform while you have the breathing room, the resources, and the credibility with your stakeholders. Don't be discouraged when it takes a long time, or even when it feels like a torment that will never end. As I'd whispered to Emma (and to myself) on that dark and difficult night, it will all be worth it when you emerge in the bright new morning of the future—renewed, revitalized, and ready to compete.

Unlike Vince Lombardi, I didn't run out of time. Panera's investors were patient, and by the third quarter of 2016, we finally began to see our hard work pay off. I knew we'd reached an inflection point when I started waking up early each morning with excitement to check our same-store sales, rather than with dread. I even found myself looking forward to our upcoming earnings release—something I hadn't felt in a long time. I could feel the progress and momentum flowing through me like my own blood.

The epic Panera 2.0 digital access rollout was nearing completion by the end of 2016. Digital orders accounted for 24 percent of sales. The catering business achieved double-digit sales growth, and we launched a national rollout of Delivery. A revised loyalty program, MyPanera, was taking off (and would go on to account for over 50 percent of transactions and reach 36 million members by the end of 2016, becoming the largest loyalty program in the industry at the time). Our stock price rose 24 percent that year. By October 2016, Panera was the ninth most valuable restaurant company in America, with a market capitalization approaching $5 billion.

The next month, I got the joyful news that Luxor had decided to cash out. We'd triumphed again, but for how long? The only way to protect yourself against activists is to keep the stock price up while also protecting long-term innovation. It's always a treacherous balancing act. The currency of an innovator is control and time: the ability to play out your idea and the time to do it. Activists aim to take both those things away. I was grateful we'd managed to buy the time we needed to complete our work—at least for now.

By Christmas 2016, we'd removed every one of the ninety-six items on the no-no list from our menu. Many others copied us, which was a good thing. In fact, it was part of our intention. We knew we were a leader others would follow. By going clean, we changed the economics of doing so and enabled others to make the leap, which was a win all through the supply chain from farm to consumer.

In early 2017, on my annual vacation, my reflections were filled with a great deal of pride—and more than a little disbelief. I marveled at the six-year journey since I wrote the transformation memo and where it had taken me. What started as a vision for improving customer access had evolved to encompass an overhaul of our production systems, an expansion of our business channels, evolution in our management team, and a fundamental rethinking of our Concept Essence. Ultimately, we changed everything, including every product we sold. I'd never worked so hard or suffered through so many moments of doubt. Along the way, many questioned me, and many abandoned ship. But many more had trusted me and my vision and had worked tirelessly beside me. I was so happy and proud to have proven those people right.

In the end, it was all worth it because I was able to look back and say that I had integrity. Integrity is about getting the job done—whether that means getting a guest the sandwich she ordered or completing a massive, multiyear organizational transformation. And you do it not just so your customers or stakeholders will be happy—you do it so you'll be able to respect yourself.

Our transformation represented a duty and a promise to me. A promise is personal. A promise implies a relationship—one of trust and one of potential. Making a promise is a demonstration of commitment, respect, and moral strength. Keeping a promise reflects one's integrity and one's honor. To this day I look back on those years of massive transformation as the best work of my life.

Know When to Sell

I could hear my dad's voice as clearly as if he'd been sitting beside me. "Just take the money!" he would tell me. I knew it. It was April 2017, and I was staring at a very long row of zeros on the purchase and sale agreement I was about to present to my board. We were preparing to sell Panera Bread to a European investment group, for a lot of money: $7.5 billion, or $315 per share. We'd been working on this deal for a few months, and I was the one who had initiated the negotiations, pushed for a higher price, and been determined to get it done. I felt confident that it was the right next step for the company. But on the morning of the board vote, I was hesitating—which was why my long-gone dad's voice popped into my head.

In case you can't tell by now, I'm not a "just-take-the-money" kind of guy. For most of my career, I'd resisted this kind of advice—resolutely pursuing long-term value creation over short-term profit taking. I'm a business builder, a creative entrepreneur who finds his greatest joy in figuring out where the market is going and being the first to get there. I love finding a solution to a problem that customers haven't even articulated yet, and seeing their faces light up when they discover it. Sure, profits matter, but they're the by-product, not the end. Profits matter because they create possibilities; they allow me to keep doing what I love. And yet, this time, I was ready to take the money. I was ready to sell the company.

Every successful entrepreneur will face this question at some point: to sell or not to sell? Knowing when the time is right to harvest—for yourself, for your stakeholders, and for the company—is never easy. I'd toyed with the idea of selling a couple of times over the years, but it had been decades since I received a serious offer. Offers for billion-dollar companies are rare and should never be treated casually. You'll respond emotionally, but the decision on selling must be made rationally, taking into consideration where the company is at, how it's valued at that moment, the interests of all your stakeholders, and where you're at in your own life's journey.

For Panera, the timing wasn't perfect, but it wasn't bad. I'd started seriously considering a sale the previous summer as our epic transformation neared completion. Our stock price was climbing; analysts could see and feel what was coming. If we could get an offer that was priced substantially above the market, it would mean we could deliver value to our shareholders and team members that would otherwise take three or four more years to attain and in any case wouldn't be guaranteed. They'd been patient and generous during the long years of upheaval while we remade the company, and I wanted to reward them. On the other hand, I was torn. If I sold now, I knew I'd be cheating myself out of a victory lap.

Some people might have counseled me to wait a couple of years, to enjoy the fruits of one of the largest, most significant, and most impactful transformations ever completed in the restaurant industry. Sit back and watch the stock go up. But they didn't know me well enough. I knew that even before the Panera 2.0 transformation was completed, I'd need to start thinking about the next one. It's what the market demands. My lead independent director, Dom Colasacco, had already shared his belief that if we hoped to keep up our extraordinarily high multiples well into the future, we would have to have a new growth plan developed and in test in just a few years. Our stock price already reflected that expectation. The stock market ultimately values the future much more than the present. Investors wouldn't care about what we had just accomplished; they would be asking what we would do for them next.

Panera's power had always lain in its ability and willingness to transform. I'd led the company through four major transformations, each one requiring us to confront a hard truth, figure out a new solution based on learning what mattered to our customers, and then put that solution into action and see it through, no matter how long it took. *Tell the truth, know what matters, get the job done.* That was the essence of each reinvention.

Our first transformation was evolving Au Bon Pain (our predecessor company) from a simple French bakery to a chain of bakery cafés—a platform shift that set the stage for new opportunities in the space between fast food and fine dining. The hard truth I told myself was that Au Bon Pain's future as a bakery was limited. The learning, as I watched our customers transforming baguettes into gourmet sandwiches, was that we could be much more than a bakery. Our bread and croissants could become a platform for the lunches people craved. We got the job done by reinventing Au Bon Pain and reengaging growth in urban locations across the East Coast.

Our second transformation was the discovery, through careful observation of customer behavior, of a whole new paradigm within the restaurant category that became the $100 billion–plus fast-casual segment. The hard truth we told ourselves was that Au Bon Pain was becoming pedestrianized in an evolving market, and we needed to understand what forces in the marketplace would shape the future. The learning was about a deeper trend—about decommodification and the desire for specialty food that elevated rather than depleted our guests' self-esteem. For us, this understanding took form as we created Panera Bread, which would become the poster child for fast casual.

Our third transformation was the recognition of the potential of Panera Bread to become a nationally dominant brand and the decision to bet everything on that brand. The hard truth we told ourselves was that we couldn't do everything. And without significant financial and human capital, along with leadership and focus, Panera would never fulfill its promise. The learning was that the potential inherent in Panera was to be protected at all costs. We got the job done by selling off the company's legacy divisions, including my "first child," Au

Bon Pain, shedding the past and betting it all on the company's as-yet-unproven future as Panera Bread.

Our fourth and final transformation was reinventing Panera completely, when we had more than two thousand stores and were feeding one in thirty Americans every week. The hard truth we told ourselves was that despite our success, we were losing competitive advantage. The learning was that what mattered to our customers was being able to get the food they craved in the ways that fit their lifestyles—through multiple channels, both digital and physical. And we got the job done by not only transforming our ordering systems but completely overhauling our back end as well, to ensure we could deliver. And then we went further, building out several potentially $1 billion–plus businesses and eventually rewriting the very essence of our concept to meet the evolving market's desire for "craveable wellness."

• • •

We were wrapping up this final transformation when I began seriously considering a sale. There were many compelling reasons to sell. At sixty-two, I still had living to do outside the office, and I couldn't imagine living through the agony of yet another company reinvention—the stress, uncertainty, expectations, and loneliness, wondering if it would ever be done. In fact, I'd informed the board in 2015 that I wanted to step out of the CEO role. Now, I asked myself the question I always ask in the pre-mortem: What can I do in the next three to five years that I will respect, looking back from my deathbed?

A sale seemed like a great answer. Given our most recent brush with activists, I was more wary than ever of the pervasive short-termism of the public markets—and concerned about what would happen to the company without my super voting stock and my credibility to protect it if I simply retired. Being private, I believed, was a competitive advantage. It would allow the company to keep doing what it did best—innovate for the long term. If I could find the right partner, I'd feel good about harvesting at this time.

The truth was, however, with our stock price rising and the company getting more valuable every day, that there were very few candidates. In fact, when the board had done a strategic review in 2015, Goldman Sachs had told us the likeliest potential acquirer out there was Starbucks. So, when I got an email in the summer of 2016 telling me that my old friend Howard Schultz, founder of Starbucks, wanted to visit me in Boston, I knew exactly what it meant, and I was ready to talk.

Starbucks was in many ways our closest competitor, having tapped into the same drive for specialness and self-esteem that was at the core of Panera's Concept Essence. I thought of Schultz as my oldest "frenemy"—the guy whose proverbial rear end I'd been chasing for three decades, ever since we met when Au Bon Pain was a handful of cafés in Boston and he had seven coffee shops in Seattle. I'd never hesitated to play hardball with Starbucks, but Howard and I also liked each other, coming from similar backgrounds and sharing an entrepreneurial passion. I knew he was a guy who thought like I did—an opportunist in the best sense of the word.

I told Dom Colasacco, "Howard doesn't come up on a Saturday afternoon just to hang out. It's likely he is going to make a serious offer to buy the company." What I didn't say out loud, but knew in my heart, was that if the offer was good enough, it was time to accept it.

Howard's new Gulfstream jet landed at Hanscom Field, an airport outside Boston, that Saturday afternoon. We talked for three or four hours about our lives, the business, and where each of our companies were headed. It seemed like we talked about everything except the thing I thought he'd wanted to talk about. No offer was discussed. Instead, Howard proposed a partnership opportunity. Panera would make soup, salad, and sandwiches and distribute it to Starbucks locations across the country. Starbucks would provide coffee to our cafés. And then he got back on his jet and returned to the Hamptons.

I was a little disappointed. But when I discussed it with my board, we concluded that this proposal was the first step in the dance. We decided to stay open and see what came next. Later that week Howard called and extended an invitation for me to come to Seattle and see their new roastery with him, visit the Starbucks headquarters, and meet with his team. I accepted.

It was a lovely tour. I enjoyed watching Howard pull my first nitro cold brew. Howard and I had a private Lebanese dinner at one of his favorite restaurants. We spent the day with his senior team comparing restaurant strategy. But again, the only thing not discussed was the thing I'd flown across the country to talk about: how we might merge the companies. I hopped back on my plane and returned to Boston, still a little puzzled. When I got on a conference call with my board members, they asked me the obvious question—"What does Howard want with Panera?" I simply couldn't answer them. There was only one thing to do: ask Howard.

So I called him and put my cards on the table: "This is going to be way too complicated if you're buying some salads and sandwiches from Panera and we are buying coffee from Starbucks. If we want to do this, the only way to go is a merger of the companies."

Howard was full of enthusiasm—like it was the best idea he'd never thought of. "Let's get a group of people to work on it," he said. He proposed his CFO and strategic consultant, and I proposed Bill Moreton.

On paper, a deal looked very attractive. It could generate as much as $1 billion in incremental EBITDA, or more. But we also began to see a problem. Panera 2.0 was completing rollout across the country, our transformation was gaining traction, and the stock kept going up—and when you're trying to do a deal, that's the one time you don't want the stock going up! By the fall the stock was pushing $222 a share. During the Thanksgiving break, one of our Panera directors, Larry Franklin, and his wife, Cheryl, joined my family at our home in the Caribbean. On our last Sunday afternoon, I remember floating in the warm ocean with Larry and telling him, "I know we're going to get this Starbucks deal done; I can feel it. When we get back tomorrow morning, Howard and I have a call scheduled and he's going to make us an offer. There's way too much incremental EBITDA for him not to."

Monday came. I got Howard on the phone. "Ron, I'm sorry, we've given it serious thought but we're not going to be able to go forward with this," he said.

It was a kick to the stomach. The stock had gone up too much, he explained. They couldn't even get to our public market price, let alone pay a premium. It was clear something had gone awry. I usually know my customer, and I'd been sure this thing was headed to a deal. I'd misjudged this by a long shot. Later, we learned of another factor that may well have played a role in the decision: Schultz, like me, was feeling the time had come to let go of the reins. He'd made the decision to step down as CEO, and his successor, Kevin Johnson, likely didn't want to take on such a major acquisition as he stepped into the role.

It was a bitter disappointment—I really thought I had this one. I could taste it. But sometimes things don't work out as you planned, even when they make great business sense. Your only choice is to pack away your disappointment, get a good night's sleep, and know that tomorrow the sun rises again and there will be other buyers out there.

Except, in this case, were there any others? Goldman had thought it unlikely. I knew I was psychologically ready for a deal. I was ready to let go—indeed, internally I'd already begun to loosen my emotional attachment to this company I loved. But where else could I turn?

There was one other organization out there that I thought could pull off, and might be interested in, a deal as big as Panera: JAB Holding Company, a German fund that already owned Krispy Kreme, Einstein Bros. Bagels, Peets Coffee, Keurig, Coty, and multiple other assets around the world. I had put out feelers for a meeting with the JAB folks before the Starbucks conversation began. Now, I reengaged the connection, and in February of 2017, Olivier Goudet, JAB's CEO, called and invited me to meet him at the company's offices in Washington, DC. Our planned one-hour lunch turned into a five-hour meeting, and when I finally left, I knew Olivier and his associate David Rose were falling in love with Panera.

I liked them too. They sold themselves as long-term thinkers who had the mindset and the patience to shepherd the company through the final stages of our transformative agenda, fulfill the promise of our five-year plan, and take care of our team members and investors. That's the kind of thing I loved to hear because that's what mattered to me.

In March, we were again holding our Panera Family Reunion at Nashville's Grand Ole Opry, one of my favorite venues. It was on that very stage that I'd made my first "farewell" speech, with the "sail on" theme, back in 2009, even though no one had known at the time that's what it was. The irony did not escape me that I was once again seriously considering leaving the company, even as I stepped onto that beloved stage and poured my heart into my speech. As I soaked up the swell of applause from our people, I was filled with emotion. I'm a sentimental guy; Panera was a part of me. But I knew it was the right time to harvest if I could get the right offer. I'd told JAB I didn't want to hear about an offer until after the reunion. So I had made an appointment to fly to DC the day after the reunion ended to meet with Olivier and David and hear what JAB had to say.

When I'd written my reunion speech, I hadn't been thinking about an impending sale. But I wouldn't have written it any differently if I had. Its theme—keeping the promise of Panera—would have made sense if I'd planned to stay there forever, but it also resonated powerfully now that the possibility of a serious offer was on the table. What I was telling our assembled Panera family was this: *the transformation that that we have been working on for more than half a decade is now in full rollout and its ultimate success is now in your hands. It's up to you to keep the promise of Panera, to our customers and all of our stakeholders, including yourselves.* I used my own kids as an example—how Nancy and I had dreams for them when they were young, but they grew up and we had come to realize that their lives were now in their hands.

I didn't say goodbye in so many words—that would have been premature—but that speech was a transference of responsibility. The applause seemed to go on forever, lifting me up on a wave of love that carried through until 3 a.m. as we danced and celebrated the company.

The next day, absolutely exhausted, I dragged myself from Nashville to Boston to drop off my family and then down to DC for my meeting with JAB. I listened for several hours as Olivier made a bid to buy the company. JAB's initial offer wasn't bad: $286 a share, which represented a 21.7 percent premium on our stock price. But I wasn't satisfied. I wanted more than $300, and the board and my investment banker, Michael Boublik of Morgan Stanley, encouraged me. I stayed up till 3 a.m. yet again—this time not dancing but reading everything I could get my hands on about JAB's historical bidding approach. I became convinced we could get a higher price. I emailed Bill Moreton, my closest colleague, telling him I wanted to push. I'll never forget how he responded: "Don't get greedy," he said, because "pigs get fat, hogs get slaughtered." I wasn't sure I like being referred to as either a pig or hog. But I knew I could get a better offer from JAB.

After three tense weeks of negotiations, JAB eventually made a final offer of $315 per share. It was a good price. I called a board meeting for the following day, April 4, to vote on the deal.

That's when all hell broke loose in my mind. That night before the vote, I didn't sleep a minute. I tossed and turned, agonizing over the decision. What was I doing? Could I really sell Panera? Was I selling out my child? As all our hard work was just paying off, could I actually walk away?

For decades, I'd been emotionally wired to the beating heart of the company. Keeping the company going, not letting down our investors, taking care of our people—these imperatives had become as instinctive to me as feeding my family. It was hard to unwind all that pressure and obligation, to wrest my own identity away from the company I'd created. I wasn't planning to leave immediately—the deal stipulated that I'd stay on as CEO, at least for a while. But I knew that it wouldn't be the same once I signed the purchase and sale. Was I really ready to let go? My deceased father's exasperated voice in my head was impatiently telling me, "Get the damn thing done already!" But still, I hesitated. As dawn broke, I gave up any pretense of trying to sleep and opened my email, where I found a new message from Bill Moreton. It was as if he was reading my mind.

> Ron—
> I imagine that you have thought about Louis and your dad more than a few times these past few days. I am sure they are resting peaceful and are incredibly proud of you. You have touched so many lives . . . especially mine.

I hope you have a great day today telling the wonderful story you
have created.
Bill

With tears in my eyes, I typed a brief reply:

Dad always told me to "just take the money." Though it has never
been my way, this is probably the right time . . .

Bill's response flashed onto my screen:

Sometimes it's good for sons to listen to their fathers.

So I did. Galvanized, I went to the board meeting and asked each
board member individually: Should we go through with this sale or
not? Each one said yes. They were unanimous in their conviction that
this was an extraordinary outcome for all of our stakeholders, and we
should do the deal. The JAB folks were waiting at their lawyers' offices, a few blocks away. I grabbed a bottle of champagne and went
over there.

"We're ready to accept the offer," I told them. "But it's not just a matter of price. It's a matter of what you are going to do with the company." And then I asked each of the senior partners in turn: "Are you
going to take good care of our concept and people?" Each one of them
answered yes. I took them at their word. We toasted, and it was done.

The only thing left to do was tell the world. So we drafted a press release, announcing what ended up being the largest US restaurant deal
ever done up until that point, at among the highest multiples ever. My
CFO Mike Bufano and I ended up writing the release ourselves, feeling
that none of our high-priced outside PR people could capture what the
company was about and what the sale represented.

When the announcement was done and released, I felt strangely
empty. I went through the motions, taking congratulatory calls, but it
wasn't until I went on CNBC the next morning that my mood lifted.
The anchors, David Faber, Sara Eisen, and Jim Cramer, with whom
I'd done dozens of shows over the years, came to the studio to greet

me. I was soon feeling more celebratory—especially when they seemed perplexed by my decision to take the company private at this moment when Panera was doing so well. Their questions reminded me of why I was doing the deal at all—I was tired of being a slave to the short term.

"It's an opportunity to do even better work," I told them.

"Well, yes," Faber challenged me, "but you're not going to have a stock price to judge that work by any longer. How are you going to measure yourself?"

That comment said it all. "We've never judged ourselves by the stock price," I retorted. "The stock price is a by-product of the work we've done. We're going to measure ourselves the way we've always measured ourselves—by our ability to make a difference and take market share." I used the moment to deliver a message that I would share many more times in the years to come: that our economy—and our politics—are not served by this focus on the short term. My old friend Jim Cramer got the message. "You've got a soul, Ron!" he declared.

Their final question: "How does it feel to have the biggest restaurant deal in US history?"

My answer: "This deal is simply a by-product of our good work."

What felt great, I explained, was to have led a company that figured out what mattered and delivered for its shareholders as the best-performing restaurant stock over its last two decades as a public entity, to have a company that was really taking care of its associates, to have a company that was genuinely serving its customers. That's how we valued ourselves, not in dollars per share.

The day had begun with a "message" from my father, reinforced by Bill. It ended with an email from my son, then eighteen and spending his gap year before college traveling in Asia. That day, he was in China, half a world away, but he knew what a big moment it was for me and had taken the time to reach out with his own reflections. "It's hard to part ways," he began, noting that he himself was also in a moment of transition, "parting ways with you and Mom and home."

"I keep reminding myself," Michael wrote, with a wisdom beyond his years, "I am not actually parting ways with you guys. There is never an end. The 'end' is just a word. The relationships you have made with the people at Panera over the last thirty years do not end on Monday, just like my relationship and my traditions I have with you won't end when I go to college and one day you die. Our relationships and customs and frankly our repetitive experiences just take place in different forms."

I've never been prouder of my son. Panera had been a part of his family since the day he was born. He and Nancy and his sister, Emma, had made real sacrifices for it, sharing me with the company more times than they would have liked. But he'd learned the most important lesson I could have taught him—to focus on what matters; to build a life, not just a business. And now he was teaching it to me.

What I told myself then, and I still tell myself today, is that the notion of "legacy" is pointless. My legacy isn't a company or anything else I've created. After I've gone, I can't control any of that. My only legacy is in what I've done, and the person I've become as a result of what I've done.

"You will always be part of Panera, and more importantly Panera will always be a part of you," Michael's note concluded. "It's time to move on: not an ending but a time to cherish the past experiences/relationships you made at Panera and embark on new experiences and memories. Maybe that means politics, maybe it means new businesses, maybe it means conscious capitalism, and it definitely means one day helping me with my own creation! Have a good day and sending good vibes from Tiger Leaping Gorge! Love you. Michael."

As I finished an intense day of media tours in Boston that evening, I knew that I had let go. I'd relinquished the control I'd fought so hard to keep over all these years. I'd always been the primary author of Panera's story, weaving the narrative of where we'd come from and where we were going. I felt, at that moment, like I'd written a pretty damn good ending to this chapter—one that benefited all of our constituents. But as Michael reminded me, it wasn't an end to my story. Held between the wise words of my father and my son, I was ready to embark on the next chapter in my life's journey.

Transformation Never Ends

It's a glorious day in June 2023, and I'm sitting on the very same beach in the Caribbean where I've done some of my best thinking over the years. It was here that I made the wrenching decision to sell off the legacy divisions of Au Bon Pain—my first child—and bet everything on Panera. I've gazed out at this stretch of white sand as I envisioned the potential of a new restaurant paradigm—fast casual. The soft sound of these lapping waves accompanied me as I considered whether to return to Panera and take on the largest transformation of my career. Now, more than six years after the company's sale, with my seventieth birthday approaching, here I am again. You might be wondering, am I finally kicking back and enjoying the view and easy breezes?

To be honest, no. Don't get me wrong—I'm grateful for this place and appreciate my home in the sun. But I don't seem to be wired to retire—at least not just yet. In fact, I'm currently reflecting on another company: Cava, the fast-growing Mediterranean food concept for which I'm a lead investor and chairman. I'm immensely proud of Cava's breakthrough IPO, with its stock more than doubling on the opening day of trading and the company reaching a market cap in excess of $4 billion. But beyond the big numbers and the glowing headlines, the real satisfaction comes from knowing that we *figured it out*—indeed, we discovered half a decade ago what would matter today and got it done. Again. The set of principles and strategies I've shared in this book—the very same ones that built Au Bon Pain and Panera—have now brought Cava to *its* launch as a public company. I've come a long way from the young CEO I was at my first IPO, thinking about all my new stakeholders with a sinking feeling in the pit of my stomach.

Even with Cava's IPO under my belt, my attention is on the future. I know that an IPO is just a one-day event, like a wedding. Cava's job now is to build a successful marriage—always a long-term endeavor— with its stakeholders. And I know CEO Brett Schulman and his team have the knowledge and skills to beat the odds and do just that.

I'm also thinking about the other companies that I'm guiding and in which I'm the lead investor—each created and being developed to dominate some of the most important niches in the hospitality industry today. These include Tatte, an upscale European- and Mediterranean-infused café that achieves authority not only as an artisan bakery but in third-wave coffee and food as well. And Life Alive, a concept that I believe has the potential to be the preeminent brand in plant-forward food—one of the most exciting segments in the restaurant industry of tomorrow. And then there's Level99, which I expect will be a dominant concept in immersive entertainment—over 35,000 square feet of mental and physical challenges combined with a craft beer hall and a wonderful restaurant. In the end, any one of these has the potential to be more impactful than Cava or even Panera. But whether each company ultimately has that impact depends on what we do with it and how we care for it.

As I sit on the beach, I'm asking myself: Is this a powerful consumer niche with long-term tailwinds, and does our concept have the potential to dominate that niche? In sum, do we have competitive advantage?

My mind is also occupied with political and social concerns. Never have the perils of short-termism been more apparent, in both business and civic society, and never has the need for long-term thinking been clearer. Our cities, institutions, economies, nations, and ecosystem are all crying out for us to tell the truth, know what matters, and get the job done. And for better or for worse, I continue to find myself called to play a part in that effort.

Now, as I sit staring out at the blue horizon and wrestling with these challenges, I wonder, idly, why am I still driving transformation while so many of my friends are retired? But I already know the answer. I'm doing this because, even though it's not an easy road, this is what makes life meaningful to me. This is what I'll look back on and respect. Transformation never stops because transformation is the essence of what I love to do.

I have spent much of my life and career looking ahead to a point in the future and then attempting to reflect, from the future back, on how to get there. And yet the point of it all is not to arrive. Some people feel compelled to climb mountains, cure diseases, or build cathedrals. My greatest joy in life comes not from reaching a goal I've set for myself, but from the creative process of figuring out new solutions and then bringing them into the world. To quote one of my favorite Bruce Springsteen songs, I'm "working on a dream." But in the end, it's not just the dream that contains the meaning; it is the work itself. I don't just sit around and hope for my dreams to come true; I work on them, every day, with discipline and focused intention. And what sustains me is not just my love of the dream; it's my love of the work—my love of the lifelong quest to tell the truth, know what matters, and get it done.

—Ron Shaich, June 2023

NOTES

Chapter 2

1. Clayton M. Christensen et al., "Know Your Customers' 'Jobs to Be Done,'" *Harvard Business Review*, September 2016.

2. Clayton M. Christensen, Scott Cook, and Taddy Hall, "What Customers Want from Your Products," *HBS Working Knowledge*, January 2006, https://hbswk.hbs.edu /item/what-customers-want-from-your-products.

Chapter 3

1. Viktor E. Frankl, *Man's Search for Meaning: An Introduction to Logotherapy* (Boston: Beacon Press, 1992), 140.

Chapter 4

1. Jane Fulton Suri, *Thoughtless Acts* (San Francisco: Chronicle Books, 2005).

Chapter 9

1. Simon Sinek, *Start with Why* (New York: Penguin, 2009), 45.

Chapter 13

1. Jillian D'Onfro, "Steve Jobs Used to Ask Jony Ive the Same Question Almost Every Day," *Business Insider*, October 8, 2015, https://www.businessinsider.com/this -is-the-question-steve-jobs-would-ask-jony-ive-every-day-2015-10.

Chapter 16

1. Albert Einstein, *The Ultimate Quotable Einstein* (Princeton, NJ: Princeton University Press, 2010), 480.

2. David A. Garvin and Lynne C. Levesque, "Emerging Business Opportunities at IBM (A)," Case 9-304-075 (Boston: Harvard Business School, 2005).

Chapter 20

1. Jack Rosenthal, "A Terrible Thing to Waste," *New York Times*, July 31, 2009, https://www.nytimes.com/2009/08/02/magazine/02FOB-onlanguage-t.html.

Chapter 21

1. Larry Bossidy and Ram Charan, *Execution: The Discipline of Getting Things Done* (New York: Crown Business, 2002), 19–20.

Chapter 23

1. Mark Turner, *The Literary Mind* (New York: Oxford University Press, 1996), 4–5.

Chapter 30

1. Jack Rosenthal, "A Terrible Thing to Waste," *New York Times*, July 31, 2009, https://www.nytimes.com/2009/08/02/magazine/02FOB-onlanguage-t.html.
2. Gary Hamel, *The Future of Management* (Boston: Harvard Business Review Press, 2007), 43.
3. Robert Greifeld, *Market Mover* (New York: Grand Central Publishing, 2019), 236.

INDEX

accountability, 87, 103, 140, 142
activist investors, 131–136, 215–217, 220
adjacent markets, growth in, 91, 92
advertising campaigns, 49, 126, 218
agile software development, 100
alignment, with vision, 55–61
Allen, Bill, 137, 139, 148
Amazon, 184
annual financial planning, 146–148
antibiotic-free chicken, 208–209
Apple, 218, 219
Applebee's, 90, 207
area franchise model, 91
artificial additives, 217–218, 220
artisan bread, 23, 41, 47–48, 51–52, 54,
    63, 207
artisan pizza, 125–129
asset-light models, 90
assets, turbocharging, 63–65
Au Bon Pain, x, 19–25, 75, 225
    decline of, 63, 70, 72, 76
    expansion of, 37–40, 71–72
    frozen dough at, 121
    IPO, 27–31, 37, 132
    sale of, 76, 78–80, 99, 225–226
    shareholders of, 33–34
    stock classes, 36
    stock price, 45
    success of, 25, 27–28
authority, 110, 116, 120, 123
    building, 128
    competitive advantage and, 120, 122,
        123, 168, 200
    loss of, 168, 207
    in niche, 51, 54, 63, 88, 126
    source of, 56, 57, 58, 60, 92, 119, 207

barriers to entry, 88, 114, 119–124, 166
benchmarking, 196–197

Bloomin' Brands, 137
board members, 39, 69, 72, 78, 133, 136
Borland, Mark, 41, 121, 154
Bossidy, Larry, 139, 148
Boublik, Michael, 230
brands, 38, 49, 56, 58, 65–66, 128, 168
bread, 23, 41, 51–52, 54, 63, 119, 120,
    121–122, 207
Bruckmann, Rosser, Sherrill & Co. (BRS),
    79–80
budgeting, 146–148
Bufano, Mike, 232
Buffett, Warren, 164
Bunge, 79
bureaucracy, 102, 155
business models, 30, 38, 48, 72, 92, 105,
    120, 124, 236
by-products, 15–18, 88, 114, 141, 223

calendars, 142–144
California, 37–38
calorie counts, 209
capital, 23, 24, 34–36, 76
catering, 200, 201, 220
Cava, 207, 235–236
Chapman, Chuck, 191, 196
Charan, Ram, 139, 148
Cheesecake Factory, 120
chicken, 208–209
Chick-fil-A, 35, 209
chief executive officer (CEO), 103–104,
    107, 137–138, 188–189
Child, Julia, 21–22
Chipotle, 52, 90, 208
Christensen, Clayton, 10, 100
Chrysler, 218
Circle of Warmth, 160
Citizens Bank, 71–72
Class A stock, 36

Class B stock, 36, 132
clean food, 217–218, 220
CNBC, 232–233
Colasacco, Dom, 224, 227
Coleman, Tony, 67
college years, 9–12
companywide memos, 159
compensation system, 95–97
competitive advantage, 7, 9–18, 49, 88
    barriers to entry and, 119–124, 166
    contrarian thinking and, 167–168
    desire-friction ratio and, 184
    growth and, 92
    loss of, 206, 226
    maintaining, 30–31, 92–93, 116, 123,
        166
    rules for, 123
    smart bets and, 110, 112, 114, 119–120
    as transient, 123–124
Concept Essence, 55–61, 66–68, 88, 104,
    145, 206–208, 211, 217–218
Constitution, US, 58
consumer behavior, 47–48, 63–65
consumer packaged goods, 200, 202
continuous improvement, 197
contrarian approach, 30, 163–169
control, 34–36, 132, 135
Cookie Jar, 18, 19, 24
corporate culture, 104, 161–162
cost management, 147
Covid-19 pandemic, 166
Cramer, Jim, 232–233
craveable wellness, 209, 226
credibility, 66, 104, 109, 127, 131–136,
    219, 226
credit card sales, 114–115
Crispani, 125–129, 132, 133
culture, 104, 161–162
customer experience, 117, 165, 180–183,
    185–187
customer needs, 21–24, 54, 102
customers
    learning about, 53–54
    observation of, 47–48, 63–65, 208
    target, 123, 168

Danoff, Will, 134
Davis, Scott, 47, 57, 122, 126

death, 3
decision-making, 89, 116–117
    See also smart bets
decommodification, 49
delivery, 100–102, 200–202, 220
desire-friction ratio, 179–189, 206
differentiation, 13, 114, 116–117, 168,
    206
digital ordering, 191–196, 202, 203, 220,
    226
discovery, 100–104, 107
Disney, Roy, 131
disruptive innovation, 104
Domino's, 202
Donatos, 99
dual classes of stock, 36, 132
Dyer, Jeff, 100

efficiency, 102
Einstein, Albert, 103
Eisen, Sara, 232–233
Eisenberg, David, 208
Eisner, Michael, 131
Elbogen, Noah, 216, 217
Ells, Steve, 52
empathy, 42–43, 53–54, 64, 118, 208
employees
    engagement of, 162
    firing, 153, 154
    incentivizing, 95–97, 152–153
    managing, 151–155
employee turnover, 95, 96
entrepreneurs
    decision to sell for, 224
    desire for control by, 34, 36, 132
    as doers, 78
    going public and, 36
    myths about, 24–25
    as opportunists, 23–25
entrepreneurship
    challenges of, 72–74
    downsides of, 69–73
execution, 123, 138–149, 195–196

Faber, David, 232–233
Facebook, 132
fail fast, 65–66

failure
    breaking cycle of, 95–97
    erosion of trust and, 111
    learning from, 127–128
family, 171, 212
Family Reunion, 74, 160, 171–173, 179,
    206, 229–230
fast casual, x, 23, 52, 54, 171, 207,
    225
fast food, 50–51, 64
financial plans, 145–148
five-year plans, 145–146
fixed costs, 127
Fleming's Prime Steakhouse, 137
focus groups, 54
food insecurity, 209
food service delivery. See delivery
franchisee meetings, 160
franchising, 89–91, 95
Frankl, Viktor, 17
Franklin, Larry, 228
future-back process, 5–8, 10–11, 139,
    148–149, 164, 174, 186

gambling, 109, 115
gathering places, 64–65, 112, 114
General Foods, 90
generalizations, 105, 118, 201, 208
General Mills, 90
General Store, 9–14, 18
Gerstner, Lou, 104
Gibson, William, 47
Gold, Stanley, 133
Golden Chain award, 45
Goldman Sachs, 227, 229
Google, 132
Goudet, Olivier, 229–230
Great Recession, 90, 163, 164–166,
    169
Gregerson, Hal, 100
Greifeld, Robert, 219
growth
    as by-product, 88–89
    declining, 71–72, 205–206, 212
    demand for, 37–40
    discipline and, 91–92
    new runways for, 199–203
    of Panera, 87–93

during recession, 165, 166
    rules for, 92

Hamel, Gary, 218
Heckler, Terry, 57, 67
Howley, Tom, 80
human capital, 80, 82, 165–166, 203, 225
Hurst, Blaine, 191

Iacocca, Lee, 218
IBM, 104
initial public offering (IPO), 27–31,
    35–37, 132, 235
innovation
    culture for, 104
    customers and, 100
    disruptive, 104
    essence of successful, 10, 59–60
    leaders, 67
    process, 105–106
    sustained, 67
    top-down, 103–107, 188–189
    transformative, 103
institutional investors, 133–134, 136
integrity, 6, 194, 221
intent, 7–8
investors, 33–36, 38–39, 78, 87, 205–
    206, 219, 224
    activist, 131–136, 215–217, 220
    institutional, 133–134, 136
Ive, Jony, 77

JAB Holding Company, 229–231, 232
JCPenney, 219
Jewson, Dwight, 47–49, 53, 57, 208
Jimmy John's, 202
Jobs, Steve, 35, 77, 199, 218
Johnson, Kevin, 229
Johnson, Ron, 219
Joint Venture Partner program, 96–97

K&N, 196–197
Kane, George, 20
Kane, Louis, 19–21, 27, 30, 45, 72,
    73, 80

Key Initiatives (KIs), 139–143, 144, 174
Kip, Jeff, 131
Kiper, Chris, 133
Kipling, Rudyard, 164
Klein, Gary, 5

la Madeleine French Bakery & Café, 137, 192–193
Laporte, Jack, 134
leaders
    credibility of, 127, 132, 135
    execution by, 148–149
    meaning-making by, 157–162
    smart bets by, 109–118
leadership, 138
    innovation and, 103–107, 188–189
    loneliness of, 72–73
    of public company, 137–149
    servant, 154
Leavening Committee, 159, 160
legacy, 234
Level99, 236
Levitt, Theodore, 10
Life Alive, 236
Lombardi, Vince, 212, 219
long-term perspective, 166–169, 236
long-term results, 134–135
loyalty program, 220
Luxor, 215–217, 220

Maguire, John, 121
Malcolm Baldrige National Quality Award, 196
marketing, rules for, 128
market tests, 126
Master Calendar, 142–144
McDonald's, 99–102, 120, 209
McManus, Jim, 79
meaning-making, 157–162
means, ends, and by-products framework, 15–18, 88, 141
meetings, 142–144, 157–162
metrics, 143, 145–148, 197
mobile ordering, 192–194, 202
Moreton, Bill, 82–83, 87–93, 100, 172, 173, 179, 188, 200, 203, 214, 228, 231–232

mortality, 3–5
Munger, Charlie, 164
MyPanera, 220

niches, 12–13, 30, 88, 123
No Labels, 180

Obama, Barack, 174, 175
observation, 21–22, 48–49, 63–65, 105, 118, 208
one-on-one meetings, 144
operational integrity, 194–198, 203
opportunists, 23–25
opportunities, 10, 21–25
opportunity costs, 81
order accuracy, 194–195
ordering system, 180–187, 191–192, 196, 202, 220, 226
Outback Steakhouse, 137

Panera Bread, ix–xi
    bread at, 121–122
    challenges facing, 205–209, 211–214
    Concept Essence for, 56–61, 66–68, 88, 206–208, 211, 217–218
    contrarian strategy at, 163–169
    crisis facing, 184–185
    Crispani, 125–129
    design of, 66–70
    franchising, 89–91, 95
    growth of, 87–93, 199–203, 205–206, 212
    launch of, 75
    naming of, 68
    ordering system at, 180–187, 191–192, 196, 220, 226
    reinvention of, 206–209
    retirement from, 171–175, 179–180, 188, 203
    return to, 188–189
    sale of, 223–234
    smart bets at, 111–118
    success of, 163, 169, 220
    transformations of, 186–189, 191–203, 205–209, 211–221, 225–226
Panera Cares, 174, 179–180, 209

Panera Family Reunions, 74, 160, 171–173, 179, 206, 229–230
Papa John's, 202
partner/managers, 95–97
patterns, 105, 208
Pausch, Randy, 157
people management, 151–155
performance reviews, 144
personal challenges, 69–74, 79, 82
pizza, 125–129
politics, 10–12, 15–16, 180, 189, 236
Postle, Rick, 89
Powell, Mike, 121
pre-mortem, 5–8, 80, 186, 226
priorities, 80–81
production systems, 193–198
profits, 17–18, 211, 223
profit sharing, 95–96
prototypes, 106
public companies, 28–29, 33, 35, 36, 87, 129, 137
    demand for growth for, 38–40

Real Estate Learning, 91
relationships, 5–6, 43, 72, 134, 233–234
reorganizations, 218–219
research, 105–106
resources, 75–76, 79–81, 90, 101, 103, 110, 127, 164, 225
restaurant industry
    challenges of, 87–88
    copycats in, 120
    evolution of, 50–51, 54
    franchising in, 89–90
retirement, 171–175, 179–180, 188, 203, 226, 235
risk aversion, 13, 24, 167
risk-taking, 109–118
Romer, Paul, 136, 217
Rose, David, 229–230
Rosenthal, Ken, 41–42, 43

same-store sales, 72, 206, 211, 212, 219
Schrotberger, Jason, 205
Schultz, Howard, 52, 227–229
Sears, 207
self-respect, 5, 6, 16, 80, 221

senior management team, 203, 211–212, 214–215
sermons, 159–161
servant leadership, 154
Shaich, Emma, 126, 181, 211, 213–214, 234
Shaich, Joseph, 3–5, 72, 73, 109
Shaich, Michael, 126, 171, 181, 211, 233–234
Shaich, Nancy Antonacci, 82, 126, 191, 211, 230, 234
Shaich, Pearl, 4, 71
Shamrock Holdings, 131–136
shareholders, 29, 30, 33, 38, 212, 224
short-term thinking, 180, 236
Sinek, Simon, 54
skepticism, 29–30
smart bets, 109–120
specialness, 49–55, 101, 168, 227
speeches, 157–162, 171–173
staffing, 196
stakeholders, 159, 219
Staples, 201
Starbucks, 52, 64–65, 112–114, 193, 227–229
St. Louis Bread Company, x, 41–45, 63–68, 72, 88, 121
stock buyback plan, 166–167, 216
stock price, 29, 33–34, 39, 40, 45, 79, 88, 125, 127, 132, 134, 138, 200, 220, 224, 227–229, 233
strategic reviews, 144
Subway, 168
Suri, Jane Fulton, 22
Sweetgreen, 207

talent, 80, 82, 138, 165–166
target customers, 123, 168
Tatte, 236
TCBY, 120
technology adoption, 186–187
testing, 65–66, 126
therapists, 154
third space, 64–65, 112
time management, 80, 81, 82, 110–111, 138, 142–143, 212
top-down innovation, 103–107, 188–189
total quality management (TQM), 197

trans fats, 209
transformations, business, x–xi, 30, 236
  execution and, 195–196
  making operational, 191–197
  at Panera, 186–189, 191–203, 205–209,
    211–221, 225–226
treasury, 80, 81–82, 138, 141
trends, 48–53, 55, 125
turnarounds, 218–219
Turner, Mark, 161
Turner Investments, 205

valuation, enterprise, 38–39
value creation, 17, 23, 165, 172, 223

value investing, 164
venture capitalists, 23, 28
vision, 139, 145
  See also Concept Essence
  alignment with, 55–61
  capturing your, 106

Wegiel, Dan, 201
Wendy's, 207
Wheat Store, 66–68, 75
Wi-Fi, 111–114, 118
work-life balance, 73–74, 173

ACKNOWLEDGMENTS

Writing this book has taken more than a decade, and the journey that gave rise to the ideas it contains has lasted a lifetime. So I have many people to thank.

I'll begin with my collaborator, Ellen Daly. Ellen has extracted the lessons of my life's work, sensitively captured my voice, and patiently dragged me over the finish line. Quite simply, this book would not exist without her.

Ellen was not the first writer to take on the daunting challenge of helping me put my stories and ideas on the page. Bill Breen put several years into the effort, and his research and many of his beautifully crafted words found their way into the final product.

Kate Antonacci McConnell and Robin Allen each worked as my special assistant and speechwriter for many years. Each was profoundly committed to this project and understood what this book meant to me and what I hoped to accomplish with it. Together, we wrestled with more versions of the outline and early drafts than I can count. Kate and Robin, along with Anene Hauschultz, gave voice to my heart and soul and helped me write some of the best speeches of my career. Along the way, each became a dear friend and confidante.

When it came time to seek a publisher, this book found a natural home at Harvard Business Review Press. My editor, Scott Berinato, understood this project from day one, supported it, pushed for it, and helped ensure the words we brought to paper were powerful. Pete Garceau designed a beautiful jacket, art directed by Stephani Finks. Anne Starr guided the book through production with a steady hand, and the rest of the HBR Press team brought discipline to the process.

Many friends and colleagues took the time to read the manuscript and offer feedback along the way, including Scott Davis, Rosalind

Franklin, Dwight Jewson, Jason Karam, Bill Moreton, and James White.

My deep gratitude also goes to the dozens, even hundreds, of people who walked alongside me at different stages of this journey. These include:

My late father, Joseph Shaich, the man who taught me how to think like a businessperson and the one individual I've been trying to prove myself to since I was born and for the quarter century since his death. Are we good yet, Dad?

My late mother, Pearl Shaich, who taught me how to love unconditionally and gave me the characteristics I like best about myself.

Louis Kane, who early on allowed me the space to be me and taught me what it meant to be a citizen of the world and a gentleman above reproach.

Bill Moreton, my business partner of three decades, who always had my back and often understood me better than I understood myself. I couldn't have wished for a better friend or a more capable partner.

Mark Borland, also my dear friend, who literally dedicated his life to Au Bon Pain and Panera, dying because of exposure to flour dust after serving as our chief operations officer and running our manufacturing and supply chain for decades. Mark was the heart of our company and a living expression of what it meant for a business to be "family."

Scott Davis, who for many decades was my closest innovation partner, started as my student, and became my teacher.

Dwight Jewson, my strategic consultant, who always made me smarter. To be honest, many of the things I have been acknowledged for emerged from his mind and our discussions.

Chuck Chapman, a former Panera chief operations officer and board member who has been a rock of operational integrity and a beacon of personal integrity in our company. Special thanks to Chuck for maintaining a long and ever-expanding list of "Ronisms" that helped to ensure my most memorable expressions found their way into this book.

Then there is Mariel Clark, my longtime head of HR, who hired almost every one of the folks who worked with me and was always an astute judge of character and a very protective friend.

Frank Aquila, Peter Cowden, David Eisenberg, Alisa Levine, Andrew Liazos, and Mark O'Connell, each an adviser and friend, who helped me to do my best work.

I also want to acknowledge some of my original colleagues from Au Bon Pain, including Louis Basile, Laura Betlow, Jon Billingsley, Ted Borland, Tony Carroll, Sue Morelli, Jim Rand, and Len Schlesinger. And the original Panera management team, including Tony Coleman, Irene Cook, Becky Fine, Greg Godfrey, Marianne Graziadei, Tom Gumpel, Archie Karel, Jeff Kip, Dan Kish, Tom Kish, Mike Kupstas, John Maguire, Mike Nolan, Phil O'Connell, Michael Simon, Hank Simpson, John Taylor, Pat Tures, and Rick Vanzura. And the final management team at Panera, including Mike Bufano, Rich Crannick, Louis DiPietro, Chris Hollander, John Meister, Pat Mellor, Keith Pascal, Rob Passanisi, Doug Schnell, Michael Simon, Bill Sleeth, Rick Ste. Marie, Shawn Utke, and Dan Wegiel. I grew up through my interactions with each of you. You taught me far more than I ever taught you.

I want to also acknowledge the thousands of Au Bon Pain and Panera folks who sat through meeting after meeting with me and put up with my love of metaphor for nearly forty years. We did our best thinking while learning and laughing together. Thank you.

I also want to thank the tens of thousands of Panera people who did the hard work of making Mother Bread proud. In so many ways it was the store managers and associates of Panera who most energized me and to whom I felt the greatest sense of responsibility. I think about the smiles and support I got from people like Helen Canale, Joanne Collyer, Tim Cross, Christina Kelleher, Melonie Robinson, Kathy Sinnott, Cathy Todisman, Corrina Vratny, and so many others. You know who you are, and I am profoundly appreciative of your friendship and your confidence in me.

Thanks are also due to Ken Rosenthal and Doron Berger, who entrusted me with St. Louis Bread Company, and believed that I would care for their baby with all the love and respect it deserved.

I want to acknowledge Rick Postle, the first president of Panera Bread and the individual who built out the Panera franchise network.

Rick's willingness to play multiple roles in St. Louis Bread Company and then Panera was fundamental to our success.

I also want to thank Panera's many long-serving board members, including our lead independent director, Dom Colasacco, and Fred Foulkes, Larry Franklin, Thomas Lynch, Diane Hessan, and James White. You knew how to make a board work. You asked hard questions and held us to the highest standards, and yet you avoided micromanaging.

My gratitude also extends to our Panera franchisees. You always challenged me and made me think that much harder, but in the end, you invested your money and executed my vision, and I am forever thankful. And so many of you grew to become great friends on the journey. I am so thankful for franchisees like Greg Anderson, Joe and Diane Bastian, Jeff Burrill, Chuck Cain, Dan Cooke, Lewis Cosby, Sam Covelli, Ed Doherty, Greg Flynn, Gavin Ford, Mike Hamra, Don Harty, Dennis Hitzeman, Tom and Lee Howley, Brian Lemek, Phil MacDonald, Jim Magers, John Oudt, Kevin Ricci, Mitch Roberts and David Peterman, Paul Saber, John Sapp, Randy Simon, Moe and Helen Sinclair, Tom and Sue Stees, Don Strang, Earl Taylor, Mark von Waaden, and Steve Wolfe.

I also need to thank the portfolio managers who invested billions of dollars in my vision for Panera and hung in there with me when times got difficult. In particular, I'm thinking of Frank Alonso, Ashley Woodruff, and the late Jack LaPorte of T. Rowe Price, Greg Wendt and Jason Karam of Capital Group, and Will Danoff, Peter Lynch, and Peter Saperstone of Fidelity.

I would also like to acknowledge Niren Chaudhary, the present CEO of Panera, who has done everything in his power to keep the culture of Panera and Mother Bread alive.

I also want to thank my partners at Act III Holdings, including Noah Elbogen, Bryan Griffith, Dwight Jewson, and Keith Pascal, who help me bring to life the ideas and philosophy expressed in this book at our investments today.

I want to acknowledge the CEOs and leaders of some of our present investments, including Brett Schulman at Cava, Chuck Chapman and

Tzurit Or at Tatte, Bryan Timko and Leah Duboir at Life Alive, Matt DuPlessie at Level99, Greg Levin at BJ's, Savneet Singh at Par, and Tim Rowe at Cambridge Innovation Center (CIC). One of the original purposes of this book was to share the many lessons I've come to learn and want to pass on. I hope this book provides powerful food for thought for you and thousands of other leaders trying to build a better competitive alternative and a life you can respect.

On a personal level, I would never have been able to live the life I did without the love and support of my close friends and family.

Lisa Weintraub, my chief of staff, has been my protector, excuse maker, researcher, voice, and confidante for nearly fifteen years. My life simply would not operate without you, Lisa, and your involvement, your insight, and your encyclopedic knowledge of what has transpired over the years helped enable this book to come to life.

Neil Leifer has been my best friend for over half a century—through high school, college, and my entire career. I've lost count of how many nights we stayed up late, talking and trying to make sense of life, family, and the world.

Then there's Alex Ponomarenko, my trainer and friend. I've met with Alex at 5:30 a.m. three times a week for the last 15 years. Though not a businessman, he taught me more about business and life and what it means to be a stand-up guy than he will ever know.

I would like to acknowledge Rana Chudnofsky, who has been a consistent source of emotional support and perspective over the last several years. Rana, you're the very definition of someone whom I can always count on—and do.

I want to thank my sister Marcia, who was there at the beginning. And her two amazing daughters, Hannah and Jesse—I'm so grateful to have you in my life.

Nancy Antonacci Shaich, you walked through this journey with me in a way no one else experienced or saw. Your sacrifice, your commitment, and your love allowed me the space to work on my dream. You put your own dreams on hold for me and our family, and for all of that I'm eternally grateful.

Michael and Emma, you graciously shared your dad with my very demanding "third child," Panera. I am so thankful that you also shared the joy of the business, were always ready to help me understand what mattered to customers, and never shied away from serving as my toughest critics. I love you both dearly and I wanted this book for you.

In so many ways each of the people mentioned on these pages and the thousands of people not mentioned have enabled the creation of this book. You're the people I've grown up with and evolved with. You're the people with whom I have shared so much—births and deaths, successes and mistakes, spats and reconnections, pain and triumph. And you are the people who helped me articulate the dream that has defined my life: to leave the world a better place than I found it and to truly make a difference in the lives of those around me. Our interactions and conversations have given me the opportunity to experience and learn the lessons I share in these pages. To all of you, I am grateful beyond words.

ABOUT THE AUTHOR

RON SHAICH is the founder and former chairman and CEO of Panera Bread, a groundbreaking restaurant brand that today has more than 2,400 bakery cafés, over 120,000 associates, and nearly $6 billion in annual systemwide sales. In addition to founding Panera, which established the high-growth fast-casual restaurant segment, Ron earlier in his career founded and grew Au Bon Pain, establishing the bakery-café segment. With both brands, he disrupted an existing industry paradigm and found new pathways to building companies of value and with values. The result: Panera generated annualized returns of more than 25 percent over the last two decades of Ron's tenure, and delivered a total shareholder return forty-four times better than the S&P 500. In 2017, Ron led a $7.5 billion sale of Panera in what was the largest US restaurant deal done up to that point and at among the highest multiples on record.

Ron is now the managing partner and CEO of Act III Holdings, investing in public and private restaurant and consumer companies that are driving long-term value creation and have the potential to significantly dominate their market niches. Act III is a lead investor in Cava, Tatte, Level99, and Life Alive, among other companies, and Ron serves as chairman of each.

Ron has been recognized repeatedly for his visionary leadership. In 2020, he was listed as one of Boston's Most Influential People by *Boston Magazine*. In 2018, he was named Restaurant Leader of the Year by *Restaurant Business*. In 2017, he received the Legend in Leadership Award from the Chief Executive Leadership Institute at the Yale School of Management. He was also named the second most influential leader in the restaurant industry by *Nation's Restaurant News* in its 2017 Power List. Earlier, he received the *Nation's Restaurant News* Pioneer Award for being one of the most significant contributors to the history of the restaurant industry. Past winners have included Colonel Harland Sanders, Ray Kroc, Norman Brinker, and J. Willard Marriott Sr. Ron was awarded IFMA's Gold Plate Award for being the industry's outstanding leader in 2005. And he twice received the *Nation's Restaurant News* Golden Chain Award, recognizing industry leadership and success. In addition, Ron was named Ernst & Young Entrepreneur of the Year for the New England region in 1998, Ernst & Young Entrepreneur of the Year for the Midwest region in 2003, and a finalist for the Ernst & Young National Entrepreneur in 2003.

Ron sits on the boards of Clark University, Farmers Business Network, Cambridge Innovation Center (CIC), Cava, Life Alive Organic Cafe, Tatte Bakery and Café, and Level99. He formerly served as chairman of the board of trustees of Clark University and on the boards of Conscious Capitalism, Inc., Unite America, Whole Foods Market, the Rashi School, the Lown Cardiovascular Foundation, and the Alliance for Business Leadership. Ron is also a cofounder of No Labels, an organization that promotes bipartisan political problem-solving and the development of a long-term strategic plan for the country.

Ron received a bachelor of arts degree from Clark University and a master of business administration degree from Harvard Business School. He is also the recipient of an honorary doctor of humane letters degree from Clark University. Ron lives in Brookline, Massachusetts, and is the proud father of Michael and Emma.